THE WORD IS Improvement

Common Core Connection

High-Utility Vocabulary

Proven Instructional Model

Blended Approach to Learning

Just 15 Minutes a Day

THE KEYS TO Improvement

Vocabulary for Success, Common Core Enriched Edition reflects the most up-to-date research in vocabulary instruction for today's middle and high school students. The word lists, instructional design and technology components bring success to every classroom.

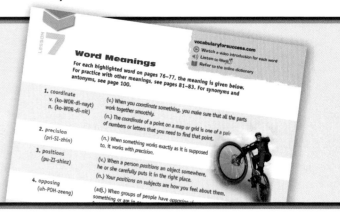

High-Utility Vocabulary

Explicit instruction for Academic and Domain-specific words ensures students learn words vital to comprehension.

Proven Instructional Model

Move students to independent learning through support with the effective Gradual Release of Responsibility model.

Every lesson includes teacher modeling, guided instruction, productive group work, and independent learning.

Teacher Launches Vocabulary in Context — "I do it"

Blended Approach to Learning

Support differentiated instruction with online videos and audio program that blends multi-media approaches.

Watch

Videos Introduce Reading Passages

Just 15 Minutes a Day

Designed to improve your students' vocabulary in just 15 minutes a day with flexible pacing guides to fit every classroom.

Douglas Fisher

Nancy Frey

Program authors Douglas Fisher and Nancy Frey have selected 210 words for each level from the most respected research-based word lists:

Academic Word List
(Coxhead, 2000) e.g., area, maintenance, triggered

Basic Word List
(Marzano, Kendall, Paynter, 2005) e.g., confer, haphazard, superlative

Background Knowledge Word List
(Marzano, 2004) e.g., hypothesis, molecule, photosynthesis

Vocabulary for Success aligns with the Common Core State Standards for English Language Arts. For a full correlation, go to vocabularyforsuccess.com.

"We do it" → **Peer Collaboration Towards Mastery** → "You do it together" → **Reinforce Through Independent Practice** → "You do it" → **Results in Vocabulary Mastery**

Listen

iWords Audio Program for Every Word

Watch

Videos Introduce Each Lesson Word

The pacing for incorporating vocabulary instruction into your classroom depends on the amount of time available for instruction and the background knowledge of your students. Suggested plans in The Teacher's Edition help teachers fit vocabulary instruction into every classroom.

THE PATH TO
Improvement

Vocabulary for Success, Common Core Enriched Edition incorporates the proven instructional model: Gradual Release of Responsibility to encourage students to work with their peers and use their social skills for vocabulary learning.

Teacher models and guides instruction

"I do it"

Scaffolded Instruction Helps Students Keep On Track

"We do it"

Peer Collaboration Towards Mastery

"We do it together"

> **"** *I give credit to this program for* **raising ALL** *of my students' vocabulary acquisition scores significantly.* **"**
> —Amy Anglin,
> Language Arts teacher, Westerville City School

Reinforce Through Independent Practice

"You do it"

Results in Vocabulary Mastery

Gradual Release of Responsibility Model in *Vocabulary for Success, Common Core Enriched Edition*

In *Vocabulary for Success, Common Core Enriched Edition*, lessons are based on the Gradual Release of Responsibility model, in which scaffolded instruction begins with explicit guidance and modeling by the teacher. Instruction then transitions to teacher-supported group work by students. Each lesson concludes with independent student practice and learning.

Teacher-Directed Instruction begins with introducing the words in a **Reading Passage**. The passage can be introduced first by a video to build background knowledge. Audio and video introductions provide multi-modal learning. Each Lesson is labeled with the genre of text represented in the opening passage. **Talk About It** encourages discussion of topic and vocabulary to get students involved.

Units are organized around Science or Social Studies themes.

UNIT **3**

Your AMAZING Body

LESSON **7** **Performing an O**
You can use your body to amazing things.
balance maneuver
contract opposing
coordinate plane
extend

LESSON **8** **Buy the Best**
Good sunglasses can help your eyes.
constrict millennia
distort organs
exposure prevention
external

LESSON **9** **Just Like an Oly**
Proper training and exerc you excel in sports.
collapse mechanism
consist obvious
evaluate react
function

vocabularyforsucc

All pages from Student Edition Grade 7

Video introduction to each Reading Passage— supplies background knowledge and brings the print passage to life.

Audio Recordings of the Reading Passage—allows students to revisit the passage at their own pace.

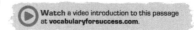 Watch a video introduction to this passage at vocabularyforsuccess.com.

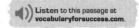 Listen to this passage at vocabularyforsuccess.com.

LESSON **7**

Performing an Ollie
<how-to>

Perform any skilled move in a sport and you'll need to coordinate your muscles, joints, and bones—your musculoskeletal system. When you perform an ollie, like the skateboarder in the picture, the muscles, bones, and joints in your body are working with precision, or exactness, to complete a difficult move.

Look at the skateboarder. To nail the trick, he first pushes off to get a rolling start. Then he positions his body over the center of the skateboard so that his rear foot is on the tail (the back portion) of the board and his front foot is in the center. Then he bends his knees. When knees bend, the opposing leg muscles

work together in a coordinated way: some muscles contract while others extend. All of this happens without the skateboarder even thinking about it.

When the skateboarder pushes his rear foot down on the board's tail, pressure rises under his other foot. The harder he pushes, the more pressure he feels. As the back of the skateboard hits the ground, the skater's foot slides up the board and he leans over. His front knee bends until it's near his chest while his back knee straightens. To shift his weight, the skateboarder moves his hips, which are ball-and-socket joints. This shift helps him balance

"I do it"

Tvi

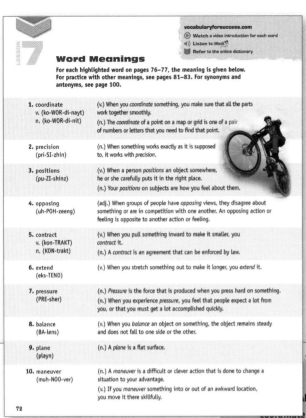

Word Meanings

LESSON 7

vocabularyforsuccess.com
▶ Watch a video introduction for each word
◀ Listen to iWords
📖 Refer to the online dictionary

For each highlighted word on pages 76–77, the meaning is given below. For practice with other meanings, see pages 81–83. For synonyms and antonyms, see page 100.

1. coordinate
v. (ko-WOR-di-nayt)
n. (ko-WOR-di-nit)

(v.) When you *coordinate* something, you make sure that all the parts work together smoothly.

(n.) The *coordinate* of a point on a map or grid is one of a pair of numbers or letters that you need to find that point.

2. precision
(pri-SI-zhin)

(n.) When something works exactly as it is supposed to, it works with *precision*.

3. positions
(pu-ZI-shinz)

(v.) When a person *positions* an object somewhere, he or she carefully puts it in the right place.

(n.) Your *positions* on subjects are how you feel about them.

4. opposing
(uh-POH-zeeng)

(adj.) When groups of people have *opposing* views, they disagree about something or are in competition with one another. An opposing action or feeling is opposite to another action or feeling.

5. contract
v. (kon-TRAKT)
n. (KON-trakt)

(v.) When you pull something inward to make it smaller, you *contract* it.

(n.) A *contract* is an agreement that can be enforced by law.

6. extend
(eks-TEND)

(v.) When you stretch something out to make it longer, you *extend* it.

7. pressure
(PRE-sher)

(n.) *Pressure* is the force that is produced when you press hard on something.

(n.) When you experience *pressure*, you feel that people expect a lot from you, or that you must get a lot accomplished quickly.

8. balance
(BA-lens)

(v.) When you *balance* an object on something, the object remains steady and does not fall to one side or the other.

9. plane
(playn)

(n.) A *plane* is a flat surface.

10. maneuver
(muh-NOO-ver)

(n.) A *maneuver* is a difficult or clever action that is done to change a situation to your advantage.

(v.) If you *maneuver* something into or out of an awkward location, you move it there skillfully.

72

Video introduction to each word— takes learning to a new level by showing students the vocabulary in a real-world context.

iWords Audio Recordings of each Lesson Word—provide word meanings, parts of speech, and an example of usage.

Word lists originate from Academic and Domain-Specific words.

- 10–12 words in each Lesson
- Multiple-meaning words in each Lesson
- Explanations of meanings
- Informal dictionary definitions (Grades 9–10)

...BULARY

coordinate	extend
precision	pressure
positions	balance
opposing	plane
contract	maneuver

his full weight on the large bones of his back leg. Here's where the tricky part comes in. The skateboarder leaps into the air using the opposing muscle groups of his legs and torso. The board follows, and looks as if it is sticking to his feet.

Now the hard part—landing! The skateboarder bends both knees and comes down on the horizontal plane of the board so that his weight is balanced in the center of the board. He can thank his musculoskeletal system for allowing him to make this incredible maneuver.

TALK ABOUT IT

With a partner, answer the questions below. Use as many of the highlighted words in the selection as you can.

1. Why is it important to *coordinate* different parts of your body when you perform an ollie?

2. What do you think are the best ways to prepare for a new *maneuver* like this?

Research suggests that if students are going to grasp and retain words and comprehend text, they need incremental, repeated exposure in a variety of contexts to the words they are trying to learn.

(Common Core State Standards for English language arts & literacy in history/social studies, science, and technical subjects)

"We do it"

Performing an ollie correctly requires precision and balance.

Peer Collaboration

Students transition to teacher-supported group work and collaborate with each other. Today's students are very social, and we want them to collaborate with peers to better understand these new vocabulary words through engaging activities.

Students collaborate to begin using the new vocabulary words in a speaking activity called Word Talk.

- This is a collaborative peer activity with teacher guidance.
- Activities encourage students to talk about word meanings, building on background knowledge.

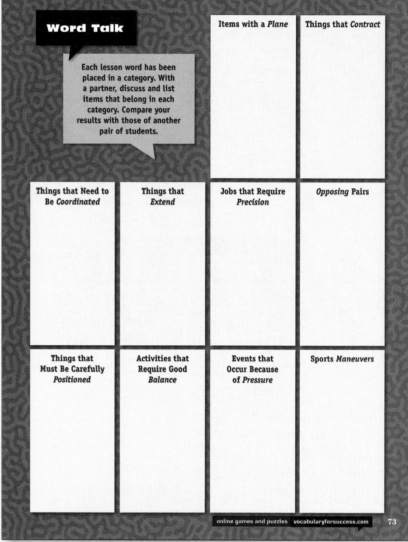

Word Talk

Each lesson word has been placed in a category. With a partner, discuss and list items that belong in each category. Compare your results with those of another pair of students.

Items with a *Plane*	Things that *Contract*

Things that Need to Be *Coordinated*	Things that *Extend*	Jobs that Require *Precision*	*Opposing* Pairs

Things that Must Be Carefully *Positioned*	Activities that Require Good *Balance*	Events that Occur Because of *Pressure*	Sports *Maneuvers*

online games and puzzles vocabularyforsuccess.com 73

"You do it"

Interactive Games and Puzzles—make studying vocabulary fun.

Online *Vocabulary for Success* Dictionary— includes formal definitions, synonyms and antonyms, and derivations for all Lesson Words.

Practice Worksheet for each Lesson—supplies additional practice.

Check for Understanding

Choose the lesson word that completes each sentence. Write the word on the line provided. Some words will be used twice.

balance	extend	positions
contract	maneuver	precision
coordinate	opposing	pressure
	plane	

1. The _____ armies prepared for battle.

2. Turning on her ballet shoes with _____, the ballerina executed her moves perfectly.

3. The pattern of the floor boards created a/an _____ that made the room feel wider.

4. Since I was sick for three days, my teacher decided to _____ the due date for my report.

5. The lack of _____ in the tire caused it to deflate.

6. Due to our busy schedules, it was difficult to _____ all of our activities without looking at our calendars.

7. How does a seal _____ the ball on the tip of its nose?

8. A toddler _____ the blocks so that the tower doesn't fall.

9. To wrinkle your nose, _____ the muscles in your fa

10. The runner made a clever _____ that put her in the lead.

11. The coach always _____ the players on the field before the game begins.

12. Accordions expand and _____ to make music.

74

All pages from Student Edition Grade 7

Students move from talking about the words to using them to complete written activities.

With Check for Understanding, teachers can immediately assess the progress students are making in understanding the meaning of new vocabulary words.

Expand Word Meanings

Read the paragraph below to learn other meanings for some of the lesson words.

I was very nervous about this week's math test. Since my grades on the last two tests were not so great, I felt a lot of pressure to do well. I was confused about a coordinate and how to maneuver the number onto a grid. However, I got extra help after school, so when it came time to take the test I felt a lot more confident. Also, our teacher, Mr. Preston, made a contract with the class. It said that if we all got at least 80% correct, he would give us a pizza party on Friday. One of his positions on academic success is that it helps to give rewards.

> Notice that the lesson's words are used in a different way here. For example, look at *contract*. Here it means an agreement between the teacher and the students. Look at the other highlighted words. Can you figure out the meanings of the words as they are used here? Refer to page 72 to confirm meanings.

Students are introduced to multiple-meaning Lesson Words in context to provide practice.

Apply Other Meanings

Complete each sentence with a highlighted word from the paragraph above.

1. After all the _____ my mother put on me to win, I felt very nervous at the swim meet.

2. Since the obstacle course was very complicated, I had to _____ very carefully so I would not fall down.

3. The math problem on the last _____ of the series was the toughest one yet.

4. Tonja's _____ on school policies were unclear, so we did not vote for her for class president.

5. Before signing any _____, make sure you read the fine print or show it to a lawyer.

6. It's not easy finding the airport on a map without at least one _____.

7. Taking too many after-school classes can add a lot of _____ to a student's life.

8. When my mom took the part-time job, she had to sign a _____ with the company.

9. When the bus is very crowded, it is hard to _____ to the door.

10. My father kept changing his mind on whether I could host a party, and he never really explained his _____ on the matter.

Tix

Independent Practice

Students develop understanding of vocabulary words through engaging independent activities that allow them to think critically and practice words in a variety of ways.

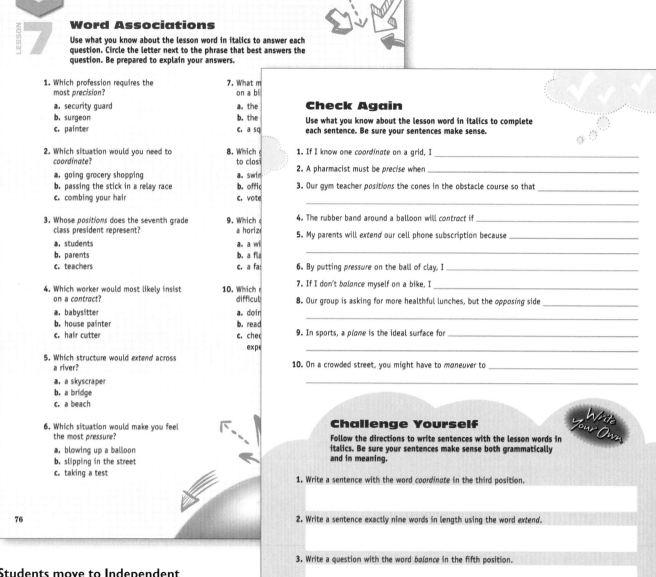

LESSON 7

Word Associations

Use what you know about the lesson word in italics to answer each question. Circle the letter next to the phrase that best answers the question. Be prepared to explain your answers.

1. Which profession requires the most *precision*?
   a. security guard
   b. surgeon
   c. painter

2. Which situation would you need to *coordinate*?
   a. going grocery shopping
   b. passing the stick in a relay race
   c. combing your hair

3. Whose *positions* does the seventh grade class president represent?
   a. students
   b. parents
   c. teachers

4. Which worker would most likely insist on a *contract*?
   a. babysitter
   b. house painter
   c. hair cutter

5. Which structure would *extend* across a river?
   a. a skyscraper
   b. a bridge
   c. a beach

6. Which situation would make you feel the most *pressure*?
   a. blowing up a balloon
   b. slipping in the street
   c. taking a test

7. What m
   on a bi
   a. the
   b. the
   c. a sq

8. Which g
   to closi
   a. swi
   b. offi
   c. vote

9. Which
   a horizo
   a. a wi
   b. a fla
   c. a fa

10. Which
    difficul
    a. doin
    b. read
    c. che
       expe

76

Check Again

Use what you know about the lesson word in italics to complete each sentence. Be sure your sentences make sense.

1. If I know one *coordinate* on a grid, I _____

2. A pharmacist must be *precise* when _____

3. Our gym teacher *positions* the cones in the obstacle course so that _____
   _____

4. The rubber band around a balloon will *contract* if _____

5. My parents will *extend* our cell phone subscription because _____
   _____

6. By putting *pressure* on the ball of clay, I _____

7. If I don't *balance* myself on a bike, I _____

8. Our group is asking for more healthful lunches, but the *opposing* side _____

9. In sports, a *plane* is the ideal surface for _____
   _____

10. On a crowded street, you might have to *maneuver* to _____
    _____

Challenge Yourself

Write Your Own

Follow the directions to write sentences with the lesson words in italics. Be sure your sentences make sense both grammatically and in meaning.

1. Write a sentence with the word *coordinate* in the third position.

2. Write a sentence exactly nine words in length using the word *extend*.

3. Write a question with the word *balance* in the fifth position.

Students move to Independent Practice starting with a Word Association activity. This activity assesses the ability to apply meanings that students have learned.

During Check Again, students have an opportunity to demonstrate understanding of meanings in a writing exercise.

In Challenge Yourself, students are asked to challenge themselves by demonstrating understanding of meaning, grammar, and syntax.

Tx

Word-Solving Strategies: Context Clues

Synonyms

Sometimes an author helps you by defining unfamiliar words with a synonym. Reread this sentence from "Performing an Ollie."

When you perform an ollie, like the skateboarder in the picture, the muscles, bones, and joints in your body are working with precision, or exactness, to complete a difficult move.

Note that after the word **precison** the synonym *exactness* is set off by commas. Similarly, the word *or* sometimes signals that a synonym may follow.

The word *or* does not always signal that a synonym will follow. Sometimes *or* is used to connect items in a series. Read this sentence:

What makes skateboarders improve most—big skateboards, good coaches, or new parks?

Notice that a comma separates *big skateboards* from *good coaches*. A comma and the word *or* separates *good coaches* from *new parks*.

BE CAREFUL!

Practice

A. Write the highlighted vocabulary word and its synonym in the first two boxes. In the third box, write another meaning for the word.

How difficult is it to invent a new skateboard maneuver? Not very difficult if you are an innovative, or creative, 15-year-old who happens to live near an imperfect skateboard park. That's how the ollie was invented. In 1978, Alan Gelfand spent many hours at a skateboard park in Hollywood, Florida. He noticed the skateboard park's imperfections, and used these defects to invent the ollie. Can you imagine his friends' incredulity as they watched with amazement while Alan performed his new maneuver?

WORD	SYNONYM	WORD MEANING

B. Write a sentence for each of the highlighted words from the paragraph above. Use a synonym as a context clue. You will use one word twice.

1. _____

2. _____

3. _____

4. _____

78

Vocabulary for Success does more than introduce new vocabulary words to students. It also teaches striving readers how to unlock the meaning of unfamiliar words.

Students have the opportunity to apply word-solving strategies to infer meaning by using context clues, analyzing parts of speech, and using print and online resources.

"You do it"

END-OF-UNIT
Enrichment

Continue Learning

After every three Lessons comes **Enrichment** and **Word Study**. **Enrichment** offers opportunities to use and respond to new vocabulary words, facilitating understanding.

LESSONS 7–9 ENRICHMENT

Synonyms and Antonyms

In the following Word Bank, you will find synonyms and antonyms for some of the words in Lessons 7–9. (Remember: Some words have both synonyms and antonyms.) Study these words; then complete the exercises below.

expand	compress	reduce	assess	internal	clash
perform	contort	clear	accuracy	situates	obscure

A. For each sentence, fill in the blank with a SYNONYM for the word in boldface.

1. Sometimes things that you think are **obvious** are not _____ to anyone but you.

2. The pianist played with great **precision**, but _____ alone is not enough make someone a great musician.

3. Multiple choice tests can **evaluate** someone's knowledge of the facts, but an essay te is a better way to _____ a student's deeper understanding of a subject.

4. In summer, he **positions** the chair by the window so he can look out at the garden. I winter, he _____ himself by the fireplace because it's warmer and cozier.

5. This bike will **function** well on city streets, but don't expect it to _____ rough terrain.

B. For each sentence, fill in the blank with an ANTONYM for the word in boldface.

6. The library hoped to **extend** the hours it stayed open, but budget constraints forced director to _____ the number of hours instead.

7. Gemma's mom thinks everything in a room should **coordinate**, but Gemma prefers co and shapes that _____.

8. A bungee cord will _____ to wrap around the package on your bike rack then **contract** to hold it in place.

9. The **external** wal_____shed were covered with ivy; rakes and other garden tools hung o_____ walls.

10. The meani_____us to me, but everyone else seemed to think was _____

100

Word Study: Proverbs

A proverb is a short, well-known saying that expresses a common truth or rule. For example, you might explain why you don't want to waste money on expensive shoes with the proverb "Money doesn't grow on trees." You might say, "Money is the root of all evil" if you think greed is the cause of many problems.

Some of the words in Lessons 7–9 can be used to help explain the meaning of proverbs. For example, the proverb "Don't judge a book by its cover" means don't judge something by its *external* (Lesson 8) appearance alone.

Practice

Read each sentence. Use context clues to figure out the meaning of each proverb in boldface. Then write the letter of the definition for the proverb.

_____ 1. People who often interrupt others should remember to be **swift to hear and slow to speak.**

_____ 2. When I got really upset about missing a TV show, my friend said, "**Don't make a mountain out of a molehill.**"

_____ 3. Before Mia agreed to do the huge project, I reminded her, "**Look before you leap.**"

_____ 4. Whenever you work on a project, remember to **measure twice, cut once** for best results.

_____ 5. It's a good idea to wash your hands before a meal because **an ounce of prevention is worth a pound of cure.**

_____ 6. When people wonder why my quiet father and our noisy neighbor are best friends, I explain that **opposites attract.**

a. People who have very different characteristics are often drawn to each other.

b. Listen carefully before you say something.

c. Take time to do things right so you won't have to redo them.

d. Don't make a situation worse than it really is.

e. Before you take action, think carefully about what might happen.

f. It's easier to stop a problem from happening than to fix it later.

g. Doing a task too fast is wasteful.

Apply

Work with a partner to find out the meaning of each proverb. (Use an online or print dictionary.) Then work together to write a sentence for each item.

1. Great minds think alike.
2. Home is where the heart is.
3. Little strokes fell great oaks.
4. Go from the frying pan into the fire.
5. Truth is stranger than fiction.
6. Necessity is the mother of invention.
7. The pen is mightier than the sword.
8. It's always darkest before the dawn.

LESSONS 7–9 ENRICHMENT

Word Study activities meet Common Core State Standards.

- Idioms
- Adages
- Denotation and Connotation
- Proverbs

Meet the Needs of Struggling Students in Grades 9 and 10

Vocabulary for Success, Common Core Enriched Edition was designed specifically for struggling students, increasing their vocabulary as well as developing their word-solving strategies to unlock unfamiliar words. Older students may need further instruction in word meaning and writing, so Grades 9 and 10 have unique features to address the needs of the older student.

Direct instruction of multiple-meaning words

warrant the attention of a dentist. **SYNONYMS:** merit, justify, necessitate; **n** a written order giving authority to do something. Police officers had a *warrant* to search the house.

More on Meanings: Multiple-Meaning Words

Some multiple-meaning words have meanings that are close but not exactly the same. Compare these sentences:

When you exhale, you **expel** air from your lungs.

The college dean had to **expel** the student for breaking the rules.

In the first sentence, *expel* means "to send out." In the second, it means "to force to leave."

Now compare these sentences:

Experts concluded that the issue did not **warrant** further investigation.

Authorities issued an arrest **warrant** for the accused thief.

In the first sentence, *warrant* is a verb. In the second, it is a noun with an unrelated meaning.

Some multiple-meaning words have literal and figurative meanings:

The sun cast a **golden** light on the landscape.

Hearing the good news, Gordon felt that everything was **golden**.

Challenge

1. Choose two of the multiple-meaning words below. For each, write two sentences that illustrate different meanings of the word.
   bluff   revolution   format
   baste   poach

2. Choose one multiple-meaning word below. Use the word in two sentences that illustrate its literal and figurative meanings.
   flexible   stretch   lend

vocabularyforsuccess.com **155**

Showing word-meaning video can help students understand multiple-meaning words

Word Study activities meet Common Core State Standards.

- Additional words per level (252)
- **More on Meanings** covers confusing word pairs, denotation and connotation, and multiple-meaning words.
- **Write Your Own** prompts students to perform a close reading of a nonfiction text and use evidence from the text to support a position.
- Common Core State Standards are identified at point of use in Teacher's Edition.

Meet the Needs of English Language Learners

Vocabulary for Success, Common Core Enriched Edition supports English Language Learners with a variety of resources:

- iWords online audio program, including pronunciations and examples of usage
- Model readings of each Passage
- Videos that support instruction with students demonstrating word meanings
- Explicit instruction in figures of speech (idioms and proverbs), denotation and connotation
- Special attention to multiple-meaning words

It is a good idea not to *divulge* _____

Showing *tact* in social situations suggests that you are _____

9. A detail that would be *tangential* to a discussion of popular music is _____

10. An *intangible* result of an act of charity would be _____

11. One step to joining the *workforce* is _____

12. An *inconclusive* medical test might cause some patients _____

Write Your Own

Reread the passage on pages 162–163. Then, on a separate sheet of paper, write a one-paragraph response to the question, "How has the use of social media affected the way in which epidemiologists work?" Use at least two words from the lesson word list, and support your answer by referring to the text of the passage.

vocabularyforsuccess.com **169**

After a close reading of a nonfiction text, students write their own response using evidence from the text.

BUILT-IN
Assessment

Ensure Mastery

Assessments are available after each Lesson, mid-year, and at the end of the year. Frequent assessment allows teachers to monitor progress and adjust instruction for every student to be successful. All assessments are in standardized-test format, giving students the practice they need.

Common Core Connection

Vocabulary for Comprehension

Read the following passage, in which some of the words you have studied in Lessons 7–9 appear in boldface type. Then answer items 1–6.

How SCUBA Works

SCUBA stands for Self-Contained Underwater Breathing Apparatus. It was invented by the U.S. military in 1939. Scuba equipment is worn by the diver and can **consist** of one or two
5 tanks of compressed gases. The diver **positions** the equipment carefully on his or her back so it doesn't fall off or get tangled in seaweed. The scuba **mechanism** makes it possible to dive hundreds of feet below the water's surface.
10 Scuba equipment works as an **external** respiration system. It holds the gases for the diver to breathe in and out.

It is important that the diver be aware of the depth of the water. Injuries and illness can

15 result from the **pre**
diver moves into d
maneuver slowly
the recommended
surface. The diver
20 adjust for changes
in the **prevention**
lungs or a case of t
that results from t
and other body **tis**
25 death. That's why
how to scuba dive
proper the **techni**

1. In sentence 3, **consist** means
   - ○ **A** made up of
   - ○ **B** texture
   - ○ **C** carry
   - ○ **D** heavy

2. An example of a **mechanism** (line 8) is
   - ○ **A** a car mechanic
   - ○ **B** a railroad track
   - ○ **C** the gears of a bicycle
   - ○ **D** a boat

3. When you feel **pressure** (line 15), you
   - ○ **A** are weak or ill
   - ○ **B** feel the force of an object
   - ○ **C** cannot stand or move
   - ○ **D** are in the dark

4. Another word
   - ○ **A** hurry
   - ○ **B** move
   - ○ **C** trick
   - ○ **D** breathe

5. Something tha
   (line 21) would
   - ○ **A** crumble
   - ○ **B** fall apart
   - ○ **C** be strong
   - ○ **D** be weak

6. A person who
   technique (lin
   - ○ **A** ask the
   - ○ **B** perform
   - ○ **C** learn mo
   - ○ **D** serve as

102

Practice for Tests

Fill in the bubble next to the answer that best completes the sentence or answers the question.

1. Read this sentence.
   I am thankful that the dentist used his instruments with *precision* to fill my cavity.
   Precision means:
   - ○ **A** accuracy
   - ○ **B** speed
   - ○ **C** painlessness
   - ○ **D** preciousness

2. A bicycle tire will *contract* when:
   - ○ **A** it's brand new
   - ○ **B** you pump air into it
   - ○ **C** you park it in the garage
   - ○ **D** it leaks air

3. The opposite of *extend* is:
   - ○ **A** balance
   - ○ **B** pressure
   - ○ **C** withdraw
   - ○ **D** pretend

4. In which group can *all* the items be described as having a horizontal *plane*?
   - ○ **A** football field, table, skateboard
   - ○ **B** skateboard, soccer ball, skis
   - ○ **C** ocean, waterfall, wave
   - ○ **D** airplane, sunset, skyscraper

5. A word closely associated with *maneuver* is:
   - ○ **A** handy
   - ○ **B** pleasant
   - ○ **C** skillful
   - ○ **D** patient

6. Read this sentence.
   The *pressure* of the heavy wind against my chest made it hard to walk.
   Pressure means:
   - ○ **A** size
   - ○ **B** pain
   - ○ **C** push
   - ○ **D** force

7. Two activities are said to *coordinate* if:
   - ○ **A** there are mix-ups everywhere
   - ○ **B** everything is running smoothly
   - ○ **C** no one is careful
   - ○ **D** they're on a map

8. When you *balance* an object, it does NOT:
   - ○ **A** fall over
   - ○ **B** remain steady
   - ○ **C** have control
   - ○ **D** stay in place

9. You would most likely state your *positions* about a topic in:
   - ○ **A** a game
   - ○ **B** a g
   - ○ **C** a c
   - ○ **D** a c

10. A perso
    - ○ **A** ag
    - ○ **B** aro
    - ○ **C** no
    - ○ **D** say

Students read high-interest passages and use context and word study skills to unlock the meaning of unknown words.

Students practice Lesson Words in performance-based tasks for periodic formative evaluation.

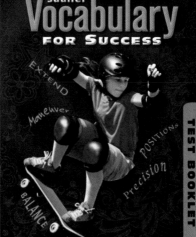

Student Test Booklet provides opportunities for additional formative assessment.

WHAT'S ONLINE?

Watch

Videos Introduce Lesson Passages

Age-appropriate and relevant, each video can be viewed before the informational passage by the whole group, in pairs, or individually.

Watch

Videos Introduce Each Lesson Word

Students demonstrate meaning and usage of each Lesson Word. English Language Learners will be able to see and hear the words in action.

Online Practice Pages and Interactive Quizzes

Monitor student progress throughout the year with additional practice pages and quizzes.

Online Dictionary

Provide formal definitions of Lesson Words with online dictionary.

Listen

iWords Audio Program for Every Word

Audio recordings of all Reading Passages and every Lesson Word with its meaning, part of speech, and example of usage.

Common Core State Standards Correlations

To review how *Vocabulary for Success, Common Core Enriched Edition* aligns to the Common Core State Standards, go to vocabularyforsuccess.com.

Interactive Games

Reinforce word meaning and usage by inviting students to use words in engaging and motivating activities.

Professional Development Videos

Seven Professional Development videos presented by Douglas Fisher and Nancy Frey support English Language Arts teachers, build word knowledge, and develop vocabulary skills.

Online Student Assessment System, Grades 6–10

Beyond the built-in program assessments—including comprehension checks, performance-based tasks, online quizzes, Mid-Year and End-of-Year Summative Assessments—an *Online Student Assessment System* is now available for *Vocabulary for Success, Common Core Enriched Edition*. This secure, web-based system makes it easy to:

- Customize practice and tests with question types that align with Common Core, or choose from preformatted Lesson, Mid-Year and Final Mastery Tests in the Test Bank
- Scramble questions and answer choices within a test for additional security
- Assess students online, after which automatic scoring will provide them with immediate feedback
- Track students through the comprehensive reporting system that provides detailed reports on class and individual student results

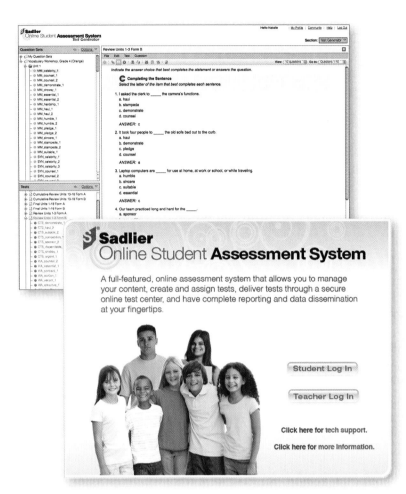

Vocabulary For Success For Grades 6–10

CHECK IT OUT!

Sadlier.com/previewVFS

Experience **Vocabulary for Success, Common Core Enriched Edition** online. View the array of print and online resources that helps teachers personalize student learning and build an extensive vocabulary for students while improving their word-acquisition skills.

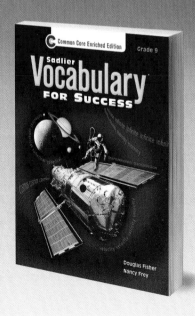

- Preview Program
- Dowload eBook Sample
- Introductory Video
- White Paper
- Find Your Sales Representative
- Request a Sample Copy

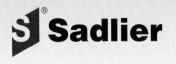

TEACHER'S EDITION

Grade 10

Sadlier Vocabulary FOR SUCCESS

C Common Core Enriched Edition

Douglas Fisher, Ph.D.
Professor of Education
San Diego State University
San Diego, CA

Nancy Frey, Ph.D.
Professor of Education
San Diego State University
San Diego, CA

PROGRAM CONSULTANTS

Ernest Morrell, Ph.D.
Professor of English Education
Teachers College, Columbia University
New York, NY

Ann Marie Ginsberg, Ed.D.
Director of the Office of Field Placement
School of Education,
Hofstra University
Hempstead, NY

Rosalie M. Quiñones, M.A. Edu. Lead
ESOL/ELL Consultant
Assistant Principal, Language Arts & Reading
Colonial High School
Orlando, FL

MaryBeth Webeler, Ph.D.
English Language Arts Consultant
Assistant Superintendent for
Curriculum & Instruction
Downers Grove Grade School District 58
Downers Grove, IL

S® Sadlier

Advisers

The publisher wishes to thank the following teachers and administrators, who read portions of the series prior to publication, for their comments and suggestions.

Laura Brumley
English Teacher
Dolores Huerta
  Preparatory High
Pueblo, CO

Sharon Fischer
English Teacher
John Adams High School
Ozone Park, NY

A. Xan Kahn
Literacy Coach
Orange County
Orlando, FL

Sarah McKenna
Independent Contractor
Del Valle ISD
Del Valle, TX

Sarah Brown Wessling
English Teacher
Johnston High School
Johnston, IA

Alison Callaghan
English Teacher
Proviso West
Hillside, IL

John Goodwin
Senior English Teacher
Health Sciences High
San Diego, CA

Rushie McLeod
English Teacher
Friendship Academy
  of Sci/Tech
Baltimore, MD

Ivana Orloff
English Teacher
Whittier High School
Whittier, CA

Photo Credits:
age fotostock/Somos Images: T30. Alamy/William Casey: T15 *left*. Blend Images LLC/ImageSource: T31; Radius Images: Tii. Depositphotos.com/Darrin Henry: Tv *right*, Txii. Getty Images/Purestock: Tv *left*, Txi; Rubberball/Alan Bailey: Tiii *bottom*; iStockphoto.com/Abejon Photography: Tiv *right*, Tviii; CAP53: Tiv *left*, Tvi. Masterfile: T17, 15 *right*. Punchstock/Purestock: Tiv *center*, Tvii. Used under permission from Shutterstock.com/Monkey Business Images: Txvi.

Cover: age fotostock/Richard Dirscherl: *top left*. Alamy/Brandon Cole Marine Photography: *bottom right*. Dreamstime/Golli: *background*. gtphoto/Hall: *center*. Interior: Alamy/Paul Abbitt: 75; Blend Images LLC: 69 *bottom*; Caro: 12 *top right*; Simon Cook: 221 *bottom*; Corbis Premium RF: 92, 232; GlowImages: 129; Golden Pixels LLC: 37 *bottom left*; Jeff Greenberg: 58, 114 *bottom left*, iv *bottom left*; hacohob: 167; imagebroker: 141, 177 *bottom*; itanistock: 103 *inset*; Johner Images: 164; Sebastian Kaulitzki: 230–31 *background*, vi *background*; Keystone Pictures USA: 242; Lyroky: 115 *bottom right*; Ilene MacDonald: 56, 212; MARKA: 197 *right*; MedicalRF.com: 91 *left*; moodboard: 154; Myrleen Pearson: 230; Chuck Pefly: 24; PhotoStockFile: 95; Radius Images: 222, 225; RIA Novosti: 215; Jeff Rotman: 143; Science Photo Library: 69 *background*, 71 *background*, 162 *bottom*, 163 *bottom*, 163 *top center*, iv *background*; Ian Shaw: 36; Stocktrek Images, Inc.: 13 *bottom*, iii *bottom right*; Tetra Images: 17; Tommy E Trenchard: 23 *top right*; Michael Ventura: 114–15; Jim West: 116; Claudia Wiens: 187; ZUMA Press, Inc.: 186 *left*; ZUMA Wire Service: 186–87 *background*. AP Photo/Gemunu Amarasinghe: 3 *background*; Frank C. Curtin: 186 *right*; Andrew England: 104; PRNewsFoto/Texas Back Institute: 81 *right*; Markus Schreiber: 176. Clemson University: 90. Corbis/National Photo Company: 126; Wendy Stone: 105; Xinhua Press/Han Chuanhao: 80 *left*. Dreamstime/Rdantoni: 41; Rjmiz: 68. Getty Images/AFP/Arash Khamooshi: 197 *left*; AFP/Behrouz Mehri: 196; AFP/Paul J. Richards: 14; Blend Images/Dave & Les Jacobs: 106; CSA Images/Mod Art Collection: 174 *hand*; DigitalGlobe: 2 *left*, 2 *left*; Frederic Dupoux: 23 *background*; Dante Fenolio: 142, v *bottom left*; Gamma-Rapho/Patrick Piel: 177 *top*, v *bottom right*; Chris Hondros: 125; Kidstock: 57 *bottom*; John Lund: 103 *background*; PhotoStock-Israel: 72; Brandi Simons: 80 *right*; The Christian Science Monitor/Mary Knox Merrill: 22; Alex Turton: 82. iStockphoto/Daniel Bendjy: 124; Özgür Donmaz: 136; Daniel Laflor: 61; Klaas Lingbeek-van Kranen: 208; Jacom Stephens: 198; YangYin: 27; Anna Zielinska: 47 *bottom right*, iii *bottom left*. NASA/JPL-Caltech: 152 *top left*; Cornell: 153 *top*; Cornell/ASU: 153 *bottom*, v *background*. National Geographic Stock/Emory Kristof: 143 *top left*. Photo Researchers/Philippe Psaila: 81 *left*. Phototake/ISM: 91 *right*. Shutterstock/almondd: 51; Baloncici: 211; Bananaboy: 178; Blend Images: 103 *inset*; Stephen Bonk: 188; Booka: 175 *background*; Cardaf: 114 *bottom left*; chaoss: 152; CLIPAREA/Custom media: 91 *background*, iv *bottom left*; cobalt88: 46; Andrea Crisante: 46 *center*; DESmith Photography: 201; Dinga: 175; East: 48; Stasys Eidiejus: 3; Johan W. Elzenga: 109; EpicStockMedia: 1 *left*; Felixdesign: 70; Iakov Filimonov: 90; Juan Gaertner: 102; Gelpi: 115 *background*; Givaga: 209; Natalie Glado: 147 *top left*; Warren Goldswain: 85; graja: 47 *bottom right*; James Horning: 144 *top left*; Eric Isselée: 191; Michal Kowalski: 211 *right*, vi *bottom right*; kuleczka: 209; Andrey Kuzmin: 105; LanKS: 35 *background*, 35, _Lonely_: 209 *background*; Travis Manley: 210; Joze Maucec: 142 *inset*; mearicon: 220–21 *background*; motorolka: 209; Jun Mu: 181; Nadin_1604: 220–21; newphotoservice: 220 *inset*; M. Niebuhr: 117; R. Peterkin: 4; Mike Phillips: 38; photogl: 235; Picsfive: 22–23, 114–15, 177; Pixel Embargo: 175 *center*; Alexander Raths: 231, vi *bottom left*; rodho: 37 *background*; Andrei Rybachuk: 221 *top*; Antonio S.: 34; Klaus Sailer: 47 *background*; R. Gino Santa Maria: 209; Silver Tiger: 80–81 *background*; Jo Ann Snover: 209; TerraceStudio: 124; Tim Roberts Photography: 7; urfin: 35 *top*, 57 *background*; violetkaipa: 35 *bottom*; Marilyn Volan: 125 *inset*; Wildstyle: 37 *bottom left*; Feng Yu: 12–13 *background*; Yurchyks: 143 *top left*; Zoom Team: 157. Wikimedia Commons/Ayacop: 71 *bottom*.

Excerpts from the *Common Core State Standards for English Language Arts* © Copyright 2010, National Governors Association Center for Best Practices and Council of Chief State School Officers. All rights reserved.

For additional online resources, go to vocabularyforsuccess.com and enter the Teacher Access Code VFS13TGETRKM

Teacher's Edition
Table of Contents

ONLINE COMPONENTS
vocabularyforsuccess.com

For Students and Teachers

- Lesson Passage Videos
- Lesson Passage Audio
- Word Meanings Videos
- iWords Audio Program
- Online Dictionary
- Interactive Games
- Interactive Lesson Quizzes
- Practice Worksheets

Professional Development Videos

- Engage Students in Learning:
  A Program Overview
- Support Common Core Standards:
  Vocabulary, Reading, and Writing
- Prepare Students for Success:
  Vocabulary Instruction for High School
  Students
- Implement an Effective Teaching Model:
  Gradual Release of Responsibility
- Integrate Multimedia in the Classroom:
  Video, Audio, and Interactive Games
- Meet Individual Needs:
  English Language Learners and Striving Readers
- Monitor Progress:
  Assessment and Guided Instruction

To the Teacher

Congratulations! By virtue of the fact you're reading this, we can already make some predictions about who you are as an educator:

- You are aware of the Common Core State Standards.

- You know that learning is social.

- You realize that tapping into your students' interests and background knowledge is key.

- You understand that adolescents have unique qualities that make teaching and learning with them so dynamic and interesting.

- You are committed to student success.

In addition, there's something else you know: Vocabulary is the key to the CCSS for reading, writing, speaking, and listening. There is a simple reason for this: Vocabulary is a proxy for the concepts those terms represent. It's nearly impossible for someone to use vocabulary accurately without knowing something about the concepts and ideas behind the words. And what's more important is that strategically selected words are a gateway for learning new words. You can't be there for your students each time they encounter an unfamiliar word. That's why it is essential to teach for word *solving*, not just word *meaning*. Knowledge about how to solve for unfamiliar words is key for vocabulary (and learning) success.

Those are the fundamental ideas behind the *Vocabulary for Success, Common Core Enriched Edition* program. Because you know that learning is a social act, you understand that student interaction using the targeted vocabulary is essential. Because you know that student interest is vital, you can see the learning opportunities present in engaging topics geared to this age group. Because you know that background knowledge is important, you can appreciate why these units tap into and build student science, history, and social studies knowledge. Because you understand that a rich vocabulary is necessary for success in college and careers, you know it's critical that your students are able to explain, inform, and persuade with precision. And because you're committed to student success, you realize that equipping them with the tools to solve problems is crucial.

These core principles will help you make decisions about how to customize *Vocabulary for Success, Common Core Enriched Edition*. Every busy high school classroom presents unique challenges and strengths that shape the way lessons are taught. Is access to technology difficult? Meet with your Instructional Technology coordinator so that he or she can help you find a novel solution. Or, if that isn't possible, watch the short introductory videos outside of class for some tips on how to introduce the new words yourself. Is time a challenge? Encourage students to work together, in class and outside of class, to learn these words faster. The core principles—interaction, engagement, and word-solving strategies—allow you to make thoughtful decisions about how best to implement the *Vocabulary for Success, Common Core Enriched Edition* program.

There is no question that the demand on students' vocabulary knowledge increases in high school as content becomes more challenging. For this reason, the words in this program have been carefully selected to build academic vocabulary using content-specific, specialized, and general words that students encounter every day as they read, write, and converse. We have brought an equally thoughtful approach to the instructional design of the program, using a gradual release of responsibility framework. The dual emphasis on word meaning and word solving builds your students' capacity to make vocabulary gains. Our intent is to equip you with materials that allow you to make decisions that take your students' strengths and needs into consideration. Without question, you are the most vital element of all—a caring and talented teacher. Your students are fortunate to have such a committed educator. And we are honored to play a part in helping your students become college and career ready.

—Douglas Fisher and Nancy Frey

Content Overview

First and foremost, *Vocabulary for Success, Common Core Enriched Edition* has been built on the CCSS. *Vocabulary for Success, Common Core Enriched Edition* provides direct, systematic instruction in and multiple exposures to a rich collection of academic vocabulary—words that high-school students will find useful in their studies as well as outside of school.

As the chart below and on page T15 shows, in addition to providing instruction in and practice with 252 carefully selected words at each grade level, *Vocabulary for Success, Common Core Enriched Edition* also furnishes students with the skills and strategies that they can use to determine the meanings of unfamiliar words that they encounter in their reading in subject areas in school and in their independent reading, too. Because this program was developed with the CCSS in mind, it promotes reading, writing, speaking, and listening skills that are dependent on vocabulary.

WORD SOLVING STRATEGIES	GRADE 9	GRADE 10
Use Context Clues		
Antonyms	✔	✔
Embedded Definitions	✔	✔
Examples	✔	✔
Inferences	✔	✔
Misdirected Clues	✔	✔
Punctuation	✔	✔
Synonyms	✔	✔
Use Word Parts		
Prefixes		
re-		✔
sub-	✔	
Suffixes		
-ine	✔	
Roots		
ag		✔
apt	✔	
chron	✔	
dom	✔	
ept	✔	
fin		✔
ig		✔
pel	✔	
prot		✔
proto		✔
puls	✔	
quis		✔
tact	✔	
tang	✔	
tend	✔	
tent	✔	
vers		✔

Vocabulary for Success

WORD SOLVING STRATEGIES	GRADE 9	GRADE 10
Use Word Parts (Cont.)		
vert		✔
vict	✔	
vinc	✔	
Use Resources		
Dictionary (Print & Online)	✔	✔
Peers	✔	✔
Thesaurus	✔	✔
More on Meanings		
Multiple Meaning Words	✔	✔
Confusing Word Pairs	✔	✔
Denotations and Connotations	✔	✔
Word Study		
Adages	✔	✔
Connotation	✔	✔
Denotation	✔	✔
Idioms	✔	✔
Proverbs	✔	✔
Reading		
Use context to infer meaning	✔	✔
Read a variety of nonfiction genres	✔	✔
Speaking		
Collaborate with peers	✔	✔
Contribute to class discussions	✔	✔
Writing		
Use vocabulary words in grammatically correct sentences	✔	✔
Convey correct meaning of vocabulary words in writing	✔	✔
Listening		
Listen attentively while working with peers	✔	✔
Listen attentively during class discussions	✔	✔

Common Core State Standards

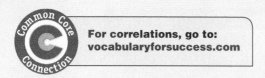

For correlations, go to:
vocabularyforsuccess.com

***Vocabulary for Success, Common Core Enriched Edition* aligns with the Common Core State Standards for English Language Arts/Literacy.**

The Teacher's Edition includes the Common Core State Standards addressed in each section of the Student Edition in abbreviated notation. For example, "CCSS Vocabulary 4.c." indicates that the vocabulary skill or skills represented on that page support Vocabulary Acquisition and Use standard 4.c. The full language of the corresponding Vocabulary, Reading, and Writing Standards for Grades 9-10 is provided below.

College and Career Readiness Standards for Language:
Vocabulary Acquisition and Use

STANDARD	*VOCABULARY FOR SUCCESS* LESSON FOCUS	GRADE 9	GRADE 10
4. Determine or clarify the meaning of unknown and multiple-meaning words and phrases based on *grades 9–10 reading and content,* choosing flexibly from a range of strategies.	Passage	✔	✔
a. Use context (e.g., the overall meaning of a sentence, paragraph, or text; a word's position or function in a sentence) as a clue to the meaning of a word or phrase.	More on Meanings, Check for Understanding, Word Associations, Check Again, Word-Solving Strategies, Practice for Tests, Synonyms and Antonyms, Word Study, Vocabulary for Comprehension, Using Context, Analogies, Word Relationships	✔	✔
c. Consult general and specialized reference materials (e.g., dictionaries, glossaries, thesauruses), both print and digital, to find the pronunciation of a word or determine or clarify its precise meaning, its part of speech, or its etymology.	Word Meanings, Word-Solving Strategies, Online Dictionary	✔	✔
d. Verify the preliminary determination of the meaning of a word or phrase (e.g., by checking the inferred meaning in context or in a dictionary).	Word Meanings, Word-Solving Strategies, Online Dictionary	✔	✔
5. Demonstrate understanding of figurative language, word relationships, and nuances in word meanings.	More on Meanings, Synonyms and Antonyms, Analogies, Word Relationships	✔	✔
a. Interpret figures of speech (e.g., euphemism, oxymoron) in context and analyze their role in the text.	Word Study	✔	✔
b. Analyze nuances in the meaning of words with similar denotations.	More on Meanings, Word Study	✔	✔
6. Acquire and use accurately general academic and domain-specific words and phrases, sufficient for reading, writing, speaking, and listening at the college and career readiness level; demonstrate independence in gathering vocabulary knowledge when considering a word or phrase important to comprehension or expression.	Word Talk, Check for Understanding, Check Again, Write Your Own, Practice for Tests, Synonyms and Antonyms, Word Study, Vocabulary for Comprehension, Analogies, Word Relationships, Generating Sentences, Extend Your Sentence	✔	✔

Vocabulary for Success

College and Career Readiness Standards for Reading:
Craft and Structure

STANDARD	VOCABULARY FOR SUCCESS LESSON FOCUS	GRADE 9	GRADE 10
4. Determine the meaning of words and phrases as they are used in a text, including figurative, connotative, and technical meanings; analyze the cumulative impact of specific word choices on meaning and tone (e.g., how the language of a court opinion differs from that of a newspaper).	Passage, Word-Solving Strategies, Vocabulary for Comprehension	✔	✔
6. Determine an author's point of view or purpose in a text and analyze how an author uses rhetoric to advance that point of view or purpose.	Passage	✔	✔

College and Career Readiness Standards for Writing:
Text Types and Purposes

STANDARD	VOCABULARY FOR SUCCESS LESSON FOCUS	GRADE 9	GRADE 10
2d. Use precise language and domain-specific vocabulary to manage the complexity of a topic.	Write Your Own, Extend Your Sentence	✔	✔

Student Edition

- Seven Units of three Lessons each, organized around high-interest science or social studies topics

- Twelve words taught in each Lesson

- Introductory nonfiction passages provide context for the words presented in each Lesson

- Direct instruction in multiple meanings, confusing word pairs, word-solving strategies, reading for comprehension, figurative language, denotation and connotation

- Opportunities for teacher-guided, collaborative, and independent work

- Engaging practice formats and test-preparation activities offer opportunities for ongoing formative assessment

- Mid-Year Review and End-of-Year Review provide summative assessment

- Also available in an eBook format

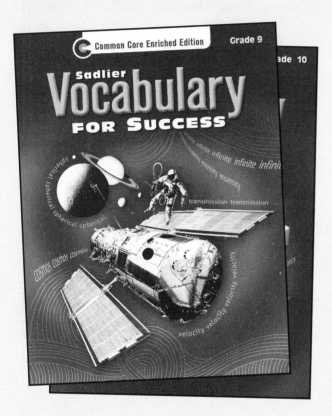

Teacher's Edition

- Common Core State Standards at point-of-use

- Suggestions for extending and differentiating instruction

- Integrates use of online resources at *vocabularyforsuccess.com*

- Full-size student pages with answers for all practice items

- Includes Answer Key to Student Test Booklet

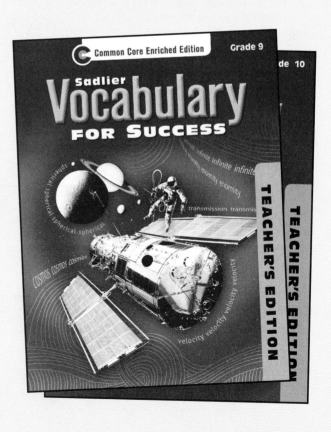

Vocabulary for Success

Student Test Booklet

- Two-page reproducible tests for each lesson
- Two-page Mid-Year Test
- Standardized test-format presentation
- Four-page Final Mastery Test

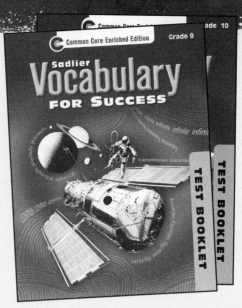

Online Resources
vocabularyforsuccess.com

Student Resources

- Reinforce CCSS through embedded rich media
- Student videos introduce Lesson passages
- Audio recordings of introductory passages and word meanings
- Student videos provide demonstrations of each word's meaning
- Online reference dictionary, games, and quizzes

Teacher Resources

- Practice worksheet for each word list
- Interactive, self-scoring quiz for each word list

Professional Development Videos

- **Engage Students in Learning:**
  A Program Overview
- **Support Common Core Standards:**
  Vocabulary, Reading, and Writing
- **Prepare Students for Success:**
  Vocabulary Instruction for High School Students
- **Implement an Effective Teaching Model:**
  Gradual Release of Responsibility
- **Integrate Multimedia in the Classroom:**
  Video, Audio, and Interactive Games

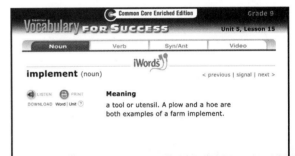

- **Meet Individual Needs:**
  English Language Learners and Striving Readers
- **Monitor Progress:**
  Assessment and Guided Instruction

Student Edition

Introduce each Unit with an engaging Unit Opener.

- Topics align with science and social studies high school courses of study.

- Opportunities to build background by introducing three related Lessons

- Twelve carefully selected words are taught in each Lesson.

Each Lesson begins with a high-interest passage to introduce the twelve new words.

- Passages represent a variety of nonfiction genres—how-to articles, biographies, personal narratives, persuasive essays, journal entries, and more.

- Lesson words are highlighted within informational passages.

- Students collaborate to discuss passages and use vocabulary words.

- A video of students introducing each Lesson passage is available at *vocabularyforsuccess.com*.

- Additional videos demonstrating meanings of all Lesson words are available at *vocabularyforsuccess.com*.

- Audio recordings of all Lesson passages are available at *vocabularyforsuccess.com*.

Research-based Lesson words meet the CCSS for vocabulary acquisition and use.

- Twelve words per Lesson are manageable for all students.

- Word meanings are given as informal dictionary definitions and as student-friendly explanations.

- Videos of students demonstrating the meanings of all twelve Lesson words are available at *vocabularyforsuccess.com*.

- Formal definitions and pronunciations, as well as synonyms, antonyms, and word histories, are available in an online dictionary at *vocabularyforsuccess.com*.

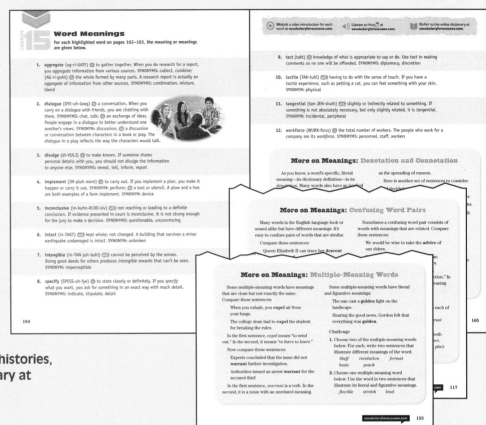

Proven instructional model for reading, writing, speaking, and listening

- Students collaborate to begin using the new vocabulary words in a speaking activity.

- Teachers can immediately assess the progress students are making in understanding the meaning of new vocabulary words.

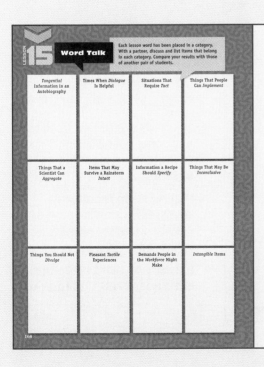

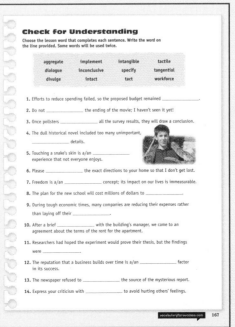

Student Edition (cont.)

Further activities require students to use higher-level thinking and to exhibit an understanding of grammar and word meaning.

- **Word-association activity** requires students to apply their understanding of the meanings of the Lesson words.

- **Open-ended writing activity** provides an opportunity for students to use all taught meanings.

- **Generative writing activity** requires students to follow directions to write sentences that make sense both grammatically and in meaning.

- **Writing prompt** allows students to demonstrate knowledge of Word Meanings in a one-paragraph response.

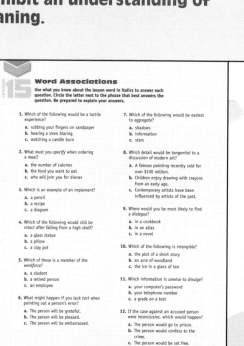

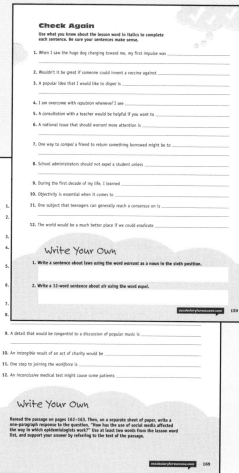

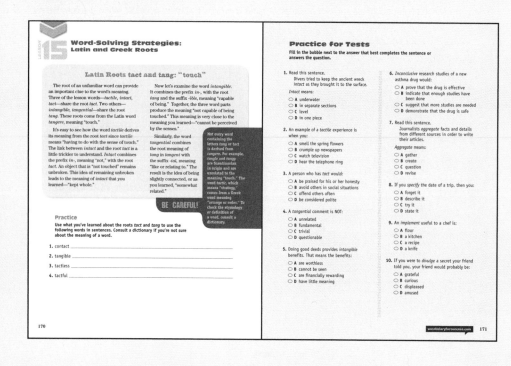

Students learn word-solving strategies and complete test-preparation activities.

- Students are taught how to use context and word parts to unlock the meanings of unfamiliar words.

- Teachers can monitor students' understanding of new vocabulary words.

- Students demonstrate mastery of word meanings in standardized-test format.

Enrichment

Synonyms and Antonyms

In the following Word Bank, you will find synonyms and antonyms for some of the words in Lessons 13–15. (Remember: Some words have both synonyms and antonyms.) Study these words; then complete the exercises below.

conversation	complicated	contribution	damaged	promptly	disclose
attraction	eliminate	accurately	rural	force	ordinary

A. For each sentence, fill in the blank with a SYNONYM for the word in boldface.

1. For a team to achieve success, each member must make a/an _____. **Input** from every individual is essential.

2. Having a guilty conscience will **compel** you to apologize. Knowing that you have hurt someone's feelings will _____ you to do what's right.

3. My little brother sometimes gets scared at night, and I have to **dispel** his fears. Turning on the light will usually _____

4. None of the plotters would _____ imprisonment, they all refu_____

5. The _____ bet_____ Through the use of **dialogu**_____

B. For each sentence, fill in _____

6. _____ living i_____ people prefer it to the nois_____

7. Some insects are fascinating _____ Centipedes and millipedes,_____

8. The tornado tore through th_____ Amazingly, some houses re_____

9. The artist had an **unconven**_____ during the night. Neverthe_____

10. The details of the accident _____ criticized for not having de_____

172

LESSONS 13–15 ENRICHMENT

Word Study: Idioms

If you ask a friend to come along to a baseball game, but he replies that baseball is "not my cup of tea," what does he mean? His response has nothing to do with drinking a hot beverage, of course. He simply means that watching baseball is not an activity that interests him. The phrase "not my cup of tea" is an **idiom**—an informal expression whose meaning is different from the literal meaning of its words.

Some vocabulary words in Lessons 13–15 have synonyms that are idioms. For example, a synonym for *unconventional* (Lesson 13) is "out in left field." If someone has an opinion that is "out in left field," that doesn't mean the opinion is on a baseball diamond. It means that the opinion is unusual.

Practice

Read each sentence. Use the context clues to figure out the meaning of each idiom in boldface. Then write the letter of the definition for the idiom in the sentence.

_____ 1. Michael was exhausted from studying, so he decided to **hit the hay**.

    a. chat informally

    b. fulfill financial obligations

    done

173

LESSONS 13–15 ENRICHMENT

Vocabulary for Comprehension

Read the following passage, in which some of the words you have studied in Lessons 13–15 appear in boldface type. Then answer questions 1–6.

The CDC Protects the Public

Whenever the topic of public health services comes up, one name frequently mentioned is the Centers for Disease Control and Prevention, or CDC. The CDC is a federal agency that
5 is part of the U.S. Department of Health and Human Services. The CDC **workforce** **implements** programs to prevent the spread of **communicable** illness and combat threats to public health. CDC workers **aggregate** data to
10 better understand factors that pose a risk to the public. Through investigations and research, they use their knowledge of **epidemiology** to try to **eradicate** diseases.

One key function of the CDC is educating the
15 public. For example, the CDC website provides information about diseases and **vaccines** that can prevent them. Because the flu is a widespread danger to the population of both **urban** and **pastoral** areas, it **warrants** special attention.
20 The CDC strives to help people understand how the flu is spread and how it can be avoided. Most people don't realize that the flu can be transmitted to a distance of about six feet, usually by airborne droplets spread by coughing, sneezing, or even
25 just talking. The disease can also be spread when people touch objects or surfaces that contain flu virus and then touch their mouths or noses. That's why it is so important to wash your hands with soap and water whenever the danger of flu
30 virus is present.

1. In sentence 3, **implements** means
   - A duplicates
   - B puts into practice
   - C collects funds for
   - D evaluates

2. In line 9, **aggregate** means
   - A convey
   - B accumulate
   - C disprove
   - D create

3. A student of **epidemiology** (line 12) would be most likely to learn about
   - A outbreaks
   - B epilepsy
   - C abrasions
   - D academics

4. When you **eradicate** (line 13) something, you do NOT
   - A eliminate it
   - B remove it
   - C destroy it
   - D preserve it

5. Another word for **pastoral** (line 19) is
   - A crowded
   - B tropical
   - C foreign
   - D countrified

6. If a proposal **warrants** (line 19) further discussion, it
   - A prevents it
   - B averts it
   - C discourages it
   - D deserves it

174

LESSONS 13–15 ENRICHMENT

An Enrichment section at the end of each Unit provides instruction and practice in word study, figurative language, and critical reading.

- **Students practice with synonyms and antonyms of Lesson words to facilitate understanding of relationships in meaning.**

- **Key vocabulary and language topics such as denotation and connotation, idioms, and proverbs are reinforced.**

- **As students read high-interest passages, they use context and word study skills to determine the meaning of vocabulary words, within a critical-reading, standardized-test format.**

Teacher's Edition

Based on the Gradual Release of Responsibility instructional model, the *Vocabulary for Success, Common Core Enriched Edition* Teacher's Edition provides just the right amount of support for teachers to effectively introduce, explain, and provide opportunities for students to learn, use, and apply new vocabulary. The Teacher's Edition enables teachers to:

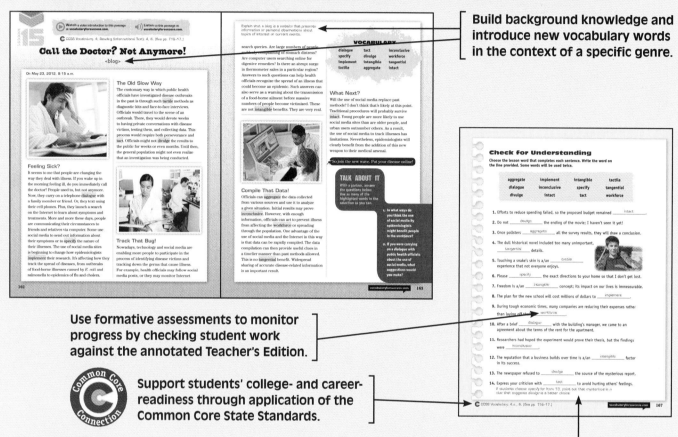

Build background knowledge and introduce new vocabulary words in the context of a specific genre.

Use formative assessments to monitor progress by checking student work against the annotated Teacher's Edition.

Support students' college- and career-readiness through application of the Common Core State Standards.

Provide specialized instruction to students.

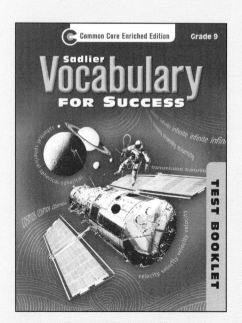

Assessment (optional)

Student Test Booklet

The *Vocabulary for Success, Common Core Enriched Edition* Test Booklet provides teachers with additional opportunities to assess students. Tests at the end of all Lessons as well as a Mid-Year Test and a Final Mastery Test offer students numerous chances to apply their understanding of new vocabulary words.

Online Student Assessment System

A Web-based system makes it easy to customize practice worksheets and tests, assess students securely online, and provide them with immediate feedback, as well as to track student progress through detailed reports on the class, a group, and individual students.

Online Resources

Everything teachers need to scaffold and differentiate instruction to meet student needs is included at **vocabularyforsuccess.com**.

Student-Generated Videos Introduce Lesson Passages

- Before students read each informational passage, decide if viewing the video will be a group activity or an independent activity.

- If it is a group activity, project the video on screen or interactive whiteboard, if available. Have students view the entire video. Then replay it, pausing at important points to have students discuss what they are learning. Have students predict how the introductory video will relate to the passage they are going to read.

- If it is an independent activity, have pairs of students view the video together on a computer. Create a simple discussion guide that students can use to discuss what they have learned.

Audio Recordings of Lesson Passages

- Encourage students to go to **vocabularyforsuccess.com** and use the Access Code VFS13SGEPYNB to read along with the audio recording, or select students whom you feel will benefit most from this kind of scaffolding.

Student-Generated Videos Introduce Each Lesson Word

- Before introducing new vocabulary words using the Word Meanings page in the Student Edition, decide if viewing the videos will be a group activity or an independent activity.

- If it is a group activity, project the video on a screen or interactive whiteboard. Have students rate their understanding of each of the twelve new Lesson words. Then focus on using the videos to scaffold the discussion for those words least familiar to students.

- If it is an independent activity, group together students who have the least familiarity with the same words.

Online Dictionary

- At the beginning of the school year, introduce the Online Dictionary to your students, and review how to locate specific words and use the word history and pronunciation keys.

- Remind students throughout the year to use the Online Dictionary as a resource.

Online Practice Pages and Interactive Quizzes

- As you monitor student progress throughout the year, identify students who will benefit most from extra practice or review.

Online Student Assessment System (Optional)

- The Web-based Online Student Assessment System allows teachers to create assessments that are automatically scored and provide students with immediate, prescriptive feedback.

Planning and Pacing

Vocabulary for Success, Common Core Enriched Edition (Grades 9–10) is designed for flexibility of use in the classroom. There are two suggested plans for using the program, depending on the amount of time available for teaching vocabulary and the background knowledge of the students in the class:

- **Five Class Days Per Week**
- **Three Class Days Per Week**

Five Class Days Per Week

By following the sample lesson plan below with homework assigned as necessary, the teacher should be able to complete one Lesson per week.

SAMPLE LESSON PLAN

DAY	STUDENT EXERCISE	SUPPORT MATERIALS
Day 1	• Introduce the Lesson words by reading the *Passage* that begins each Lesson • Encourage class discussion about the new words by answering the *Talk About It* questions	• Online video introduction to the Passage • Online audio recording of the Passage
Day 2	• Introduce the *Word Meanings* for the Lesson words • Introduce *More on Meanings* and have students complete the Challenge exercise • Encourage class participation and discussion in completing the *Word Talk* exercises	• Online video introduction for each Lesson word • Online iWords audio for each Lesson word • Online dictionary for reference
Day 3	• Have students complete the *Check for Understanding* exercises • Have students complete the *Word Associations* exercises	• Online dictionary for reference • Online Student Assessment System
Day 4	• Have students complete the *Check Again* exercises • Have students complete the *Write Your Own* exercises • Introduce *Word-Solving Strategies*	• Online interactive games to support classroom instruction • Online Student Assessment System
Day 5	• Review the Lesson • Complete the *Practice for Tests* exercises • Have students complete the Lesson in the *Student Test Booklet* (optional purchase)	• Additional practice worksheets, graphic organizers, and flash cards are available online at **vocabularyforsuccess.com**. • Online Student Assessment System • *Student Test Booklet*

For a full-year Planning and Pacing Calendar that includes:
- Enrichment Sections
- Mid-Year Review (Units 1-4)
- End-of-Year Review (Units 5-7)

} Go to *vocabularyforsuccess.com*

Three Class Days Per Week

The teacher who provides for vocabulary instruction three class days a week, and assigns parts of the Lesson as homework, should be able to complete one Lesson per week by following this sample pacing plan.

SAMPLE LESSON PLAN

DAY	STUDENT EXERCISE	HOMEWORK	SUPPORT MATERIALS
Day 1	• Introduce Lesson words by reading the *Passage* and answering the *Talk About It* questions • Study the *Word Meanings* • Introduce *More On Meanings*	• Have students complete the Challenge exercise in *More On Meanings* and the *Word Talk* exercises	• Online video introduction to the Passage • Online audio recording of the Passage • Online Student Assessment System
Day 2	• Complete the *Check for Understanding* and *Word Associations* exercises in class	• Have students complete the *Check Again* and *Write Your Own* exercises	• Online video introduction for each Lesson word • Online iWords audio for each Lesson word • Online dictionary for reference • Online Student Assessment System
Day 3	• Introduce the *Word-Solving Strategies* part of the Lesson • Review the Lesson • Have students complete the Lesson in the *Student Test Booklet* (optional purchase)	• Have students complete the Practice exercises on the *Word Solving Strategies* page and the *Practice for Tests* exercises	• Online interactive games to support classroom instruction • Additional practice worksheets, graphic organizers, and flash cards are available online at *vocabularyforsuccess.com* • Online Student Assessment System • *Student Test Booklet*

For a full-year Planning and Pacing Calendar that includes:
- Enrichment Sections
- Mid-Year Review (Units 1-4)
- End-of-Year Review (Units 5-7)

} Go to *vocabularyforsuccess.com*

Flexible Instruction Model

Vocabulary for Success, Common Core Enriched Edition can be used in a flipped classroom setting by assigning the viewing of the videos and Lesson passage to the students for homework and then providing instruction and discussion in class.

Research Base

Vocabulary for Success, Common Core Enriched Edition was built on the foundation of the CCSS. The authors of *Vocabulary for Success, Common Core Enriched Edition* conceived and designed the program to reflect the most up-to-date research in vocabulary instruction at the high school level. In its pedagogical approach, in the selection of the word list, and in its instructional model, the *Vocabulary for Success, Common Core Enriched Edition* program is supported by authoritative research and represents best practices in vocabulary instruction.

Research

Vocabulary for Success

NEED FOR DIRECT INSTRUCTION IN VOCABULARY

Research	Vocabulary for Success
"Word knowledge is directly related to a learner's content learning, especially through reading." (Flood, J., D. Lapp, and D. Fisher, 2003) *"Vocabulary is among the greatest predictors of reading comprehension."* (Baker, Simmons, and Kame'enui, 1998) *"The relationship between vocabulary and reading proficiency is so powerful that there is evidence that vocabulary size in kindergarten is an effective predictor of reading comprehension and academic achievement in the later school years."* (Scarborough, 2001)	• Ten student book pages are devoted to each Lesson's word list to provide significant opportunities for students to use and practice new vocabulary words. • Activity formats are varied and consistent, allowing students to read new vocabulary words in context, discuss word meanings, and use new words while working collaboratively and independently. • Numerous opportunities are provided to use vocabulary words while speaking and writing. • Activities that feature multiple meanings of vocabulary words help students expand their vocabularies.

WORD LISTS

Research	Vocabulary for Success
Given the importance of academic background knowledge and the fact that vocabulary is such an essential aspect of it, one of the most crucial services that teachers can provide, particularly for students who do not come from academically advantaged backgrounds, is systematic instruction in important academic terms (Marzano, 2004). In general, experts agree that there are three types of words that students need to know: Tier 1, Tier 2, and Tier 3 words (Beck, McKeown, & Kucan, 2002). In the world of secondary schooling, these words are classified as general, specialized, and technical (Vacca & Vacca, 2007).	• Words are selected from three research-based lists: Basic Word List (Marzano, Kendall, & Paynter, 2005); Academic Word List (Coxhead, 2000); Background Knowledge Word List (Marzano, 2004). • Words were selected with the needs of striving readers in mind and include high-utility academic words and content-specific words (Tiers 2 and 3). • Words are grouped around high-interest social studies and science topics to provide context that scaffolds instruction. • Each word list features twelve words, many of which have multiple meanings. • End-of-unit activities feature synonyms and antonyms. • Some words have been selected to provide context for teaching word-solving strategies.

Vocabulary for Success

Research

Vocabulary for Success

PROVEN INSTRUCTIONAL MODEL

The Gradual Release of Responsibility model stipulates that the teacher move from assuming *"all of the responsibility for performing a task…to a situation in which the students assume all of the responsibility."* (Duke & Pearson, 2002)

This gradual release may occur over a day, a week, or a semester. Stated another way, the gradual release of responsibility *"emphasizes instruction that mentors students into becoming capable thinkers and learners when handling the tasks which they have not yet developed expertise in."* (Buehl, 2005)

This Gradual Release of Responsibility model of instruction has been documented as an effective approach for improving writing achievement (Fisher & Frey 2003), reading comprehension (Lloyd, 2004), and literacy outcomes for English Language Learners (Kong & Pearson,003).

Each unit presents a structure for successful instruction that moves from "I do it" to "We do it" to "You do it together" to "You do it alone."

- Teacher models and guides instruction: Unit Opener, Introductory Passage, Word Meanings, More on Meanings

- Productive group work with teacher scaffolding: Word Talk, Check for Understanding

- Independent learning: Word Associations, Check Again, Write Your Own, Word-Solving Strategies, Practice for Tests

BEST PRACTICES IN VOCABULARY INSTRUCTION

Measurement of vocabulary knowledge has five dimensions:

- Generalization through definitional knowledge

- Application through correct usage

- Breadth through recall of words

- Precision through understanding of examples and nonexamples

- Availability through use of vocabulary in discussion (Cronback, 1942, cited in Graves, 1986), (Fisher & Frey, 2008)

- The vocabulary standards focus on understanding words and phrases, their relationships, and their nuances and on acquiring new vocabulary, particularly general academic and domain-specific words and phrases.

- Vocabulary words are clustered around topics.

- Words are embedded in high-interest informational passages.

- Explanations and informal dictionary definitions are provided for each word.

- Students use words orally before they use them in their writing.

- Written activities challenge students to show an understanding of the grammatical and semantic features of new words.

Vocabulary for Success, Common Core Enriched Edition is a vocabulary development program built on the foundation of CCSS and designed for the needs of striving readers.

Vocabulary for Success, Common Core Enriched Edition focuses on teaching the most critical words necessary for academic success.

One of the greatest challenges striving readers in high school face is reading their content area textbooks. For that reason, the authors of *Vocabulary for Success, Common Core Enriched Edition* selected vocabulary words from research-based word lists that identified words that students reading near or below grade level are unfamiliar with. Each week, students will learn:

- Key words that most striving adolescent readers are unfamiliar with (Basic Word List; Marzano, Kendall, & Paynter, 2005)

- High-utility words that appear in all content area textbooks (Academic Word List; Coxhead, 2000)

- Content-specific words that are critical to comprehension (Background Knowledge Word List, Marzano, 2004)

Vocabulary for Success, Common Core Enriched Edition teaches striving readers how to unlock the meanings of unfamiliar words.

Whether reading for school or for pleasure, most striving readers lack the skills and strategies necessary to unlock the meanings of words they do not know. For each word list, students are taught and have the opportunity to apply word-solving strategies to infer meaning by using context clues, analyzing parts of words, and using print and online resources. In addition, multiple meanings of words on each word list are taught to enable students to expand their vocabularies as quickly as possible.

Vocabulary for Success, Common Core Enriched Edition encourages collaboration and discussion among peers.
The Gradual Release of Responsibility Model at the core of the program provides significant opportunities for students to collaborate and learn from one another. As student pairs or groups are formed, keep in mind that mixed-ability pairs or groups may yield the best results.

Vocabulary for Success, Common Core Enriched Edition provides test-prep practice.
Many striving readers need to be introduced to standardized test formats before taking high-stakes assessments. That is why for each word list, one activity allows students to practice by "bubbling" responses. In addition, the Vocabulary for Comprehension activity at the end of each unit provides practice in reading connected text to infer word meaning.

Vocabulary for Success, Common Core Enriched Edition includes online support that scaffolds and supports or extends core instruction.
Each *Vocabulary for Success* student book provides all the necessary support and instruction to expand students' vocabularies. Audio and video resources at **vocabularyforsuccess.com** provide another level of support and scaffolding. Additional practice and quizzes are also provided.

Meeting the Needs of the English Language Learner

Vocabulary for Success, Common Core Enriched Edition has been built on the foundation of CCSS and is effective with English Language Learners.

Each new word is introduced in a meaningful context.

English Language Learners learn best when new vocabulary is introduced in context. In *Vocabulary for Success, Common Core Enriched Edition*, students first experience each word in the context of a high-interest informational passage. Those students who need support reading the passages can access audio recordings available at ***vocabularyforsuccess.com***. In addition, students can also access videos that provide background information for each Lesson passage.

Teachers use explanations and informal definitions to teach the meaning of each word.

After reading each new word in the context of an informational passage, teachers use the Word Meanings activity to introduce the meaning of each new word. The instruction is particularly well-suited to English Language Learners because teachers use explanations and informal definitions to teach the meaning of each word. Teachers also model using correct grammar and pronunciation during class discussions. Students needing additional practice at this stage of the learning process can access video recordings of peers demonstrating the meaning of each word at ***vocabularyforsuccess.com***.

There are significant opportunities for students to use each word orally before using the word in writing.

The Gradual Release of Responsibility model provides many opportunities during guided practice for students to use new vocabulary orally while collaborating with peers. During guided practice, teachers circulate among groups and can provide additional language support as necessary. By first using the word orally, English Language Learners will have more success using the new vocabulary in their writing.

Abundant practice and opportunities for homework ensure success.

For each Lesson, students are exposed to new vocabulary while completing ten unique and motivating activities. This repetition helps ensure that English Language Learners will have success learning and using the words taught in *Vocabulary for Success, Common Core Enriched Edition*.

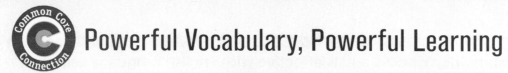

Powerful Vocabulary, Powerful Learning

by Douglas Fisher
Professor of Education, San Diego State University
Teacher Leader, Health Sciences High

and

Nancy Frey
Professor of Education, San Diego State University
Teacher Leader, Health Sciences High

To be sure, there's power in words. And, as educators, it is our prerogative to impart this power to our students. The foundation of successful vocabulary instruction first and foremost requires attending to the selection, context, and grouping of words. To deepen students' understanding of these words, the teacher models his or her thinking about using words in context, students engage in activities in which they use the words with peers, and finally, learners have multiple experiences with the words so these words can become a part of their personal vocabularies. In other words, vocabulary instruction must be intentional in order for it to be effective.

Common Core State Standards Emphasize Vocabulary

The Common Core State Standards emphasize the value of vocabulary and the importance of teaching the right words. In its language: "The vocabulary standards focus on understanding words and phrases, their relationships, and their nuances and on acquiring new vocabulary, particularly general academic and domain-specific words and phrases" (CCSS, p. 8). In fact, there are three specific standards devoted to vocabulary acquisition and use for high school students:

- Determine or clarify the meaning of unknown and multiple-meaning words and phrases by using context clues, analyzing meaningful word parts, and consulting general and specialized reference materials, as appropriate. (L4)

- Demonstrate understanding of figurative language, word relationships, and nuances in word meanings. (L5)

- Acquire and use accurately a range of general academic and domain-specific words and phrases sufficient for reading, writing, speaking, and listening at the college and career readiness level; demonstrate independence in gathering vocabulary knowledge when considering a word or phrase important to comprehension or expression. (L6)

These standards were included because, as confirmed by a cluster of 1980s research studies, vocabulary demand skyrockets as students become immersed in formal discipline-specific study. Arguably the most widely reported figures stem from the seminal research of Nagy and Anderson, who reported that by the time a student entered ninth grade, he or she would encounter 88,500 word *families* in printed school materials (1984). This staggering number would give even the most energetic teacher pause. While 500,000 individual words are too much to contemplate, the operative word—

families—gives us a glimpse of what effective instruction might look like. We'll return to this idea later.

A second cluster of vocabulary research has focused on vocabulary's influence on learning. Most secondary educators are aware of the importance of vocabulary because it serves as a proxy for conceptual knowledge (DelliCarpini, 2012; Espin, Shin, & Busch, 2005). Stated differently, the more familiar you are with the vocabulary of a content area, the more likely it is that you know something about that content. This idea is borne out in the findings of Baker, Simmons, and Kame'enui (1998) who found that vocabulary knowledge was a strong predictor of reading comprehension. By some estimates, vocabulary knowledge accounts for between 70-80% of reading comprehension (Nagy & Scott, 2000). This statistic is a significant factor at the secondary school level, where other expository reading materials increase not only in the frequency of their use, but also become increasingly dense, abstract, and technical (Alexander-Shea, 2011; Shook, Hazelkorn, & Lozano, 2011).

Devoting Time to Word Learning is Time Well-Spent

The third cluster of vocabulary research concerns comprehensive word knowledge, which is layered, and extends well beyond definitional knowledge. It includes knowledge of examples and non-examples, adept use in oral and written communication, and fluent availability and recall of words (e.g., Blachowicz & Fisher, 2000; Cronbach, 1942; Dale, O'Rourke, & Bamman, 1971; Graves, 1986). Because knowledge is multidimensional, teaching those words must be as well. Effective vocabulary instruction requires that words are taught within context, that definitional and contrastive meanings are provided, and that students have multiple, authentic experiences with using words in their spoken and written language (Beck, McKeown, & Kucan, 2002; Blachowicz & Fisher, 2000; Graves, 2006).

Taken together, these three clusters of vocabulary research provide a road map for effective vocabulary instruction. First, adolescents experience a rise in school vocabulary demand. Second, the increased influence of vocabulary directly impacts students' ability to read and converse in the language of the discipline. And third, the complex nature of word knowledge requires an instructional approach that cultivates an increasingly sophisticated understanding of the relationship between words and concepts. An effective vocabulary program offers carefully selected words that are modeled in context by the teacher, associative experiences that emphasize both the definitional and contrastive meanings of words, student interaction with words and one another, and generative experiences that allow students to make it their *own* vocabulary.

INTENTIONAL INSTRUCTION OF WORDS

Selecting Words The practice of constructing lists of words for student study and use has been a dominant feature in vocabulary instruction for more than a century. Among the lists that have influenced the field include the Dolch Word List of sight vocabulary for young readers (1936), the Academic Word List (Coxhead, 2000), the Background Knowledge Word List (Marzano, 2004), and the American Heritage dictionary 100 words every high school graduate should know list (2003). While they vary at the word level, they have one important element in common—they are all derived from what students are expected to understand.

These lists are not to be used in isolation, but rather as contextually bound to a discipline or academic behavior. For example, the AWL is comprised of 570 headwords totaling 3000 individual words from textbooks in 11 different disciplines. The researcher recorded the frequency of words, excluding the first 2000 most common words in English (the General Service List; words such as *the*, *make*, and *together*). The list is composed of high-utility academic words that occur across disciplines, such as *reinterpret*, *analyze*, and *correspond*. While the AWL draws from textbooks as its primary source, the Background Knowledge Word List uses a different set of documents. Twenty-eight national standards documents were analyzed to develop a list of nearly 8000 words for K-12, which tend to be more discipline specific, such as *monarchy* and *radiation*. One strength of this approach is that the selected words represent content-specific knowledge and its inherent conceptual understanding.

While word lists provide an excellent starting point for identifying possible words for direct instruction, their usefulness must be weighed against other factors, including their utility, opportunity for analysis, and overall cognitive capability. Drawing from the collective work of Graves (2006), Nagy and Herman (1987), and Marzano (2004), we have constructed a decision-making model for further refining the list of possibilities (Fisher & Frey, 2008b):

- Is the word representative of an essential idea or concept?
- Will the word be used repeatedly within and across units of instruction?
- Is the word transferable across other disciplines?
- Does the use of the word invite contextual analysis?
- Does the word offer an opportunity for structural analysis?
- Do the selected words honor the learner's cognitive capability?

A third consideration for selecting words is the way in which they can be clustered to ensure that they can serve as doorway words for learning new vocabulary. Given the large number of words that students need to know, and the relatively small number of words that can receive direct instruction, it is essential to choose terms that foster independent word learning. Approximately 80-85% of printed English is comprised of words from the General Service List (those 2000 common words we mentioned earlier). Many of those 15-20% of words in printed English are formed around a common base, root, or affix. These word families are constructed using the building blocks of the language: *dis-* and *-trans-*, *-ance*, and *–norm-*. By clustering and teaching these building blocks, teachers find that students are better able to transfer their knowledge of the language when they encounter unfamiliar words during independent reading (Baumann, Font, Edwards, & Boland, 2005).

Regarding the Common Core State Standards, the focus is on general academic words and domain-specific words. Relying on only one category of words and neglecting the other can compromise learners, as authors use both in the composing process (Wolsey, 2011). In the language of the Common Core State Standards:

- **General academic** words are far more likely to appear in written texts than in speech. They appear in all sorts of texts: informational texts (words such as *relative*, *vary*, *formulate*, *specificity*, and *accumulate*), technical texts (*calibrate*, *itemize*, *periphery*), and literary texts (*misfortune*, *dignified*, *faltered*, *unabashedly*). Tier 2 words often represent subtle or precise ways to say relatively simple things—*saunter* instead of *walk*, for example. Because Tier 2 words are found across many types of texts, they are highly generalizable.

- **Domain-specific** words are specific to a domain or field of study (*lava*, *carburetor*, *legislature*, *circumference*, *aorta*) and key to understanding a new concept within text. Because of their specificity and close ties to content knowledge, Tier 3 words are far more common in informational texts than in literature. Recognized as new and "hard" words for most readers (particularly student readers), they are often explicitly defined by the author of a text, repeatedly used, and otherwise heavily scaffolded (e.g., made a part of a glossary). (Appendix A, p. 33)

In sum, the selection of words for direct instruction involves analysis of research-based word lists that represent both general academic and domain-specific terms. In addition, the final selection of instructional vocabulary should incorporate both the practical utility of the words and their potential for building learners' skills in solving both the targeted vocabulary as well as related words. Once these words are identified, they are taught using a gradual release of responsibility.

Using a Gradual Release of Responsibility in Vocabulary Instruction

Learning theorists have described the importance of supports that gradually fade as the learner becomes more confident, a process referred to as scaffolding (Wood, Bruner, & Ross, 1976). Pearson and Gallagher (1983) applied this concept to reading instruction and called it a gradual release of responsibility. This model includes teacher modeling, guided instruction, productive group work, and independent learning (Fisher & Frey, 2008a). Stahl and Fairbanks (1986) described an initial phase of knowledge, which they termed the associational level, in which students know words superficially, mostly through matching definitions to terms. As they deepen their understanding, students move into the comprehension level, where they can sort and categorize. And at the highest level of word learning, the generative level, they apply what they know about words to new situations, especially using it in their writing (Stahl & Fairbanks, 1986).

Teacher Modeling

Teacher modeling allows students to witness the skilled decision-making used by an expert to make choices about how words are understood, chosen, and used in context. Many adolescents who have a monolithic view of vocabulary do not know that when a skilled reader encounters an unknown word, he or she looks inside the word for structural clues, outside the word for context use, and even further outside at resources such as a glossary (Fisher & Frey, 2008b). They remain unaware that when the word has multiple meanings, all the meanings the reader knows are activated simultaneously in the brain, and that the reader must rapidly sort through those meanings to arrive at the best choice (Swinney, 1979). Therefore, these problem-solving techniques need to be demonstrated to students for them to apply the techniques in their own learning.

The concept development research of Tennyson and Cocchiarella (1986) is helpful in modeling vocabulary, as most of us never witnessed our own teachers using this technique (Fisher, Frey, & Lapp, 2009). Consider how teacher modeling of the vocabulary term *inconclusive* works in a reading about an epidemic:

- *Label and definition:* "I know that *inconclusive* is related to *conclusive* and that the prefix *in-* means 'not or the opposite of,' so I think that that they did not get a conclusion."

- *Context:* "I'm going to reread that sentence. *'The data were inconclusive and thus the researchers had to start again to find out if their hypotheses were correct.'* Yes, I can see the definition right in the sentence."

- *Best example:* "I've heard of *inconclusive* before. I was watching a TV show about crime scenes and the detective said that they could not match the suspect's DNA to the evidence because the blood test was inconclusive."

- *Strategy information:* "When I first read that sentence, *inconclusive* jumped out at me because I don't see it very often. But I reread the sentence, looked for some context clues, and used some structural analysis to find a more familiar word and prefix within it. I also paused to remind myself of a previous experience I've had with the term."

Peer Interaction While modeling establishes the initial thinking processes that one uses when reading, writing, and speaking about vocabulary, students need opportunities to try out these processes for themselves in their everyday language. As Bromley (2007) reminds us in her article about vocabulary instruction, "Language proficiency grows from oral competence to written competence" (p. 529). All students, and especially English language learners, benefit from purposeful use of new vocabulary within the context of meaningful and engaging activities (Fisher, Frey, & Rothenberg, 2008). Peer interaction exists as part of a cohesive instructional design that follows a gradual release of responsibility (Fisher & Frey, 2008a). Students begin to assume some of the cognitive responsibility as they explain, discuss, clarify their understanding, and reflect on their learning. When a student or group is stuck, the teacher uses modeling and direct explanation (Frey, Fisher, & Everlove, 2009).

In order to promote the cognitive processes necessary for learning, many vocabulary researchers have recommended games and other activities that capitalize on a sense of play to increase learning (e.g., Beck, McKeown, & Kucan, 2002; Blachowicz & Fisher, 2002; Graves, 2006). These activities raise word consciousness and naturally encourage repeated and authentic use of the words during the course of the task, thereby reinforcing new learning (Graves, 2006). The most effective peer interaction tasks emphasize comprehension and generative learning, both of which prepare students for the more complex learning that occurs during the independent phase of instruction (Stahl & Fairbanks, 1986).

Moving to Independent Word Learning A Gradual Release of Responsibility model of instruction that provides teacher modeling, guided instruction, and productive group work decreases the likelihood that independent practice will reinforce incorrect understanding (Fisher & Frey, 2008a). However, vocabulary instruction should also deepen conceptual understanding through a process that Stahl and Fairbanks (1986) call the generative level of word knowledge, in which students use targeted vocabulary in more formal original writing. There is also an increased focus on using academic language in conjunction with academic vocabulary. Independent activities include the use of generative sentences to allow students to consider the grammatical and semantic features of the word (Fisher & Frey, 2008a). A generative sentence activity names the word, the position of its occurrence within the sentence, and the condition of the sentence itself. For example:

- Write a sentence of nine words in length using the word *levy*.
- Write a question with the word *prototype* in the sixth position.
- Write a sentence with the word *erode* in the third position.

  Cliffs slowly <u>erode</u> when water removes sand from their bases.

Students can further expand their generative sentences by selecting one for expansion to paragraph length. Generative activities provide students with the opportunity to consolidate their word learning by requiring them to utilize their associational and comprehension levels of knowledge. In turn, the vocabulary more fully becomes a part of their vocabulary as they become more confident using it in their spoken and written language.

Conclusion We can lift words from the page and ensure that vocabulary learning is an interesting part of students' instructional day. We can move beyond the "assign, define, and test" approach to vocabulary instruction and develop systems and resources that really do result in students understanding word meanings. As this comprehension happens, students will use their new-found vocabulary regularly and authentically. When we are intentional with our vocabulary instruction, students learn words that they can use in all aspects of their lives.

References

Alexander-Shea, A. (2011). Redefining vocabulary: The new learning strategy for social studies. *The Social Studies*, 102(3), 95-103.

Baker, S. K., Simmons, D. C., & Kame'enui, E. J. (1998). Vocabulary acquisition: Research bases. In D. C. Simmons & E. J. Kame'enui (Eds.), *What research tells us about children with diverse learning needs* (pp. 183-218). Mahwah, NJ: Lawrence Erlbaum.

Baumann, J. F., Font, G., Edwards, E. C., & Boland, E. (2005). Strategies for teaching middle-grade students to use word-part and context clues to expand reading vocabulary. In E. H. Hiebert & M. L. Kamil (Eds.), *Teaching and learning vocabulary: Bringing research to practice* (pp. 179-205). Mahwah, NJ: Erlbaum.

Beck, I. L., McKeown, M. G., & Kucan, L. (2002). *Bringing words to life: Robust vocabulary instruction*. New York: Guilford.

Blachowicz, C. L. Z., & Fisher, P. (2000). Vocabulary instruction. In M. L. Kamil, P. B. Mosenthal, P. D. Pearson, & R. Barr (Eds.), *Handbook of Reading Research* (Vol. III, pp. 503-523). Mahwah, NJ: Lawrence A. Erlbaum.

Blachowicz, C. L. Z., & Fisher, P. (2002). *Teaching vocabulary in all classrooms* (2nd ed.). Upper Saddle River, NJ: Merrill Prentice Hall.

Bromley, K. (2007). Nine things every teacher should know about words and vocabulary instruction. *Journal of Adolescent and Adult Literacy*, 50(7), 528-537.

Coxhead, A. (2000). A new academic word list. TESOL *Quarterly*, 34(2), 213-238.

Cronbach, L. J. (1942). An analysis of techniques for systematic vocabulary testing. *Journal of Educational Research*, 36, 206-17.

Dale, E., O'Rourke, J., & Bamman, H. A. (1971). *Techniques for teaching vocabulary*. Palo Alto, CA: Field Educational Publications.

DelliCarpini, M. (2012). Success with ELLs. *English Journal*, 101(5), 97-101.

Dolch, E. W. (1936). A basic sight word vocabulary. *Elementary School Journal*, 36, 456-460.

Editors of the American Heritage Dictionary. (2003). *100 words every high school graduate should know*. Boston: Houghton Mifflin Harcourt.

Espin, C. A., Shin, J., & Busch, T. W. (2005). Curriculum-based measurement in the content areas: Vocabulary matching as an indicator of progress in social studies learning. *Learning Disabilities Quarterly*, 38(4), 353-363.

Fisher, D., & Frey, N. (2008a). *Better learning through structured teaching: A framework for the gradual release of responsibility*. Alexandria, VA: Association for Supervision and Curriculum Development.

Fisher, D., & Frey, N. (2008b). *Word wise and content rich: Five essential steps to teaching academic vocabulary*. Portsmouth, NH: Heinemann.

Fisher, D., Frey, N., & Lapp, D. (2009). *In a reading state of mind: Brain research, teacher modeling, and comprehension instruction*. Newark, DE: International Reading Association.

Fisher, D., & Frey, N., & Rothenberg, C., (2008). *Content area conversations: How to plan discussion-based lessons for diverse language learners*. Alexandria, VA: Association for Supervision and Curriculum Development.

Frey, N., Fisher, D., & Everlove, S. (2009). *Productive group work: How to engage students, build teamwork, and promote understanding*. Alexandria, VA: ASCD.

Graves, M. F. (1986). Vocabulary learning and instruction. *Review of Educational Research*, 13, 49-89.

Graves, M. F. (2006). *The vocabulary book: Learning and instruction*. New York: Teachers College.

Marzano, R. J. (2004). *Building background knowledge for academic achievement: Research on what works in schools*. Alexandria, VA: Association of Supervision and Curriculum Development.

Nagy, N. E., & Anderson, R. C. (1984). How many words are there in printed school English? *Reading Research Quarterly*, 19, 303-330.

Nagy, W. E., & Herman, P. A. (1987). Breadth and depth of vocabulary knowledge: Implications for acquisition and instruction. In M. G. McKeown & M. E. Curtis (Eds.), *The nature of vocabulary acquisition* (pp. 19-36). Hillsdale, NJ: Lawrence Erlbaum Associates.

Nagy, N. E., & Scott, J. (2000). Vocabulary processes. In M. L. Kamil, P. B. Mosenthal, P. D. Pearson, & R. Barr (Eds.), *Handbook of reading research* (Vol. III, pp. 269-284). Mahwah, NJ: Lawrence Erlbaum.

Pearson, P. D., & Gallagher, G. (1983). The gradual release of responsibility model of instruction. *Contemporary Educational Psychology*, 8, 112-123.

Shook, A. C., Hazelkorn, M., & Lozano, E. R. (2011). Science vocabulary for all. *Science Teacher*, 78(3), 45-49.

Stahl, S., & Fairbanks, M. (1986). The effects of vocabulary instruction: A model-based meta-analysis. *Review of Educational Research*, 56(1), 72-110.

Swinney, D. A. (1979). Lexical access during sentence comprehension: (Re)considerations of context effects. *Journal of Verbal Learning and Verbal Behavior*, 18, 645-659.

Tennyson, R. D., & Cocchiarella, M. J. (1986). An empirically based instructional design theory for teaching concepts. *Review of Educational Research*, 56, 40-71.

Wolsey, T. D. (2010). Complexity in student writing: The relationship between the task and vocabulary uptake. Literacy Research And Instruction, 49(2), 194-208.

Excerpts from the *Common Core State Standards for English Language Arts* © Copyright 2010, National Governors Association Center for Best Practices and Council of Chief State School Officers. All rights reserved.

Grade 10 Test Booklet Answer Key

Lesson 1
Test Booklet pages 1–2

A.
1. tsunami
2. adjacent
3. entity
4. demographic
5. precipitous
6. series
7. infrastructure
8. buoyancy
9. deduce
10. humanitarian

B.
11. series
12. humanitarian
13. tempestuous
14. decimate
15. infrastructure

C.
16. B   21. B
17. D   22. C
18. A   23. A
19. D   24. A
20. C   25. B

Lesson 2
Test Booklet pages 3–4

A.
1. exodus
2. defuse
3. catalyst
4. diffuse
5. hubris
6. inertia
7. inverse
8. retain
9. poise
10. allocate

B.
11. poise
12. constituency
13. allocate
14. irony
15. inertia

C.
16. B   21. B
17. A   22. D
18. D   23. B
19. D   24. A
20. C   25. C

Lesson 3
Test Booklet pages 5–6

A.
1. uninterested
2. accommodate
3. inspect
4. chorus
5. nominal
6. project
7. subside
8. regime
9. disinterested
10. cardinal

B.
11. subside
12. project
13. Capitol
14. depose
15. cardinal

C.
16. D   21. D
17. C   22. A
18. C   23. B
19. A   24. A
20. C   25. B

Lesson 4
Test Booklet pages 7–8

A.
1. usurp
2. commerce
3. copyright
4. reparation
5. unlicensed
6. winnow
7. levy
8. eminent
9. imminent
10. disposable

B.
11. deregulation
12. levy
13. litigation
14. disposable
15. commerce

C.
16. D   21. A
17. B   22. B
18. D   23. C
19. A   24. A
20. C   25. B

Lesson 5
Test Booklet pages 9–10

A.
1. depressed
2. elicit
3. funder
4. subsidiary
5. illicit
6. payroll
7. specialization
8. fiduciary
9. facilitate
10. anonymous

B.
11. elicit
12. franchise
13. illicit
14. fiduciary
15. institutionalize

C.
16. B   21. B
17. D   22. C
18. A   23. D
19. C   24. C
20. A   25. B

Lesson 6
Test Booklet pages 11–12

A.
1. mode
2. persona
3. counterfeit
4. assign
5. bylaw
6. congregate
7. fraud
8. systemic
9. pose
10. clause

B.
11. pose
12. mode
13. Implementation
14. counterfeit
15. quote

C.
16. C   21. D
17. D   22. D
18. A   23. B
19. A   24. B
20. A   25. C

Lesson 7
Test Booklet pages 13–14

A.
1. articulation
2. belie
3. invert
4. channel
5. avert
6. metamorphosis
7. diversion
8. acuity
9. versatile
10. paradigm

B.
11. biotechnology
12. metamorphosis
13. restoration
14. avert
15. channel

C.
16. D   21. A
17. A   22. C
18. A   23. C
19. B   24. B
20. B   25. B

Lesson 8
Test Booklet pages 15–16

A.
1. locomotion
2. irreversible
3. practitioner
4. preliminary
5. reactivate
6. supplement
7. rigidity
8. rehabilitate
9. refinement
10. regenerative

B.
11. rigidity
12. supplement
13. refinement
14. integral
15. elasticity

C.
16. B   21. C
17. D   22. C
18. B   23. D
19. A   24. D
20. A   25. C

Lesson 9
Test Booklet pages 17–18

A.
1. deleterious
2. incontrovertible
3. screen
4. discreet
5. traumatic
6. neuron
7. stimulation
8. simulation
9. cerebral
10. chemical

B.
11. cerebral
12. discreet
13. illustrative
14. deconstruct
15. screen

C.
16. D   21. B
17. B   22. A
18. B   23. D
19. C   24. B
20. A   25. A

Grade 10 Test Booklet Answer Key

Lesson 10
Test Booklet pages 19–20

A.
1. refuge
2. friction
3. hence
4. liberate
5. cower
6. wretched
7. psyche
8. ethical
9. commemorate
10. refugee

B.
11. exhibit
12. psychological
13. friction
14. hence
15. exhibit

C.
16. D
17. A
18. C
19. D
20. A
21. B
22. C
23. B
24. C
25. C

Lesson 11
Test Booklet pages 21–22

A.
1. inaccuracy
2. ideology
3. ethnicity
4. vacillate
5. significant
6. acculturate
7. nuance
8. assimilate
9. homogeneous
10. symbiotic

B.
11. significant
12. assimilate
13. symbiotic
14. quandary
15. overgeneralization

C.
16. A
17. A
18. C
19. D
20. B
21. B
22. A
23. D
24. A
25. C

Lesson 12
Test Booklet pages 23–24

A.
1. enfranchise
2. motivate
3. concurrent
4. acumen
5. self–evident
6. acknowledge
7. subordinate
8. threshold
9. perimeter
10. parameter

B.
11. threshold
12. vehement
13. subordinate
14. append
15. parameter

C.
16. B
17. D
18. A
19. C
20. A
21. C
22. D
23. B
24. C
25. A

Mid-Year Test: Test Booklet pages 25–26

A.
1. fraud
2. concurrent
3. quandary
4. imminent
5. diffuse
6. adjacent
7. retain
8. subside
9. refinement
10. avert

B.
11. eminent
12. anonymous
13. liberate
14. simulation
15. motivate

C.
16. C
17. A
18. B
19. D
20. B
21. D
22. C
23. B
24. A
25. C

Lesson 13
Test Booklet pages 27–28

A.
1. portal
2. forthcoming
3. protagonist
4. solely
5. prototype
6. protein
7. aquatic
8. protozoan
9. postulate
10. eclectic

B.
11. Whereby
12. Migratory
13. protagonist
14. postulate
15. protein

C.
16. B
17. A
18. A
19. C
20. B
21. B
22. C
23. D
24. D
25. A

Lesson 14
Test Booklet pages 29–30

A.
1. inquisitive
2. coherent
3. optical
4. requisition
5. exquisite
6. acquisitive
7. pantomime
8. unparalleled
9. vast
10. visualization

B.
11. automate
12. pantomime
13. prerequisite
14. visualization
15. requisition

C.
16. B
17. D
18. C
19. B
20. A
21. D
22. B
23. D
24. A
25. A

Lesson 15
Test Booklet pages 31–32

A.
1. virtual
2. infinitesimal
3. ensure
4. lexicon
5. permutation
6. finite
7. nanotechnology
8. affinity
9. cyclical
10. auspicious

B.
11. virtual
12. insure
13. cyclical
14. ensure
15. revelation

C.
16. D
17. C
18. A
19. C
20. A
21. C
22. A
23. B
24. D
25. B

Grade 10 Test Booklet Answer Key

Lesson 16
Test Booklet pages 33–34

A.
1. rhetoric
2. revolutionize
3. introspection
4. arbitrarily
5. wrought
6. allusion
7. vigilante
8. diffident
9. ironic
10. status quo

B.
11. subculture
12. allusion
13. geopolitical
14. rhetoric
15. ironic

C.
16. B
17. D
18. A
19. A
20. C
21. C
22. D
23. B
24. C
25. D

Lesson 17
Test Booklet pages 35–36

A.
1. erode
2. verify
3. incidentally
4. so–called
5. albeit
6. confine
7. metaphor
8. analogous
9. impertinent
10. anecdotal

B.
11. Satire
12. confine
13. Incidentally
14. so–called
15. conversely

C.
16. B
17. A
18. C
19. D
20. A
21. C
22. D
23. D
24. B
25. B

Lesson 18
Test Booklet pages 37–38

A.
1. exemplary
2. incognito
3. paragon
4. platform
5. affect
6. effect
7. hyperbole
8. ceaseless
9. jaunty
10. inflammatory

B.
11. containment
12. simulate
13. platform
14. effect
15. affect

C.
16. B
17. A
18. D
19. D
20. B
21. C
22. A
23. B
24. D
25. C

Lesson 19
Test Booklet pages 39–40

A.
1. federation
2. proscribe
3. panel
4. deciduous
5. biochemistry
6. thereby
7. imposition
8. inhibit
9. ambience
10. pathogen

B.
11. panel
12. prescribe
13. organic
14. thereby
15. imposition

C.
16. C
17. D
18. A
19. B
20. D
21. B
22. A
23. C
24. D
25. C

Lesson 20
Test Booklet pages 41–42

A.
1. version
2. cosmetic
3. incidence
4. ambiguous
5. assurance
6. extract
7. epiphany
8. negate
9. castigate
10. seemingly

B.
11. cosmetic
12. assurance
13. coagulate
14. agitate
15. extract

C.
16. C
17. B
18. D
19. A
20. B
21. A
22. A
23. D
24. B
25. A

Lesson 21
Test Booklet pages 43–44

A.
1. averse
2. adverse
3. methodology
4. facetious
5. neutralize
6. revision
7. toxin
8. excessive
9. empiricism
10. exult

B.
11. whereas
12. averse
13. Whereas
14. adverse
15. Revision

C.
16. C
17. B
18. A
19. D
20. D
21. A
22. B
23. B
24. A
25. C

Final Mastery Test: Test Booklet pages 45–48

Part 1

A.
1. rigidity
2. significant
3. counterfeit
4. accommodate
5. metamorphosis
6. discreet
7. usurp
8. disinterested
9. elicit
10. exhibit

B.
11. Inertia
12. congregate
13. homogeneous
14. tempestuous
15. refuge

C.
16. A
17. B
18. B
19. C
20. D
21. B
22. C
23. A
24. D
25. C

Part 2

A.
1. excessive
2. impertinent
3. diffident
4. affect
5. paragon
6. eclectic
7. acknowledge
8. ambiguous
9. inquisitive
10. castigate

B.
11. auspicious
12. inhibit
13. motivate
14. neutralize
15. unparalleled

C.
16. B
17. C
18. C
19. A
20. A
21. B
22. C
23. A
24. B
25. D

Grade 10

Common Core Enriched Edition

Douglas Fisher, Ph.D.
Professor of Education
San Diego State University
San Diego, CA

Nancy Frey, Ph.D.
Professor of Education
San Diego State University
San Diego, CA

PROGRAM CONSULTANTS

Ernest Morrell, Ph.D.
Professor of English Education
Teachers College, Columbia University
New York, NY

Ann Marie Ginsberg, Ed.D.
Director of the Office of Field Placement
School of Education,
Hofstra University
Hempstead, NY

Rosalie M. Quiñones, M.A. Edu. Lead
ESOL/ELL Consultant
Assistant Principal, Language Arts & Reading
Colonial High School
Orlando, FL

MaryBeth Webeler, Ph.D.
English Language Arts Consultant
Assistant Superintendent for
Curriculum & Instruction
Downers Grove Grade School District 58
Downers Grove, IL

Advisers

The publisher wishes to thank the following teachers and administrators, who read portions of the series prior to publication, for their comments and suggestions.

Laura Brumley
English Teacher
Dolores Huerta
  Preparatory High
Pueblo, CO

Sharon Fischer
English Teacher
John Adams High School
Ozone Park, NY

A. Xan Kahn
Literacy Coach
Orange County
Orlando, FL

Sarah McKenna
Independent Contractor
Del Valle ISD
Del Valle, TX

Sarah Brown Wessling
English Teacher
Johnston High School
Johnston, IA

Alison Callaghan
English Teacher
Proviso West
Hillside, IL

John Goodwin
Senior English Teacher
Health Sciences High
San Diego, CA

Rushie McLeod
English Teacher
Friendship Academy
  of Sci/Tech
Baltimore, MD

Ivana Orloff
English Teacher
Whittier High School
Whittier, CA

Photo Credits:
Cover: age fotostock/Richard Dirscherl: *top left*. Alamy/Brandon Cole Marine Photography: *bottom right*. Dreamstime/Golli: *background*. gtphoto/Hall: *center*.
Interior: Alamy/Paul Abbitt: 75; Blend Images LLC: 69 *bottom*; Caro: 12 *top right*; Simon Cook: 221 *bottom*; Corbis Premium RF: 92, 232; GlowImages: 129; Golden Pixels LLC: 37 *bottom left*; Jeff Greenberg: 58, 114 *bottom left*, iv *bottom left*; hacohob: 167; imagebroker: 141, 177 *bottom*; itanistock: 103 *inset*; Johner Images: 164; Sebastian Kaulitzki: 230–31 *background*, vi *background*; Keystone Pictures USA: 242; Lyroky: 115 *bottom right*; Ilene MacDonald: 56, 212; MARKA: 197 *right*; MedicalRF.com: 91 *left*; moodboard: 154; Myrleen Pearson: 230; Chuck Pefly: 24; PhotoStockFile: 95; Radius Images: 222, 225; RIA Novosti: 215; Jeff Rotman: 143; Science Photo Library: 69 *background*, 71 *background*, 162 *bottom*, 163 *bottom*, 163 *top center*, iv *background*; Ian Shaw: 36; Stocktrek Images, Inc.: 13 *bottom*, iii *bottom right*; Tetra Images: 17; Tommy E Trenchard: 23 *top right*; Michael Ventura: 114–15; Jim West: 116; Claudia Wiens: 187; ZUMA Press, Inc.: 186 *left*; ZUMA Wire Service: 186–87 *background*. AP Photo/Gemunu Amarasinghe: 3 *background*; Frank C. Curtin: 186 *right*; Andrew England: 104; PRNewsFoto/Texas Back Institute: 81 *right*; Markus Schreiber: 176. Clemson University: 90. Corbis/National Photo Company: 126; Wendy Stone: 105; Xinhua Press/Han Chuanhao: 80 *left*. Dreamstime/Rdantoni: 41; Rjmiz: 68. Getty Images/AFP/Arash Khamooshi: 197 *left*; AFP/Behrouz Mehri: 196; AFP/Paul J. Richards: 14; Blend Images/Dave & Les Jacobs: 106; CSA Images/Mod Art Collection: 174 hand; DigitalGlobe: 2 *left*, 2 *left*; Frederic Dupoux: 23 *background*; Dante Fenolio: 142, v *bottom left*; Gamma-Rapho/Patrick Piel: 177 *top*, v *bottom right*; Chris Hondros: 125; Kidstock: 57 *bottom*; John Lund: 103 *background*; PhotoStock-Israel: 72; Brandi Simons: 80 *right*; The Christian Science Monitor/Mary Knox Merrill: 22; Alex Turton: 82. iStockphoto/Daniel Bendjy: 124; Özgür Donmaz: 136; Daniel Laflor: 61; Klaas Lingbeek-van Kranen: 208; Jacom Stephens: 198; YangYin: 27; Anna Zielinska: 47 *bottom right*, iii *bottom left*. NASA/JPL-Caltech: 152 *top left*; Cornell: 153 *top*; Cornell/ASU: 153 *bottom*, v *background*. National Geographic Stock/Emory Kristof: 143 *top left*. Photo Researchers/Philippe Psaila: 81 *left*. Phototake/ISM: 91 *right*. Shutterstock/almondd: 51; Baloncici: 211; Bananaboy: 178; Blend Images: 103 *inset*; Stephen Bonk: 188; Booka: 175 *background*; Cardaf: 114 *bottom left*; chaoss: 152; CLIPAREA/Custom media: 91 *background*, iv *bottom left*; cobalt88: 46; Andrea Crisante: 46 *center*; DESmith Photography: 201; Dinga: 175; East: 48; Stasys Eidiejus: 3; Johan W. Elzenga: 109; EpicStockMedia: 1 *left*; Felixdesign: 70; Iakov Filimonov: 90; Juan Gaertner: 102; Gelpi: 115 *background*; Givaga: 209; Natalie Glado: 147 *top left*; Warren Goldswain: 85; graja: 47 *bottom right*; James Horning: 144 *top left*; Eric Isselée: 191; Michal Kowalski: 211 *right*, vi *bottom right*; kuleczka: 209; Andrey Kuzmin: 105; LanKS: 35 *background*, 35; _Lonely_: 209 *background*; Travis Manley: 210; Joze Maucec: 142 *inset*; mearicon: 220–21 *background*; motorolka: 209; Jun Mu: 181; Nadin_1604: 220–21; newphotoservice: 220 *inset*; M. Niebuhr: 117; R. Peterkin: 4; Mike Phillips: 38; photogl: 235; Picsfive: 22–23, 114–15, 177; Pixel Embargo: 175 *center*; Alexander Raths: 231, vi *bottom left*; rodho: 37 *background*; Andrei Rybachuk: 221 *top*; Antonio S.: 34; Klaus Sailer: 47 *background*; R. Gino Santa Maria: 209; Silver Tiger: 80–81 *background*; Jo Ann Snover: 209; TerraceStudio: 124; Tim Roberts Photography: 7; urfin: 35 *top*, 57 *background*; violetkaipa: 35 *bottom*; Marilyn Volan: 125 *inset*; Wildstyle: 37 *bottom left*; Feng Yu: 12–13 *background*; Yurchyks: 143 *top left*; Zoom Team: 157. Wikimedia Commons/Ayacop: 71 *bottom*.

For additional online resources, go to vocabularyforsuccess.com and enter the Student Access Code VFS13SGEPYNB

Table of Contents

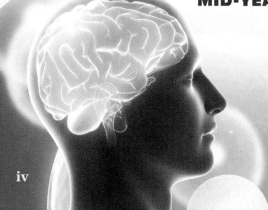

UNIT 7

The Chemistry of 21st Century Adolescence

Dear Students:

We're excited about the school year ahead, and we hope you are, too. You've got a new vocabulary book in your hands right now, and we hope you'll take a few minutes to thumb through it as you read this letter. You'll see that *Vocabulary for Success, Common Core Enriched Edition* is different from other vocabulary books you may have seen or used in the past.

The first thing that might catch your eye is the Lesson titles. Each of these topics has been selected to appeal to your interest in the social, physical, and biological worlds around you. The words you will study in *Vocabulary for Success, Common Core Enriched Edition* are related to these topics. The words will help you better understand what you read in school, and out of school, too. They will also help you better express yourself as a writer and as a speaker.

You may also notice that there are quite a few activities in this program that you can do with your classmates. One of the things educators have found is that learning can occur through games and activities.

We're also proud of the video and audio resources that are available with the program. Learning new words isn't just about someone telling you what they are; you need to experience them in many different ways. Each lesson in *Vocabulary for Success, Common Core Enriched Edition* is accompanied by a short video introduction to the words—so you can see and hear them in action. You can also listen to the words being pronounced and used in sentences. Maybe you'll be inspired to make your own vocabulary videos and podcasts!

One last thing: we organized the word lists so that you can learn words independently, too. No vocabulary program could teach you all the words you'll need to know, and that's really not how people learn most vocabulary, anyway. This program is designed to help you become a better independent word learner. People learn new vocabulary in a variety of ways. At times, figuring out an unknown word by figuring out the parts you do know is a great strategy. At other times, the clues around the unknown word can tip you off to the meaning. And don't forget resources such as dictionaries.

Whether you aspire to be an engineer, scientist, artist, musician, educator, or athlete, your ability to express your ideas is the key to your success. That's where the title came from—*Vocabulary for Success, Common Core Enriched Edition.*

Douglas Fisher and Nancy Frey

Pronunciation Key

The pronunciation is indicated for every basic word introduced in this book. Single letters or combinations of letters, as listed below, are used to represent sounds and are similar to those appearing in many dictionaries that use student-friendly pronunciations.

Of course, there are many English words for which two or more pronunciations are commonly accepted. For all such words in this book, the authors have sought to make things easier for students by giving just one pronunciation. The only significant exception occurs when the pronunciation changes with a shift in the part of speech. Thus we would show that *appropriate* in the adjective form is pronounced *uh-PROH-pree-uht*, and the verb form, *uh-PROH-pree-ayt*. Note that the major stressed syllable is represented by capital letters.

Vowels

a	hat, chance	**ee**	feet, beat	**oo**	room, rule
ah	father	**i**	sit	**or**	torn, pore
air	hair, dare	**ihr**	gear, mere	**oy**	boy, soil
ar	park	**eye**	island, tile, bye, pie, fly	**ou**	pouch, cow
ay	say, main, fade, cape	**o**	pot	**u**	put, look
aw	saw, fraught, cough	**oh**	doe, though, bone, roam	**uh**	cut, about, lotion
e	ten			**ur**	urge, heard, corner
				yoo	cue, muse, fuel

Consonants

b	bore, crib	**m**	mine, ram	**t**	tin, fit
ch	chore, hitch, which	**n**	not, thin, knife, gnome	**th**	thick, faith
d	deal, had	**ng**	thing	**th**	than, rather, clothe
f	feed, off, enough	**p**	pit, trap	**v**	vine, rave, of
g	give, rag	**r**	race	**w**	wise, wharf
h	her	**s**	sing, cellar	**y**	yam
j	jelly, bridge, giant	**ss**	mass, face, gas	**z**	zoo, is, choose
k	kid, trick, card	**sh**	shape, fish	**zh**	pleasure
l	line, fill				

Stress

The syllable receiving the major stress is capitalized:
FOH-kuhss, kon-sti-TOO-shuhn

Abbreviations

adj. adjective   *adv.* adverb   *n.* noun   *v.* verb

ONLINE COMPONENTS
vocabularyforsuccess.com

Note: A spoken pronunciation of each key word is also available at **vocabularyforsuccess.com**. The **Online Audio and Video Program** permits you to hear not only the pronunciation of each word but also its definition and an example of its usage in a sentence. You also can watch a video introduction of each word. With iWords you can listen to one word at a time or download all of the words of a Unit, and listen to the audio program at your convenience.

The Science of 21st Century Disasters

Watch a video introduction to this passage at **vocabularyforsuccess.com**.

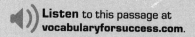 **Listen** to this passage at **vocabularyforsuccess.com**.

C CCSS Vocabulary: 4; Reading (Informational Text): 4, 6. (See pp. T16–17.)

The Indian Ocean Tsunami of 2004

<transcript>

December 26, 2004
INTRO MUSIC: (15 seconds)

COMMENTATOR: Indonesia and the Indian Ocean region are reeling this morning from the shock of a massive tsunami. Generated by what appears to have been a 9.0 earthquake centered near the island of Sumatra, this series of giant waves destroyed entire coastal communities. It then swept inland to decimate towns and villages as much as a mile or more from the sea.

Early reports suggest that the number of missing may top 50,000. From initial reports we can deduce that the scale of destruction we are seeing now may well be unprecedented. And the cost in human life and damage to infrastructure will surely mount as waves continue to pound shoreline communities throughout the region. For a deeper understanding of how this came about, let's go to our science adviser.

SCIENCE ADVISER: From the sheer power of this quake, we can deduce that what we witnessed this morning was the catastrophic release of forces deep beneath Earth's crust. As the ocean floor shifted, the shock sent waves racing across the Indian Ocean at the speed of a jet airliner.

COMMENTATOR: This just in. Indonesian authorities report the human toll of the Indonesian tsunami now tops 80,000 missing or known dead, as humanitarian aid is rushed to the region. At this point it seems that the United States Navy may be the only entity in the area equipped to provide immediate aid. Eleven countries are now reporting catastrophic losses. That number is expected to rise as the waves continue to ripple across the Pacific. Countries immediately adjacent to the earthquake's epicenter have thus far been the hardest hit. However, waves with forty-foot crests—so precipitous they would dwarf an office building— continue to pummel the region's shorelines. Reports now indicate the death toll from the Indonesian tsunami is likely to reach more than 100,000. Let's go to our correspondent on the ground in the coastal town of Banda Aceh, Indonesia. Adam, can you give us a closer look at the situation there?

CORRESPONDENT: Sam, I'm not in Banda Aceh. In fact at the moment I don't know where

A transcript is a written version of what speakers say during a television program. This transcript is what was said during a news program.

I am. I'm with a stream of refugees still headed inland, as reports of aftershocks have spooked thousands of already shaken people into what amounts to pure panic. The demographic I'm seeing here is largely poor—coastal fishing people now without homes or livelihoods. The tempestuous scene behind me is a grim reflection of the horror these people are fleeing. Many of those I've spoken to survived only by clinging to driftwood or floating cars, anything with enough buoyancy to carry them along with the flood surge—depositing some people as far as several miles inland.

COMMENTATOR: Thank you, Adam. The reports we are now getting indicate the estimated number of missing and known dead has risen to 150,000. Such a number would make this quite possibly the deadliest tsunami in history.

VOCABULARY

tsunami	infrastructure	precipitous
series	humanitarian	demographic
decimate	entity	tempestuous
deduce	adjacent	buoyancy

TALK ABOUT IT

With a partner, answer the questions below. Use as many of the highlighted words in the selection as you can.

1. **What difficulties might a news commentator face in reporting on a disaster like the 2004 *tsunami*?**

2. **What do you think was the worst damage to *infrastructure* that Indonesia and its *adjacent* countries faced in the aftermath of this disaster?**

India

Indonesia

Above: Map showing the earthquake's epicenter

Background: Massive waves crashing into villages along the Sri Lankan coastline

Word Meanings

For each highlighted word on pages 2–3, the meaning or meanings are given below.

For practice with synonyms, see page 32.

1. **adjacent** (uh-JAY-suhnt) **adj** nearby; sharing a border or wall. One building that is *adjacent* to another is right next to it. **SYNONYMS:** neighboring, against

2. **buoyancy** (BOI-uhn-see) **n** the ability to float. *Buoyancy* is critical for boats and ships. **SYNONYMS:** floatability, lightness, airiness

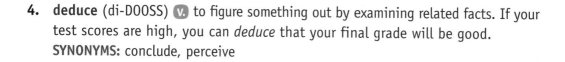

3. **decimate** (DESS-uh-mate) **v** to utterly destroy; vanquish completely. The original, Roman meaning of *decimate* was to kill one in ten soldiers to encourage the rest to surrender. **SYNONYMS:** demolish, crush

4. **deduce** (di-DOOSS) **v** to figure something out by examining related facts. If your test scores are high, you can *deduce* that your final grade will be good. **SYNONYMS:** conclude, perceive

5. **demographic** (de-moh-GRA-fik) **n** the makeup or composition of a group of people, based on a shared feature. The *demographic* of a country club is usually a wealthy one. **SYNONYMS:** composition, description

6. **entity** (EN-tuh-tee) **n** something that exists by itself and is separate from other things. The United Nations is an international *entity* that deals with disasters and other issues that cross national borders. **SYNONYMS:** thing, creature, body, organization, legal authority

7. **humanitarian** (hyoo-man-uh-TER-ee-uhn) **adj** having to do with helping people and relieving suffering. Organizing *humanitarian* aid is an urgent task after a large disaster. **SYNONYMS:** helpful, charitable; **n** someone who works to make other people's lives better. Alice, a volunteer for the Red Cross, is a dedicated *humanitarian* who helps people in need. **SYNONYMS:** philanthropist, benefactor

8. **infrastructure** (IN-fruh-struhk-chur) **n** buildings or structures such as roads and bridges that are a routine part of daily life. Every few decades we must replace our *infrastructure* to prevent the collapse of roads and bridges. **SYNONYMS:** architecture, transportation systems

▶ **Watch** a video introduction for each word at **vocabularyforsuccess.com**.

🔊 **Listen** to iWords🎵 at **vocabularyforsuccess.com**.

📖 **Refer** to the online dictionary at **vocabularyforsuccess.com**.

9. **precipitous** (pri-SIP-uh-tuhs) **adj.** high and steep. A cliff above the ocean is *precipitous* if the drop down is nearly straight. **SYNONYMS:** sheer, dizzying; **adj.** hasty, sudden. The young actor's sudden rise to fame was *precipitous*. **SYNONYMS:** quick, rash, ill-considered

10. **series** (SIHR-eez) **n.** things that happen or are present one after another, in order. The tsunami created a *series* of killer waves. **SYNONYMS:** chain of events, cycle; **n.** a set of television shows that is shown every week and features the same characters. The fall television *series* begins in September. **SYNONYM:** installments

11. **tempestuous** (tem-PEST-oo-uhss) **adj.** wild and unpredictable. Natural disasters often feature *tempestuous*, unpredictable weather. **SYNONYMS:** violent, roaring, raging, fierce, intense, turbulent, stormy, impassioned, loud, noisy, boisterous

12. **tsunami** (tsoo-NAH-mee) **n.** a giant wave caused by an underwater earthquake or volcano. If a *tsunami* reaches land, it can cause mass destruction to a region. **SYNONYMS:** tidal wave, killer wave

More on Meanings: Denotation and Connotation

A dictionary definition tells you a word's specific, literal meaning—its *denotation*. Many words also have a meaning that is suggested or implied, the word's *connotation*.

Words may have positive or negative connotations. Compare these sentences:

The two contestants had an **unpredictable** relationship.

The two contestants had a **tempestuous** relationship.

Unpredictable connotes something changeable. *Tempestuous* has stronger and more negative connotations, suggesting something wild, stormy, or out-of-control.

Now consider this pair of sentences:

Balanced on the cliff edge, Elton faced a **steep** drop into the valley below.

Balanced on the cliff edge, Elton faced a **precipitous** drop into the valley below.

Steep is a mild word, suggesting a sharp grade but not necessarily a straight drop. *Precipitous* has a much stronger, almost dangerous connotation—a cliff face impossible to scale.

Challenge Choose two of the words below. For each, suggest two synonyms, one with a positive connotation, one with a negative connotation. Then use each synonym in a sentence that demonstrates the feeling associated with it.

curious	*weak*	*cool*
sweet	*verbal*	*proud*

Have students brainstorm synonyms and discuss the connotations of each.

 CCSS Vocabulary: 5.b. (See pp. T16–17.)

vocabularyforsuccess.com 5

Word Talk

Each lesson word has been placed in a category. With a partner, discuss and list items that belong in each category. Compare your results with those of another pair of students.
C CCSS Vocabulary: 6. (See pp. T16–17.)

Events That Call for *Humanitarian* Aid

wars, tornados, hurricanes, tsunamis, epidemics, earthquakes

Examples of Different Types of Population *Demographics*

ethnic origin, race, age, sex, income level, education level

Reasons a Warning System for a *Tsunami* Might Pay for Itself

lives saved, property saved, total disaster avoided

Objects with a *Precipitous* Slope

mountains, cliffs, roller coasters, ski slopes

Things That May Happen in a *Series*

events, TV shows, comic books, meetings

Things That Have *Buoyancy*

swim floats, kickboards, life jackets, boats, ships, canoes, kayaks, corks

How You Can *Deduce* What the Weather Will Be Like

temperature, clouds, wind

Examples of an *Entity*

school, athletic team, club, organization

Examples of Things That Are *Tempestuous*

wild crowd at a concert, fans at a soccer match, ocean during a storm

Things That Might *Decimate* a City

earthquake, volcano, fire, bomb

Things That Are *Adjacent* to a Street

sidewalk, buildings, offices, houses, schools, post offices, restaurants

Examples of *Infrastructure* You Use on a Daily Basis

streets, roads, sidewalks, water pipes, sewer pipes, telephone poles, electric poles, gas lines

Check for Understanding

Choose the lesson word that completes each sentence. Write the word on the line provided. Some words will be used twice.

adjacent	deduce	humanitarian	series
buoyancy	demographic	infrastructure	tempestuous
decimate	entity	precipitous	tsunami

1. The fancy shopping center's customers had a wealthy ___demographic___.

2. Early life vests were made of cork and other light materials to ensure ___buoyancy___.

3. I gave my sister a whole ___series___ of excuses, each more far-fetched than the last.

4. ___Infrastructure___ is vital for getting massive numbers of people where they need to go.

5. A wildly contagious disease could easily ___decimate___ the closely packed population of a city.

6. Some coastal towns in Japan have erected high walls against the threat of a/an ___tsunami___.

7. The slope was far too ___precipitous___ to descend without a rope.

8. ___Adjacent___ offices often share expenses for things they both order regularly.

9. The political rally began with a subdued tone but grew to be loud and ___tempestuous___.

10. In our state more than one ___entity___ is responsible for managing the parks.

11. I can ___deduce___ from your red-rimmed eyes that you were up very late studying last night.

12. The volcano's eruption displaced so many people, they required ___humanitarian___ aid.

13. The shattered sailboat was kept afloat by the ___buoyancy___ of its fuel tanks.

14. To properly tax a population, you first need an accurate ___demographic___ for income and property ownership.

If students choose *infrastructure* for Item 10, remind them that *infrastructure* refers to buildings and structures, whereas *entity* can include people who are part of a group.

Word Associations

Use what you know about the lesson word in italics to answer each question. Circle the letter next to the phrase that best answers the question. Be prepared to explain your answers.

1. Faced with a *precipitous* rock face, what might a climber most need?

   a. detailed maps
   b. a rope and harness
   c. a weatherproof tent

2. Which of these would most likely be *tempestuous*?

   a. a commuter train
   b. weather
   c. party clothes

3. Which of these would best describe a population's *demographic*?

   a. They are between 40 and 60 years old.
   b. They may participate in elections.
   c. They have a king as ruler.

4. What sort of *entity* might be useful in helping out in a global disaster?

   a. a fire department
   b. an international relief agency
   c. a government bureau

5. What do things that happen in a *series* have in common?

   a. They cannot be undone.
   b. They do not conflict with one another.
   c. They occur in a given order.

6. If two homes are directly *adjacent* to each other, where are they most likely located?

   a. a city
   b. the countryside
   c. a village

7. What does any given *tsunami* have in common with all the rest?

   a. It is the worst disaster in history.
   b. It is caused by an undersea earthquake.
   c. It occurs in distant regions.

8. What sort of *infrastructure* allows you to travel great distances by car?

   a. a street
   b. a bridge
   c. a highway

9. How does a detective *deduce* who committed a crime?

   a. by watching a movie
   b. by gathering clues at the scene
   c. by trusting a gut feeling that won't go away

10. Which of these would be considered *humanitarian* aid for victims of a disaster?

    a. fast vehicles
    b. food and shelter
    c. guns and ammunition

11. When might it be vital to find something with *buoyancy*?

    a. on a sinking ship
    b. while playing tennis
    c. during a critical battle

12. Which of these would be most likely to *decimate* an economy?

    a. a strong leader
    b. increased banking fees
    c. high unemployment

C CCSS Vocabulary: 4.a. (See pp. T16–17.)

Check Again

Use what you know about the lesson word in italics to complete each sentence. Be sure your sentences make sense.

1. Moving from one apartment into an *adjacent* one might be easy because _____ they are so close. _____

2. You can often *deduce* people's feeling about what you have just said by _____ looking at their expression. _____

3. A sailor relies on *buoyancy* to _____ keep a boat afloat on the water. _____

4. The Girl Scouts is an *entity* that _____ is separate from other groups. _____

5. When you watch a *series* of games, you watch _____ several in a row. _____

6. It is often said of musical geniuses that they are *tempestuous* rather than _____ mild-mannered. _____

7. The state of our *infrastructure* affects everyone because _____ we all use it daily. _____

8. A *precipitous* drop in sales would be bad for a record company because _____ it would lose profits. _____

9. The underwater volcano caused a *tsunami* that _____ sent a series of violent waves onshore. _____

10. A rock star running for president might appeal to a *demographic* that _____ is young. _____

11. A person would be considered a *humanitarian* if he or she _____ helps serve food at a soup kitchen. _____

12. Wildfire can *decimate* an entire forest if it is not _____ put out. _____

Write Your Own

Reread the transcript on pages 2–3. Then, on a separate sheet of paper, write a one-paragraph response to the question, "How might government and other entities be better prepared for disasters such as the 2004 tsunami?" Use at least two words from the lesson word list and support your answer by referring to the text of the passage.

Word-Solving Strategies:
Context Clues

Punctuation

Punctuation can signal a clue to the meaning of an unknown word. Reread this sentence from "The Indian Ocean Tsunami of 2004":

> The demographic I'm seeing here is largely poor—coastal fishing people now without homes or livelihoods.

The dash signals that words that shed light on the meaning of *demographic* will follow. Commas, quotation marks, italics, and parentheses can also be used as signals. Here's an example:

> Since she hadn't slept well for a while, she suffered from *narcolepsy*. (She fell asleep at inappropriate times throughout the day.) Her job performance suffered as a result.

BE CAREFUL!

Sometimes an unknown word may be illuminated by the words that come before it—as here:

> *However, waves with forty-foot crests—so precipitous they would dwarf an office building—continue to pummel the region's shorelines.*

Precipitous is clear when you scan back to the words before the dash. Remember that it helps to look both ways—forward and back—for help.

Practice

Write a highlighted word and the punctuation that helps define it in the first two boxes. Then write the meaning of the word in the third box.

The flood came out of nowhere. The devastation was immediately obvious—our barn was washed away, and our truck was upside-down. We started scouring the area, searching quickly, making sure no one was missing. Everyone was accounted for, but the havoc was terrible, chickens and cows running everywhere. The stark terror in their eyes (wide and pleading, horrified) was awful to see.

WORD	PUNCTUATION	WORD MEANING
devastation	dash	damage and destruction
scouring	comma	looking everywhere
havoc	comma	wild confusion
stark	parentheses	very obvious, easily seen

CCSS Vocabulary: 4.a.; Reading (Informational Text): 4. (See pp. T16–17.)

Practice for Tests

For a quiz and additional practice for this lesson, go to vocabularyforsuccess.com.

Fill in the bubble next to the answer that best completes the sentence or answers the question.

1. In order to *deduce* anything, you need:
   - ○ **A** authority
   - ● **B** clues
   - ○ **C** witness statements
   - ○ **D** fingerprints

2. To be considered a *humanitarian,* you must:
   - ○ **A** be brave in the face of danger
   - ○ **B** work for an aid agency
   - ○ **C** organize resources
   - ● **D** help people in need

3. A collapsing *infrastructure* hurts business because:
   - ○ **A** people spend money closer to home
   - ● **B** products are harder to transport to markets
   - ○ **C** repairing broken bridges costs more than replacing them
   - ○ **D** shipping by sea is expensive

4. Which of these is a *precipitous* act?
   - ○ **A** buying a bicycle from a friend
   - ● **B** shaving off your hair on a dare
   - ○ **C** hiking in a national park
   - ○ **D** looking out the window of an airplane

5. Read this sentence.
   > Staring angrily, Aki sneered and shook her fist in that *tempestuous* way of hers.

   Tempestuous means:
   - ● **A** passionate
   - ○ **B** gale-force
   - ○ **C** sweaty
   - ○ **D** stubborn

6. When several things happen quickly in a *series* with disastrous results, it is sometimes known as a:
   - ○ **A** joyous celebration
   - ○ **B** championship game
   - ○ **C** broken promise
   - ● **D** cascade effect

7. Read this sentence.
   > We finally managed to *decimate* the team that kept us from the championship.

   Decimate means:
   - ● **A** soundly defeat
   - ○ **B** get revenge upon
   - ○ **C** strike fear into
   - ○ **D** pull equal with

8. For anything to have *buoyancy,* it must have:
   - ○ **A** wood
   - ● **B** air
   - ○ **C** rubber
   - ○ **D** heat

9. Which of these would NOT be considered an *entity*?
   - ○ **A** a state agency
   - ○ **B** a nongovernmental organization
   - ○ **C** an alien life form
   - ● **D** a group of friends

10. The word *tsunami* is often used to describe:
    - ○ **A** international events
    - ○ **B** a world war
    - ● **C** a set of huge waves
    - ○ **D** surprising behavior

If students choose D for Item 5, have them look at the base word *tempest*, meaning "storm," and explain that *stormy* and *passionate* are synonyms.

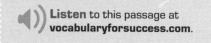
Watch a video introduction to this passage at **vocabularyforsuccess.com**.

Listen to this passage at **vocabularyforsuccess.com**.

C CCSS Vocabulary: 4; Reading (Informational Text): 4, 6. (See pp. T16–17.)

Katrina's Perfect Storm

\<editorial\>

When Hurricane Katrina made landfall on the Louisiana coast on August 29, 2005, it was not the most powerful storm to hit U.S. shores. Its wind speeds clocked at 125 miles per hour, a Category 3. It had nowhere near the force of previous hurricanes in Florida and the Carolinas. But Katrina was still a monster. It was poised in the Gulf, carefully picking its target: the city of New Orleans.

In what can only be seen as an act of hubris, New Orleans had been built below sea level, making the city flood easily even without a major storm. However, still at least wary of the nearby sea, the builders had constructed levees around the shallow basin. These stout floodwalls were meant to retain high waters brought by floods and hurricanes. Instead Katrina's powerful tidal surge breached these levees with ease, and the city was inundated. But it wasn't just geography that laid New Orleans open for disaster.

Mother and daughter, victims of Hurricane Katrina

Human failures on a scale as diffuse and far-reaching as the storm itself led to the costliest and most destructive natural disaster in the history of the United States. The origin of those human failures is still being hunted down. Seven years after the hurricane, the city is still picking up the pieces. The aftermath saw an exodus of the very population that gave New Orleans its rhythm and life, the people who contributed to its identity as a music and tourist attraction. Residents of hard-hit neighborhoods such as the Lower Ninth Ward, a neighborhood near the Mississippi River, fled the state and even the region, many of them permanently.

Certainly there were national failures to blame. The Federal Emergency Management Agency (FEMA) failed to allocate vital resources, such as food and water that were already in the region ready to distribute. Some local government leaders were guilty of failure as well. They did not use the hundreds of school buses available for evacuation before the levees broke. Thousands of people were left stranded in a convention center and at the Superdome, a large sports arena. At least 200 police officers simply walked off the job when things were at their worst, leaving no one to defuse rising tensions and give a sense of order.

An editorial is an essay in a print or an online publication that gives opinions about a topic and may suggest actions.

But what strikes any careful observer is the most obvious irony of all. The failures of the Katrina response did not begin after the hurricane struck, but long before.

Widespread corruption between the city and the Army Corps of Engineers had led to substandard construction on the levees. The poor neighborhoods that were most vulnerable were already catalysts for crime and lawlessness. Lack of public transit had doomed many residents to stay and face the storm and the flood that followed. For years there had been a strong constituency in the city objecting to all these conditions. That body of concerned citizens was ignored repeatedly, leading to a fatal state of inertia.

As so often is the case, before the disaster, the discussion about preparedness occurred in inverse proportion to actual deeds. Many people talked about the problem but failed to act. Rosy promises continue to be made. But governmental inaction, powerful construction lobbies, and special interests prevented any real progress. What was and remains devastation for many has become a golden opportunity for a few—and a lesson for all of us.

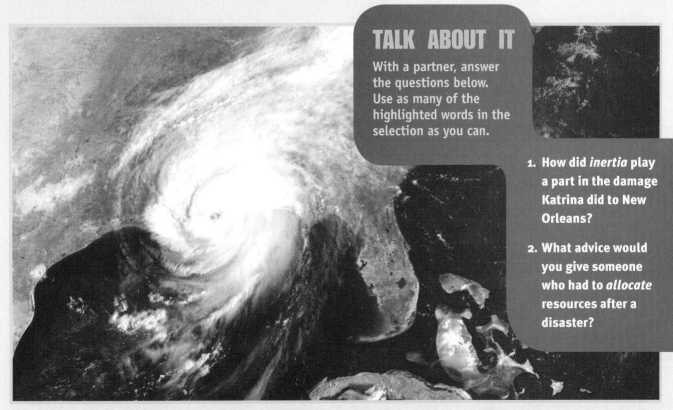

Hurricane Katrina moves ashore over southeast Louisiana.

TALK ABOUT IT

With a partner, answer the questions below. Use as many of the highlighted words in the selection as you can.

1. How did *inertia* play a part in the damage Katrina did to New Orleans?

2. What advice would you give someone who had to *allocate* resources after a disaster?

Word Meanings

For each highlighted word on pages 12–13, the meaning or meanings are given below.

For practice with synonyms, see page 32.

1. **allocate** (al-oh-KATE) **v.** to decide that something should be used by a particular person or for a particular purpose. The government must decide how to *allocate* federal resources. **SYNONYMS:** distribute, give, assign

2. **catalyst** (KAT-uh-list) **n.** a person or thing that is the cause of a major change or action. The protest group that worked hard to bring about change was the *catalyst* for the new law that was passed.

3. **constituency** (kuhn-STICH-oo-uhn-see) **n.** people who live and vote in an area. A legislator generally must please his or her *constituency* to stay in office. **SYNONYMS:** population, supporters, citizens

4. **defuse** (dee-FYOOZ) **v.** to make something less tense or serious. You might need to *defuse* tensions to prevent a fight. **SYNONYMS:** ease, mollify, curb, buffer, release

5. **diffuse** (di-FYOOSS) **adj.** spread over an area. A *diffuse* population would be found across a wide territory, not concentrated in a small area. **SYNONYMS:** disparate, spread out, scattered; **adj.** being wordy and not well-organized. If you have not written and practiced a speech you have to give, it may be *diffuse* and hard to follow. **SYNONYMS:** lengthy, long, rambling, vague, pointless

6. **exodus** (EK-suh-duhss) **n.** a vast population movement, usually leaving one place for another because of poverty, hunger, or war. A large movement of people out of a famine-stricken area could be described as an *exodus*. **SYNONYMS:** migration, mass escape, population shift

7. **hubris** (HYOO-briss) **n.** excessive pride or self-confidence. To prepare an expensive victory celebration before a close contest would be an act of *hubris*. **SYNONYMS:** pride, arrogance

8. **inertia** (in-UR-shuh) **n.** lack of energy or movement. Political *inertia* is often blamed for lack of action on critical problems. **SYNONYMS:** stasis, doldrums, inaction; **n.** a property of matter that means something in motion stays in motion and something at rest stays at rest until acted upon by an outside force. A sled's *inertia* will carry it forward until it strikes a solid barrier. **SYNONYMS:** energy, force

C CCSS Vocabulary: 4.c., 4.d. (See pp. T16–17.)

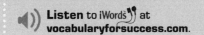

Watch a video introduction for each word at **vocabularyforsuccess.com**.

Listen to iWords🎵 at **vocabularyforsuccess.com**.

Refer to the online dictionary at **vocabularyforsuccess.com**.

9. **inverse** (IN-vurss) **adj.** opposite. Multiplication and division are *inverse* operations. **SYNONYMS:** reversed, backward, counter; **n.** the opposite of something. The *inverse* of up would be down. **SYNONYMS:** reverse, converse, contrary

10. **irony** (EYE-ruh-nee) **n.** a strange or funny situation caused when things that happen are the opposite of what was expected. A criminal solving a crime would be an *irony*. **SYNONYM:** paradox

11. **poise** (POIZ) **v.** to hold suspended. The ballet dancer can *poise* motionless on one foot. **SYNONYM:** hover; **n.** grace under pressure, an easy confidence. It takes great *poise* to accept a disappointing defeat in front of others. **SYNONYMS:** tact, composure, dignity

12. **retain** (ri-TAYN) **v.** to hold. When you *retain* something, you keep it. **SYNONYM:** reserve

More on Meanings: Confusing Word Pairs

Confusing word pairs are words that look or sound alike but have different meanings. Compare these sentences:

The reasons for the failure of the enemy invasion were varied and **diffuse**.

When war threatened, UN diplomats were called in to **defuse** the situation.

In the first sentence, *diffuse* is an adjective meaning "widespread." In the second sentence, *defuse* is a verb meaning "to resolve tensions."

This word pair has the same part of speech:

I **concur** with my opponent on this matter.

The dictator will **conquer** any nation that stands in his way.

Both *concur* and *conquer* are verbs. However, *concur* here means "to agree with," while *conquer* means "to defeat or to subjugate."

Sometimes a confusing word pair contains related meanings. Compare these sentences:

This mineral may **emit** radiation.

We can **admit** only a few new students.

In the first sentence, *emit* is a verb meaning "to give off, let out." In the second sentence, *admit* is a verb meaning "to let in."

Challenge

1. Choose two word pairs below. Use each of the words in a sentence.

   cellar, seller *climatic, climactic*
   aisle, isle

2. Choose one word pair below. Use both words correctly in the same sentence.

   course, coarse *tortuous, torturous*

If students need help using both words in the same sentence, brainstorm situations in which both meanings could apply.

C CCSS Vocabulary: 4.a., 5. (See pp. T16–17.)

vocabularyforsuccess.com

15

Word Talk

Each lesson word has been placed in a category. With a partner, discuss and list items that belong in each category. Compare your results with those of another pair of students.

C CCSS Vocabulary: 6. (See pp. T16–17.)

Resources a City Government Might *Allocate*

tax dollars, tax breaks, road crews, emergency equipment, police, firefighters

Ways to *Defuse* Tensions Between Nations

peace talks, treaties

Examples of *Inertia*

watching TV on the couch instead of going outside, thinking about exercising but not exercising

Personal Characteristics That Might Lead to *Hubris*

selfishness, pride, egotism

Ways a Company Might Seek to *Retain* Workers

higher pay, better benefits

Conditions That Might Be a *Catalyst* for Crime

poverty, unemployment, overcrowding

Things That Might Lead a Population to Experience an *Exodus*

famine, drought, flood

Ways a Politician Might Please His or Her *Constituency*

fix roads, create jobs, build schools

Examples of People, Animals, or Things That Can *Poise*

a hummingbird, a pen above paper, an acrobat on a wire

Examples of Things That Are *Diffuse*

large storms, weather systems, galaxies

Ways *Irony* Can Be Instructive

to make a point, to create humor, to reveal the unexpected

Examples of an *Inverse* Relationship

multiplication and division, a seesaw

Check for Understanding

Choose the lesson word that completes each sentence. Write the word on the line provided. Some words will be used twice.

allocate	defuse	hubris	irony
catalyst	diffuse	inertia	poise
constituency	exodus	inverse	retain

1. After winning the lottery, I tried hard to _____retain_____ a sense of reality.

2. The origins of the war are _____diffuse_____ and therefore complicated.

3. She tried to spend less on groceries by eating fresh vegetables, but she achieved the _____inverse_____ result.

4. _____Inertia_____ in Congress often means that no laws are passed and nothing is accomplished.

5. Celebrating before he crossed the finish line was an act of _____hubris_____.

6. Our school decided to _____allocate_____ its funds to clubs rather than to sports.

7. The famine led to a vast _____exodus_____ of people from the stricken region.

8. "_____Poise_____ the X-ray machine directly over the patient," the technologist directed, "then lower it slowly."

9. The senator's immoral actions struck everyone as a powerful _____irony_____, since he was always lecturing about morality.

10. The meeting of inventors became a rich _____catalyst_____ for hundreds of new ideas.

11. As neighborhood crime increased, the legislator's _____constituency_____ became angry.

12. The coach managed to _____defuse_____ the tense situation before a fight developed.

13. The _____irony_____ was that the firehouse was the first building to burn down.

14. There is a strong anticrime _____constituency_____ in that inner-city district.

In Item 8, students may have difficulty with this meaning of *poise*. Suggest they think in terms of the word *position* (a word that means very nearly the same thing) as a mnemonic.

Word Associations

Use what you know about the lesson word in italics to answer each question. Circle the letter next to the phrase that best answers the question. Be prepared to explain your answers.

1. If you step off a moving skateboard, what will *inertia* cause it to do?

   a. keep rolling
   b. stop suddenly
   c. flip over

2. Which of these would most likely cause an *exodus*?

   a. a political movement
   b. worsening economic conditions
   c. a bloody civil war

3. Of these, which best illustrates the meaning of *diffuse*?

   a. something that is everywhere
   b. something that stays in one place
   c. something that can calm others down

4. Who would most likely be guilty of *hubris*?

   a. a thief
   b. a braggart
   c. a liar

5. What is the *inverse* of getting good grades?

   a. studying
   b. failing
   c. exercising

6. If you spent a lot of effort getting ready for a harsh winter, which of these events would best show *irony*?

   a. The mittens you bought are not warm.
   b. The season lasts longer than usual.
   c. It is the mildest winter on record.

7. When would it be hardest to show *poise*?

   a. while tutoring a foreign-language student in English
   b. while doing an interview after a major sports loss
   c. while bargaining for a lower price on a purchase

8. When taking a history test, what would be most helpful to *retain*?

   a. a big breakfast
   b. a good night's sleep
   c. facts about the topic

9. Who would most need to *defuse* things?

   a. a nurse
   b. a diplomat
   c. a secretary

10. Which is the best *catalyst* for political change?

    a. voting a new party into power
    b. re-electing the current leader
    c. deciding not to vote at all

11. Which initiative would most likely have the greatest *constituency*?

    a. a movement to lower crime rates
    b. a movement to rename a building
    c. a movement to restrict travel

12. What is the most important thing a program manager at a radio station must *allocate*?

    a. acting talent
    b. microphones
    c. time slots

CCSS Vocabulary: 4.a. (See pp. T16–17.)

Check Again

Use what you know about the lesson word in italics to complete each sentence. Be sure your sentences make sense.

1. Sam showed a lot of *poise* when he made the tragic announcement at the assembly, because he _____ kept a cool head/remained calm.

2. The *constituency* banded together to vote out their do-nothing _____ representative.

3. In a wild act of *hubris*, the rookie chess player declared that for his entire career he would remain _____ undefeated.

4. The *exodus* out of the war-torn country involved thousands of _____ people.

5. The *inverse* of love is _____ hate.

6. If a dam were to *retain* too much water, it might _____ burst.

7. When a speeding car's engine turns off, *inertia* keeps it _____ moving.

8. When the two players squared off to fight, an umpire stepped in to *defuse* _____ the tension.

9. In lean financial times, it becomes much trickier for legislatures to *allocate* _____ money/funds.

10. For the driven young scholar, the vast new library was a perfect *catalyst* for _____ learning.

11. He convinced nobody with his *diffuse* argument that _____ was pointless and full of excess language.

12. The *irony* was that although the company president himself was bankrupt, _____ he ran a very profitable business.

Write Your Own

1. **Write a sentence using the word *hubris*.**

   His hubris caused many problems, including a lack of friends.

2. **Write an eleven-word sentence using the word *exodus*.**

   The exodus of the unemployed workers from the city was massive.

Word-Solving Strategies:
Context Clues

Examples

Sometimes an author provides an example to illustrate the meaning of an unfamiliar word. Reread this sentence from "Katrina's Perfect Storm."

The Federal Emergency Management Agency (FEMA) failed to allocate vital resources, such as food and water that were already in the region ready to distribute. Some local government leaders were guilty of failure as well. They did not use the hundreds of school buses available for evacuation before the levees broke.

"Vital resources such as food and water" that were "ready to distribute" and "school buses" that were "available" are examples of things that might have been allocated. A reader could visualize these examples and understand that *allocate* means "to provide, distribute, or make available."

BE CAREFUL!

Examples that give clues to meaning usually follow an unfamiliar word, but don't be misled. Look at this fragment from the passage:

...leaving no one to defuse rising tensions and give a sense of order.

Here, the word *defuse* does not mean "give a sense of order." The author is making a related but different point. The tensions need to be eased or lessened, which is how *defuse* is used.

Practice

Write a sentence using each of the highlighted words from the paragraph below. Use examples to illustrate the meaning of the word.

As he helped out in the search and rescue, Shawn wanted to maximize his efforts by using his resources in the most efficient way possible. The atrocious storm had destroyed so much property and flooded such a large area that it had left widely scattered pockets of refugees. Shawn thought that the most crucial factor was to save time, to make only one trip in his boat. The sturdy rowboat could hold six people safely. However, if people clung to the sides, he could consolidate the rescue of twice as many, bringing everyone to the shelter together.

1. ___Willy thought he could maximize his odds by taking as many shots as possible at the basket.___

2. ___An atrocious tornado, terrible and unimaginable, might touch down and destroy the town.___

3. ___We should agree on a plan of action that includes crucial details such as important deadlines.___

4. ___The way to consolidate our efforts is to put all our resources together to accomplish this task.___

CCSS Vocabulary: 4.a.; Reading (Informational Text): 4. (See pp. T16–17.)

Practice for Tests

For a quiz and additional practice for this lesson, go to **vocabularyforsuccess.com**.

Fill in the bubble next to the answer that best completes the sentence or answers the question.

1. A *constituency* is usually united by:

- ○ **A** military force
- ○ **B** temporary laws
- ● **C** a shared issue
- ○ **D** a variety of leaders

2. A population becomes *diffuse* when it:

- ○ **A** values cities over towns
- ○ **B** develops its industrial base
- ○ **C** turns against its leadership
- ● **D** covers a large area

3. Boasting goes along with *hubris* because boasting:

- ○ **A** is often loud
- ● **B** involves overconfidence
- ○ **C** is what bullies do
- ○ **D** requires effort

4. In a sense, you are overcoming *inertia* when:

- ○ **A** you buy expensive clothing
- ● **B** you get up off the couch
- ○ **C** you win a lottery
- ○ **D** you look out a window

5. Read this sentence.

> The disastrous result proved the exact *inverse* of Johnson's expectations.

Inverse indicates that Johnson's expectations were:

- ○ **A** negative
- ● **B** hopeful
- ○ **C** silly
- ○ **D** fulfilling

6. To *defuse* a bomb is to:

- ○ **A** determine its origin
- ○ **B** wedge it in place
- ○ **C** spread out its explosive parts
- ● **D** render it harmless

7. Read this sentence.

> When the water holes dried up, the elephant herds began their *exodus*.

Exodus means:

- ● **A** mass departure
- ○ **B** loud trumpeting
- ○ **C** desperate hunting
- ○ **D** death throes

8. The *catalysts* for fire are:

- ○ **A** dry leaves
- ● **B** a spark and tinder
- ○ **C** oil and gas
- ○ **D** a stone hearth and a chimney

9. Which of these would NOT require *poise*?

- ○ **A** losing a spelling bee everyone thought you'd win
- ○ **B** making a birthday cake no one likes
- ○ **C** facing angry voters after a scandal
- ● **D** taking a victory lap for a home run

10. If you *allocate* part of your paycheck to savings, you:

- ○ **A** will avoid all taxation
- ○ **B** will make slightly less than you did before
- ● **C** will see your money accumulate
- ○ **D** will soon earn a profit

If students chose C for Item 6, it may be because of the homophonic confusion that can happen between *defuse* and *diffuse*. Explain that *defuse* contains the word *fuse*—as on a bomb—giving a hint to its meaning.

Watch a video introduction to this passage at **vocabularyforsuccess.com**.

Listen to this passage at **vocabularyforsuccess.com**.

CCSS Vocabulary: 4; Reading (Informational Text): 4, 6. (See pp. T16–17.)

The Earthquake That Rocked My World

\<first-person narrative\>

On January 12, 2010, I was rushing to make a 5:00 PM appointment at the Hotel Caribe, but because my car was with the mechanic, I had taken a cab, and we were stuck in rush-hour traffic. The cabdriver was shouting; I was sweating. We were within sight of the hotel when the first tremor of the earthquake hit. For me, it seemed that boys were jumping on the bumpers, making the car a seesaw. Then I saw the hotel begin to dance. For three seconds or so it did this, the monster quake utterly disinterested in the building's human contents, shaking the structure until it crumbled. From the street we heard a chorus of wails.

Searching through a building's remains

A crowd of people who looked and moved like zombies emerged, covered in white dust and seeking the nominal safety of the streets. Continued tremors caused rubble to project over our heads, sending pieces flying like missiles.

I shook the cabdriver, who was wailing himself, expressing shock and disbelief with his high shriek. But his tone actually calmed me and eased the sheer terror I felt. The cardinal point when so distressed is to do something, anything, and he was doing something. As the shaking of the earth continued, I urged him to see if we could turn around, since my daughter was not far away, near the capitol. I could see the top of the building leaping up and down like everything else. Amazingly, the car was undamaged. Nevertheless, the cabby was uninterested in

helping me, and the broken streets would hardly accommodate our car anyway.

As I found my way through the panic and rubble, my rage grew. What if something had happened to my daughter? I resented the ruling regime that had allowed such weak structures to be built, especially in a city as large as Port-au-Prince. As the tremors began to subside, I saw with great relief that our house, only a two-story affair, was undamaged. Yet I vowed to make it my mission to fight to depose anyone in authority whose inaction or neglect had made this day more terrible than it needed to be. Regulations must be put in place to require building codes and establish an authority to inspect structures. Measures must be taken so that buildings can withstand such quakes in the future and lessen the damage to life and property. Our future depends on it.

A first-person narrative is writing that describes an experience or event from the writer's point of view.

Above: People walking through the streets after the earthquake

Below: Ruins of the presidential palace in Port-au-Prince, Haiti

TALK ABOUT IT

With a partner, answer the questions below. Use as many of the highlighted words in the selection as you can.

1. Why might the narrator have felt such strong and sudden rage at Haiti's ruling *regime*?

2. Did you feel *uninterested* in this account of the Haiti earthquake? Why or why not?

Word Meanings

For each highlighted word on pages 22–23, the meaning or meanings are given below.

For practice with synonyms, see page 32.

1. **accommodate** (uh-KOM-uh-date) **v.** find or make room for, take care of. A narrow footpath would not be wide enough to *accommodate* a city bus. **SYNONYMS:** put up, allow, enable

2. **capitol** (KAP-uh-tuhl) **n.** the building in which a government is housed. The United States *Capitol* is a building that is often copied in smaller scale by other states and nations.

3. **cardinal** (KAR-duh-nuhl) **adj.** of most importance. The main idea of a paragraph is the *cardinal* point that the writer is making. **SYNONYMS:** crucial, vital, basic; **n.** a songbird with a large beak. The male *cardinal* is bright red, and the female is grayish brown with a red tint.

4. **chorus** (KOR-uhss) **n.** a sound made by many voices joined together. At many sporting events one can hear a *chorus* of cheers for the favorite team. **SYNONYMS:** choir, concert; **n.** the part of a song repeated after each verse. When you are learning to sing a song, it is always easier to learn the *chorus,* since it is repeated often. **SYNONYM:** refrain

5. **depose** (di-POZE) **v.** to topple from office, remove from power. The first step in a coup is to *depose* the leader. **SYNONYMS:** fire, dismiss

6. **disinterested** (diss-IN-tuh-ress-tid) **adj.** not taking sides; unconcerned or uninvolved. Someone who is *disinterested* in a family argument doesn't favor one person over the other. **SYNONYMS:** fair, unbiased

7. **inspect** (in-SPEKT) **v.** to very carefully look at something to find any flaws. A city usually has a person whose job it is to *inspect* all the structures to be sure they are safe. **SYNONYMS:** scrutinize, investigate, examine

8. **nominal** (NOM-uh-nuhl) **adj.** very small, easily dismissed. A wooden fence is only a *nominal* defense against intruders. **SYNONYMS:** minor, useless, powerless, trifling, insignificant, token

9. **project** (pruh-JEKT) **v.** to throw or cast harshly. When a volcano erupts, it will *project* ash into the air. **SYNONYMS:** throw, toss, spit; (PROJ-ekt) **n.** an undertaking of some kind, a pre-arranged task. Building the highway system is a government *project*. **SYNONYMS:** task, mission

CCSS Vocabulary: 4.c., 4.d. (See pp. T16–17.)

Watch a video introduction for each word at **vocabularyforsuccess.com**.

Listen to iWords at **vocabularyforsuccess.com**.

Refer to the online dictionary at **vocabularyforsuccess.com**.

10. **regime** (ri-ZHEEM) **n.** a ruling government. In a country that is not stable, a new *regime* comes into power fairly often. **SYNONYMS:** government, ruling party, authority

11. **subside** (suhb-SIDE) **v.** to become less intense or active. Crime will often *subside* when economic conditions improve. **SYNONYMS:** quiet, lessen, diminish; **v.** to sink. Pumping too much water from underground can cause the land to *subside*. **SYNONYMS:** collapse, give way, cave in

12. **uninterested** (uhn-IN-truh-stid) **adj.** bored, uncaring. If you're *uninterested* in a show, you might turn the TV off. **SYNONYMS:** bored, unconcerned, turned-off

More on Meanings: Confusing Word Pairs

Many words in the English language look or sound alike but have different meanings. It's easy to confuse pairs of words that are similar. Compare these sentences:

Because I had nothing to gain or lose, I was a **disinterested** party in the result of the court case.

The thinly written characters and lack of action left me **uninterested** in the novel's outcome.

In the first sentence, *disinterested* is an adjective meaning "unconcerned." In the second sentence, *uninterested* is an adjective meaning "bored, uninvolved."

The two words in a confusing word pair may have different parts of speech. Here's an example:

The **bough** snapped off the tree, nearly striking my head.

He knew to **bow** very low before the empress.

Bough, meaning "a tree branch," is a noun, while *bow*, meaning to "to bend at the waist to show respect," is a verb. However, both words have the same sound and their spellings are frequently confused.

Sometimes a confusing word pair consists of words with meanings that are related. Compare these sentences:

The government decided to **censor** the edgy writer's work.

Her defiant behavior caused the government to **censure** her for her actions.

In the first sentence, *censor* is a verb meaning "to ban." In the second sentence, *censure* is a verb meaning "to criticize harshly."

Challenge

1. Choose two word pairs below. Use each of the words in a sentence.

   team, teem pedal, peddle skeptic, septic

2. Choose one word pair below. Use both words correctly in the same sentence.

   dual, duel poll, pole canvas, canvass

If students have difficulty using both words in a sentence, suggest that they write two sentences and then edit the content of each so that they can combine the two as one.

Word Talk

Each lesson word has been placed in a category. With a partner, discuss and list items that belong in each category. Compare your results with those of another pair of students.

C CCSS Vocabulary: 6. [See pp. T16–17.]

Examples of Things You Might *Project*

stones, balls, water balloons, your voice

Reasons You Might Want to *Depose* a Leader

unfair treatment, no freedom, criminal behavior

Everyday Things You Hear in a *Chorus*

birds singing, crickets chirping, frogs croaking

Examples of a *Regime* That Rules Over Parts of Your Life

city government, county government, state government, federal government

---

Things That Cost Only a *Nominal* Amount

stamps, gum, fruit

Why You Are *Uninterested* in Certain Movies

too childish, too romantic, too violent

Cardinal* Rules of Succeeding in School

study hard, pay attention, do your work

Advantages of Being *Disinterested* in a Dispute

less stress, nothing to lose

What You Might Do to *Accommodate* a Guest

provide a place to stay, serve meals, provide entertainment

Things You Might Find in a State *Capitol*

offices, tourists, legislators

Things That Someone Must *Inspect* for Safety

buildings, food, toys

Things That Can *Subside*

swelling, anger, interest

Check for Understanding

Choose the lesson word that completes each sentence. Write the word on the line provided. Some words will be used twice.

accommodate	chorus	inspect	regime
capitol	depose	nominal	subside
cardinal	disinterested	project	uninterested

1. Jeffrey was ___uninterested___ in his little brother's long, involved story.

2. The rebels finally managed to ___depose___ the dictator.

3. The manager made sure everything was in good shape when the official came to ___inspect___ the restaurant.

4. The state ___capitol___ has a high dome topped by a gold-plated statue.

5. Public support for the marginal candidate was only ___nominal___.

6. Despite how intriguing the case is, it's crucial for a judge to be ___disinterested___.

7. The quarterback hoped his powerful throw could ___project___ the football into the end zone.

8. A/An ___cardinal___ rule is to treat others as you would have them treat you.

9. The children knew that their father's loud laughter would ___subside___ as soon as he heard about the broken window.

10. We did our best to ___accommodate___ the stranded travelers.

11. The swamp frogs sounded off together in a strange ___chorus___.

12. The new ___regime___ promised the citizens peace and good times.

13. Before starting a long road trip, it's best to ___inspect___ your car's tires.

14. This small shelf will barely ___accommodate___ all our plates and bowls.

If students have difficulty with Items 1 and 6, review the meanings of *disinterested* and *uninterested*.

Word Associations

Use what you know about the lesson word in italics to answer each question. Circle the letter next to the phrase that best answers the question. Be prepared to explain your answers.

1. If you see a *cardinal*, what are you seeing?

   a. a bird
   b. someone important
   c. a large group of things

2. Which of these professions requires that one be *disinterested*?

   a. politician
   b. surgeon
   c. judge

3. If you were to *depose* a king, what might you want to do to his government?

   a. overthrow it
   b. scare it
   c. rename it

4. Which of these would have a *chorus*?

   a. a novel
   b. a song
   c. a game

5. When would you likely do a *project* for school?

   a. for the basketball game
   b. for a discussion with your teacher
   c. for the science fair

6. Which of these is something you might *inspect*?

   a. a family reunion
   b. a bicycle tire
   c. a funny story

7. What does the *capitol* of the United States have that no other building does?

   a. prominent judges and attorneys
   b. the nation's only valuable statuary and artwork
   c. the government of the nation

8. In an earthquake, you would wait for this to *subside* before leaving your shelter.

   a. faults
   b. rescue efforts
   c. tremors

9. What might you do if you were *uninterested* in a song on the radio?

   a. complain to the network
   b. switch to a different station
   c. turn up the volume

10. Which of these gives the most *nominal* protection from the sun?

    a. a shirt with no sleeves
    b. sunscreen
    c. a hat and an umbrella

11. What is a garage designed to *accommodate*?

    a. a car
    b. a stove
    c. a bed

12. In what sense is your student government a *regime*?

    a. It can sometimes be dictatorial.
    b. It is a group of one or more leaders.
    c. It is given the power to run things.

CCSS Vocabulary: 4.a. (See pp. T16–17.)

Check Again

Use what you know about the lesson word in italics to complete each sentence. Be sure your sentences make sense.

1. We marched all the way to the *capitol* to _____ express our complaints about the government. _____

2. The referee's unpopular decision was greeted by a *chorus* of boos, because _____ many people in the crowd disagreed with the call. _____

3. The referee could remain *disinterested* in the game because she _____ knew no one on either team. _____

4. It is usual for a mother to *inspect* _____ the food she buys for her family. _____

5. If the pain from your toothache begins to *subside*, you might smile because _____ it is going away. _____

6. If you are *uninterested* in an issue, it is hard to give it much _____ thought, time, or focus. _____

7. A population generally wants to *depose* a government only when it _____ lets them down or betrays them. _____

8. If you are approached by a mountain lion in the wild, you should *project* _____ rocks, sticks, or any threatening weapon to scare it away. _____

9. A *cardinal* rule for batters in baseball is _____ keep your eye on the ball. _____

10. To *accommodate* wider trains, the railroad had to _____ build wider tracks. _____

11. Faced with an unpopular *regime*, citizens in a democracy can express outrage by _____ protesting or voting for someone else. _____

12. *Nominal* support is unlikely to win a candidate very many _____ votes. _____

Write Your Own

Reread the first-person narrative on pages 22–23. Then, on a separate sheet of paper, write a one-paragraph response to the question, "What problems did the citizens of Haiti face immediately after the earthquake?" Use at least two words from the lesson word list and support your answer by referring to the text of the passage.

Word-Solving Strategies: Context Clues

Embedded Definitions

Sometimes an author helps the reader out with a difficult word by providing a definition that is embedded in the text. Reread this paragraph from "The Earthquake That Rocked My World":

> A crowd of people who looked and moved like zombies emerged, covered in white dust and seeking the nominal safety of the streets. Continued tremors caused rubble to project over our heads, sending pieces flying like missiles.

The word *project* is followed by a phrase that defines the word directly in the text: "sending pieces flying like missiles." Embedded definitions are sometimes, though not always, set off by commas. Writers often give more information about a word by including additional details that also make the writing more interesting and lively.

BE CAREFUL!

Although the word *or* can signal a synonym or a definition, it doesn't always. Read this sentence:

> *The lost hikers refused to climb any farther; every member of the party was disoriented, or exhausted.*

Here, the word *disoriented* seems to also mean "exhausted," but this is not the case, as the word *or* simply introduces another issue facing the hikers.

Practice

Write a sentence using each of the highlighted words from the paragraph below. Use embedded definitions to help define the words.

Edward was vigilant as he moved through the rubble, always on the alert so as not to displace large pieces that could bring down more of the building. He edged deeper into the ruin, even as the structure settled around him, threatening to obliterate everything that wasn't already completely destroyed. The beams groaned, and so did the survivors. Edward did what he could, offering solace, words of reassurance that kept their spirits up until the rescue teams arrived. He tried to alleviate the victims' fears and reduce their anxiety with his calm voice and encouraging presence.

1. _The archaeologist was vigilant, forever watchful to be sure he did not miss an artifact._

2. _When the tornado touched down, it did not obliterate the house, or destroy it completely._

3. _After the accident, long bicycle rides gave me solace, reassurance that the world was okay._

4. _When her leg was broken, she took medicine to alleviate her pain and take away her suffering._

C CCSS Vocabulary: 4.a.; Reading (Informational Text): 4. (See pp. T16–17.)

Practice for Tests

For a quiz and additional practice for this lesson, go to **vocabularyforsuccess.com**.

Fill in the bubble next to the answer that best completes the sentence or answers the question.

1. A hotel that can *accommodate* guests has:
   - ○ **A** a free breakfast
   - ○ **B** a swimming pool
   - ● **C** rooms available
   - ○ **D** a discount

2. A *chorus* of moans might most likely come from:
   - ○ **A** a beehive
   - ● **B** a disappointed audience
   - ○ **C** an astonished dancer
   - ○ **D** a disgruntled worker

3. When you *inspect* something, you
   - ○ **A** pass it
   - ● **B** check it
   - ○ **C** fix it
   - ○ **D** build it

4. Read this sentence.
   He began to work on the *project* after he had finalized the plans.

   Project means:
   - ○ **A** a feeling
   - ● **B** a job
   - ○ **C** a bird
   - ○ **D** a sound

5. You are *disinterested* in a spelling bee when:
   - ○ **A** you find the contest boring
   - ● **B** you have nothing to gain by who wins
   - ○ **C** you are not intrigued by the contestants
   - ○ **D** you know your side will win

6. A *cardinal* rule is one that:
   - ○ **A** is easily broken
   - ○ **B** shows direction
   - ○ **C** uses chance
   - ● **D** is most important

7. Read this sentence.
   Before his rousing speech, the general waited for his emotions to *subside*.

   Subside means:
   - ○ **A** quake
   - ○ **B** collapse
   - ● **C** lessen
   - ○ **D** swell

8. The *uninterested* queen:
   - ○ **A** laughed
   - ● **B** yawned
   - ○ **C** danced
   - ○ **D** spoke

9. Which of these could you NOT *depose*?
   - ○ **A** a state governor
   - ○ **B** a student council
   - ○ **C** a powerful king
   - ● **D** a voting constituency

10. Because his involvement was *nominal*, he:
    - ● **A** did not do anything
    - ○ **B** worked hard
    - ○ **C** paid cash
    - ○ **D** invested money

If students chose A or C for Item 5, they may be confusing *disinterested* and *uninterested*. Explain that you can be fascinated by a contest in the outcome of which you are "disinterested"—standing to gain or lose nothing.

Synonyms and Antonyms

In the following Word Bank, you will find synonyms and antonyms for some of the words in Lessons 1–3. (Remember: Some words have both synonyms and antonyms.) Study these words; then complete the exercises below.

weight	stormy	pride	awkwardness	unimportant	decrease
sheer	close	humility	possess	dethrone	excited

A. For each sentence, fill in the blank with a SYNONYM for the word in boldface.

1. To gather information about the suspect's activities, the agents put 24-hour cameras in the **adjacent** building, which was _____close_____ enough to deploy listening devices as well.

2. We were able to **retain** mineral rights to the land, so we could _____possess_____ the full benefits from that source.

3. The coach felt that whenever the cheers from the fans began to **subside**, the team's performance also began to _____decrease_____ .

4. The colt's **tempestuous** character threatened hopes that he might do well in shows— horses with such _____stormy_____ personalities rarely succeed in that finicky world.

5. No one dreamed anyone could _____dethrone_____ the powerful king. That the rebels managed to **depose** him in mere days seemed a miracle.

B. For each sentence, fill in the blank with an ANTONYM for the word in boldface.

6. Far from showing the **hubris** of his early days, the seasoned athlete approached his final contest with an attitude that showed great _____humility_____ .

7. After being wildly _____excited_____ by the novel's opening pages, I gradually became **uninterested** as the story got bogged down in tedious details.

8. Daria showed great **poise** as she walked the balance beam without her usual _____awkwardness_____ and clumsiness.

9. As the water poured into its hull, the ship lost its **buoyancy**, and the extra _____weight_____ dragged it to the bottom.

10. Keeping hydrated during the long race was a **cardinal** principle, next to which every other consideration became relatively _____unimportant_____ .

CCSS Vocabulary: 4.a., 5, 6. (See pp. T16–17.)

Word Study: Denotation and Connotation

You know that the literal meaning of a word is its denotation. Some words can have a connotation that gives the word a positive or negative feeling or tone. Words that are synonyms have basically the same denotation. For example, *cool* and *cold* both indicate a chilly attitude. However, *cool* has a relatively neutral connotation, while *cold* has a negative one. Compare the connotations of these synonyms:

POSITIVE	NEGATIVE	NEUTRAL
disciplined	obsessive	self-controlled
wise	know-it-all	intelligent
vibrant	ditzy	energetic

Look at the word *uninterested* from Lesson 3 and some of its synonyms:

aloof   **unconcerned**   **unsympathetic**
uninvolved   **indifferent**   **unemotional**

The words' common denotation is "uncaring." *Uninvolved* and *indifferent* have a neutral connotation, while *unconcerned* and *unemotional*, in some circumstances, have a positive feeling. *Aloof* and *unsympathetic* have clearly negative connotations.

Practice

A. Circle the word in parentheses that has the connotation (positive, negative, or neutral) given at the beginning of the sentence.

negative   **1.** The architect's designs for the new building were (**complicated**, (**unrealistic**)).

positive   **2.** The cowboy had a/an (**ungainly**, (**loose-limbed**)) stride.

positive   **3.** After the difficult test, I wanted to ((**trumpet**,) **boast**) my improvement.

neutral   **4.** When it comes to new artists' work, I maintain a (**reserved**, (**blasé**)) attitude.

negative   **5.** The situation was rapidly turning into a/an ((**apocalypse**,) **crisis**).

neutral   **6.** Winston's mints give you a/an ((**burst**,) **explosion**) of flavor.

negative   **7.** The journalist was reprimanded when it was discovered that he had (**invented**, (**faked**)) the entire story.

B. Work with a partner. Write a plus sign (+) if the word has a positive connotation; write a minus sign (-) if the word has a negative connotation. Put a zero (0) if the word is neutral.

1. ridiculous [−]   **3.** irresistible [+]   **5.** arrogant [−]   **7.** available [O]

2. vivid [+]   **4.** disrespectful [−]   **6.** credible [+]   **8.** financial [O]

Vocabulary for Comprehension

Read the following passage, in which some of the words you have studied in Lessons 1–3 appear in boldface type. Then answer questions 1–6.

Attack of the Sneaker Wave

There's a deadly threat on the Pacific Northwest's beaches. It is nowhere near so immense as the **tsunami** nor so terrifying as a shark attack, but it is far more common than either. This quiet
5 killer is called the sneaker wave. The sneaker wave is not caused by earthquakes or even by the weather, but rather by an unpredictable combination of factors, namely other waves and the tide. The strike of a sneaker wave is stealthy.
10 The water does not rear up in a curling wave— it's flat and **diffuse**, yet still surprisingly deep. It slides up the beach with incredible speed and is so powerful that it can **decimate** a beach.

Faced with a sneaker wave, you might quickly
15 **deduce** that leaping onto a log is a good idea.

The bigger it is, the more **buoyancy** it has, right? Forget about it. A sneaker wave can toss even a massive redwood trunk with ease, utterly **disinterested** in who or what may be on it. Avoid
20 these logs altogether. A stone jetty may seem to provide protection, but don't even think about it. Jetties are notoriously slick and slippery, and waves plus rocks equals a **catalyst** for disaster. Their assistance is only **nominal** in this situation.

25 Your best bet in any encounter with a sneaker wave is to **retain** your **poise** and head for higher ground. Better yet, follow this **cardinal** rule: Never turn your back to the sea.

If students answered A, B, or D for Item 3, they may need to review the meaning of deduce, *"to figure something out by examining related facts."*

1. Another word for **diffuse** in line 11 is
   - ○ **A** common
   - ● **B** widespread
   - ○ **C** relieved
   - ○ **D** spent

2. In line 13, **decimate** means
   - ● **A** destroy
   - ○ **B** recollect
   - ○ **C** summon up
   - ○ **D** dismiss

3. Another word for **deduce** (line 15) is
   - ○ **A** consider
   - ○ **B** hope
   - ● **C** determine
   - ○ **D** guess

4. The sneaker wave is **disinterested** (line 19) in who or what is on the log because the wave
   - ○ **A** is flat and spread out
   - ○ **B** has no way of knowing
   - ○ **C** is bored and apathetic
   - ● **D** is not able to care either way

5. In line 23, **catalyst** means
   - ○ **A** a dangerous situation
   - ● **B** a perfect condition
   - ○ **C** a stealthy trap
   - ○ **D** an impossible obstacle

6. If a rule has **cardinal** (line 27) importance, it
   - ○ **A** is at the top or bottom of a list
   - ● **B** trumps all other rules
   - ○ **C** pertains to health or safety
   - ○ **D** involves some sort of directions

Ⓒ CCSS Vocabulary: 4.a., 6; Reading (Informational Text): 4. (See pp. T16–17.)

Trade You! Commerce in the 21st Century

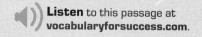

Watch a video introduction to this passage at **vocabularyforsuccess.com**.

Listen to this passage at **vocabularyforsuccess.com**.

 CCSS Vocabulary: 4; Reading (Informational Text): 4, 6. (See pp. T16–17.)

Buying Music Online

\<debate\>

Today's debate question: *Is downloading music ethical?*

Danielle: I don't see why downloading music and sharing it with my friends would be considered unethical. As long as I pay for the download, I'm not violating any copyright laws. There are plenty of sites that offer legitimate electronic commerce. Some companies offer users a one-time fee so that people can download music without fear of litigation or lawsuits. There are even a few sites that offer free music legally! Responsible users know how to winnow trustworthy companies from dishonest ones. In addition, many electronic devices make downloading easy, so how can downloading music be considered illegal?

Also, downloading a single song is more appealing than buying an entire album. If an album has only one fantastic song, it is more economical to purchase a single hit than to purchase the entire album. Music purchased with disposable income is a luxury. In difficult economic times, not everyone can afford expensive luxuries. Finally, if I decide to download a single song and share it with my friends, there is no harm done. Sharing music with friends is a way to show musical appreciation.

Jai: In my opinion, most people who download music do it illegally. In fact, most sites that offer music downloads are unlicensed; they are illegal. These corrupt online companies simply usurp musicians' songs. When you download music from unlicensed sites, it's the equivalent of stealing a CD from a store. You are taking artists' work and not paying them for their contribution.

Moreover, sharing music over networks is not legal. People need to know that every time they download free music, they are stealing by depriving the musician of his or her income. If bands object to having their music downloaded for free, then taking it is theft, pure and simple. The music

Explain that a debate is a formal discussion in which two opposing viewpoints are presented.

is the band's property, and taking it without payment is unethical.

Danielle: Some bands do not object to offering free music online. Their philosophy is that if more people hear their music, then more people will buy their music. If I share my music with a friend, isn't that the same as lending my friend a book?

Jai: The problem is that file sharing means sharing with millions of people. When you share music files, even files you have purchased, you are challenging all the copyright laws! Some music lovers consider deregulation of the music industry a fix to this dilemma, but until that happens, music is considered intellectual property that should be protected. Do you honestly believe that celebrated and eminent musicians want the music industry deregulated? Of course not, because if music were deregulated, lawsuits filed by musicians and record companies would be imminent.

However, there is a way for online companies *and* musicians to make money. Musicians and record companies could impose a levy on downloaded music in addition to the fee.

The tax could go directly to the artists. That money would be reparation to the musicians who are losing income on their CDs.

Danielle: I think musicians should decide if they want their music to be available for free downloading. After all, if they own the rights to their music, they should be the ones who decide the fate of their songs.

TALK ABOUT IT

With a partner, answer the questions below. Use as many of the highlighted words in the selection as you can.

1. Jai thinks that downloading music violates *copyright* laws. Danielle does not. With whom do you agree? Why?

2. Given the recent advances in technology, do you think *deregulation* of the music industry would be a wise thing to do? Explain your answer.

Word Meanings

For each highlighted word on pages 36–37, the meaning or meanings are given below.

For practice with synonyms, see page 66.

1. **commerce** (KOM-urss) **n.** the buying and selling of goods. Electronic *commerce*, or buying things online, has changed the way people shop. **SYNONYM:** trade

2. **copyright** (KOP-ee-rite) **adj.** related to laws protecting the rights of all artists. *Copyright* laws protect the creative work of writers and musicians. **n.** the license given to a published work, such as a book, a movie, or music. If a writer has a *copyright* for a novel, no one else can use his or her words or copy them without giving credit. **SYNONYM:** patent; **v.** to get a copyright. Writers should *copyright* their published writings so others cannot steal them. **SYNONYM:** get a patent

3. **deregulation** (DEE-reg-yuh-LAY-shuhn) **n.** the removal of government rules or control over an industry. The *deregulation* of the airline industry allowed airlines to set their own prices. **SYNONYMS:** free trade, noninterference

4. **disposable** (diss-POH-zuh-buhl) **adj.** available for use. *Disposable* income is the money a person has left over for spending after he or she pays all necessary expenses, such as bills. **SYNONYM:** nonessential; **adj.** designed to be used up or thrown away. *Disposable* gloves are widely used in the health care industry because they can be thrown away after use. **SYNONYM:** consumable

5. **eminent** (EM-uh-nuhnt) **adj.** in high standing compared to others, remarkable; striking, noteworthy. An *eminent* musician is one whose songs are widely known and much loved by audiences and critics. **SYNONYMS:** well-known, famous, distinguished

6. **imminent** (IM-uh-nuhnt) **adj.** about to happen. When you see dark clouds and hear thunder, a storm is probably *imminent*. **SYNONYMS:** approaching, looming, threatening

7. **levy** (LEV-ee) **n.** a tax or an extra charge for a product. Although food items at a grocery store are not taxed, a *levy* is often collected on nonfood items. **SYNONYMS:** tax, toll; **v.** to impose and collect a tax or extra charge. The government and the state have the power to *levy* taxes on items. **SYNONYMS:** charge, collect

8. **litigation** (LIT-uh-GAY-shuhn) **n.** legal action; a court case. A complicated lawsuit may take several years of *litigation* before a conclusion is reached. **SYNONYMS:** lawsuit, case

CCSS Vocabulary: 4.c., 4.d. (See pp. T16–17.)

▶ **Watch** a video introduction for each word at **vocabularyforsuccess.com**.

◀)) **Listen** to iWords at **vocabularyforsuccess.com**.

📖 **Refer** to the online dictionary at **vocabularyforsuccess.com**.

9. **reparation** (rep-uh-RAY-shuhn) **n.** an action that makes up for a wrong; the payment for financial losses suffered by another. A person can make a *reparation* for a wrong by paying money or by offering a service. **SYNONYMS:** compensation, damages

10. **unlicensed** (uhn-LYE-suhnssd) **adj.** not having permission; not approved. A police officer has the authority to give a ticket to an *unlicensed* driver. **SYNONYMS:** unlawful, unauthorized, illegal

11. **usurp** (yoo-SURP) **v.** to take power. People who *usurp* control of a country take it over without the consent of the citizens. **SYNONYMS:** seize, grab, confiscate

12. **winnow** (WIN-oh) **v.** to sort out or separate; to select. To *winnow* means you select some things and discard the rest. **SYNONYMS:** sift, choose, discriminate

More on Meanings: Confusing Word Pairs

Words that sound alike but have different spellings and meanings are often confused in writing. Compare these sentences:

The **eminent** actor chooses his roles with his reputation in mind.

After so many failures, surely success is finally **imminent**.

Both *eminent* and *imminent* are adjectives. However, *eminent* means "noteworthy," while *imminent* means "about to happen."

Easily confused words can be different parts of speech.

The **recent** rains have made the river flood.

I **resent** your accusation.

Recent is an adjective meaning "happening a short time ago." *Resent* is a verb meaning "to feel bitter or unhappy about something."

Sometimes a confusing word pair consists of words with meanings that are related. Compare these sentences:

My cousin in Bosnia hopes to one day **immigrate** to the United States.

Sophia's great-grandparents decided to **emigrate** from Uruguay to Canada.

Immigrate is a verb meaning "to come to a country permanently." *Emigrate* is a verb meaning "to leave one country for another." How do you know which word to use? Remember that a person immigrates *to* a place and emigrates *from* a place.

Challenge Choose one word pair below. Use both words correctly in the same sentence.

ceiling, sealing   *flaunt, flout*

mortality, morality

If students confuse *eminent* and *imminent*, provide a memory aid: An eminent person emits excellence; an imminent incident is impending.

Word Talk

Each lesson word has been placed in a category. With a partner, discuss and list items that belong in each category. Compare your results with those of another pair of students.
C CCSS Vocabulary: 6. [See pp. T16–17.]

Businesses That Might Experience *Deregulation*

auto makers, oil producers, financial institutions

Examples of Works Covered by *Copyright* Laws

books, movies, songs, poems

Eminent Writers You Like

Walter Dean Myers, Suzanne Collins, J. R. R. Tolkien, J. K. Rowling

Examples of Products That Have a *Levy*

cars, furniture, televisions, clothing, appliances

People Who Deal in *Commerce*

advertisers, business owners, bankers

People Involved in *Litigation*

lawyers, judges, plaintiffs, defendants, witnesses

Ways to Make *Reparation*

pay a fine, make an apology, do volunteer work

Signs of the U.S. President's *Imminent* Arrival

cheering crowds, band music, security and police

Consequences of Driving While *Unlicensed*

get a ticket, get into trouble with parents, have to take a driving class

Items That People Purchase with *Disposable* Income

games, jewelry, music, collectibles

Things People Can *Usurp*

a political office, the rights of others, property, a position of power

Chores You Would Like to *Winnow* from Your To-Do List

clean the bathroom, vacuum the bedroom, wash the car

Check for Understanding

Choose the lesson word that completes each sentence. Write the word on the line provided. Some words will be used twice.

commerce	disposable	levy	unlicensed
copyright	eminent	litigation	usurp
deregulation	imminent	reparation	winnow

1. With the recent _____deregulation_____ of gasoline production, gas prices are increasing.

2. I spent hours trying to _____winnow_____ out all the errors in my research paper.

3. The guidance counselor gave me a list of several _____eminent_____ universities and told me to aim high when applying to colleges.

4. When my dog tore up my neighbor's yard, I offered my mowing services for the entire summer as _____reparation_____.

5. As more companies have opened online stores, electronic _____commerce_____ has increased.

6. My brother tries to _____usurp_____ my spot on the couch when he visits home from college.

7. Many people would rather enter into _____litigation_____ than settle a dispute fairly.

8. Do you know how long _____copyright_____ protection for a published work will last?

9. The residents knew the tsunami was _____imminent_____ and quickly took shelter.

10. After we paid our bills, the money left over was our _____disposable_____ income.

11. In order to encourage healthy eating, some officials want to impose a/an _____levy_____ on foods that contain lots of sugar and salt.

12. The _____unlicensed_____ builder made a mess, because he had not had any training.

13. After the candidates made their speeches, I was able to _____winnow_____ my choices.

14. The company must pay a/an _____reparation_____ to all the customers who bought the faulty item.

If students answer *imminent* for Item 3, review More on Meanings: Confusing Word Pairs on page 39.

Word Associations

Use what you know about the lesson word in italics to answer each question. Circle the letter next to the phrase that best answers the question. Be prepared to explain your answers.

1. If you have 15 chores to do and have time for only 3, how many do you need to *winnow* from your list?

   a. 5
   b. 12
   c. 18

2. To which of the following could the word *eminent* apply?

   a. Mark Twain
   b. Veterans Day
   c. Italian cream cake

3. Why would you be unwilling to fly with an *unlicensed* pilot?

   a. It might take too long.
   b. It might not be safe.
   c. It might be the only option.

4. Why do artists get a *copyright*?

   a. to make money
   b. to keep secrets
   c. to protect their work

5. Who is most likely to *usurp* authority?

   a. a dictator
   b. a coach
   c. an elected official

6. In which situation would you expect to face *litigation*?

   a. volunteering at an animal shelter
   b. breaking a window during a baseball game
   c. wrecking a neighbor's car

7. Which of the following happens after *deregulation*?

   a. less government control
   b. more government control
   c. no change in government control

8. Which of the following items is considered *disposable*?

   a. a tree
   b. a newspaper
   c. a house

9. What would be considered reasonable *reparation* if you lost something you had borrowed from another person?

   a. replacing or paying for the item
   b. treating the person to lunch
   c. telling the person you are sorry

10. If a tornado were *imminent*, what should you do?

    a. Calmly continue what you were doing.
    b. Grab a camera and take pictures of it.
    c. Run quickly for shelter.

11. Which of the following is most directly involved in *commerce*?

    a. a business
    b. a school
    c. a government

12. Which of the following would have the highest *levy*?

    a. a magazine
    b. a video game
    c. a diamond necklace

CCSS Vocabulary: 4.a. (See pp. T16–17.)

Check Again

Use what you know about the lesson word in italics to complete each sentence. Be sure your sentences make sense.

1. This *eminent* musician likes to keep the fans happy by _____ performing in tours in cities all around the world.

2. If you *copyright* a book you wrote, no one else can _____ claim he or she wrote it.

3. If the music industry undergoes *deregulation*, then _____ more people might download free music.

4. Some products have a *levy* imposed on them, which means _____ they are taxed.

5. Someone trying to *usurp* a throne might _____ organize a group of people who would help with the takeover.

6. It is not a good idea to hire *unlicensed* workers because they _____ might not do the work correctly.

7. In order to *winnow* the best players for your team, you must _____ identify them and then choose them.

8. If someone wants to make a *reparation* for breaking a vase, he or she might _____ offer to buy a replacement.

9. When you are having a big party, a reason to use reusable cups, plates, and napkins rather than *disposable* ones is _____ disposable items may end up polluting the environment.

10. If you knew you were going into *litigation*, you would most likely want _____ to hire a good lawyer.

11. Some people dislike doing *commerce* on the Internet because _____ they think it is unsafe.

12. A sign that winter is over and spring is *imminent* is _____ a blooming flower.

Write Your Own

Reread the passage on pages 36–37. Then, on a separate sheet of paper, write a one-paragraph response to the question, "Why would musicians not want to have their music downloaded for free?" Use at least two words from the lesson word list and support your answer by referring to the text of the passage.

Word-Solving Strategies: Context Clues

Synonyms

Synonyms can help you determine the meaning of an unknown word in a passage. Sometimes, writers will include a synonym in the same sentence, setting the word off with a comma or semicolon. Reread this sentence from "Buying Music Online":

> In fact, most sites that offer music downloads are unlicensed; they are illegal.

Here, the writer uses the word *unlicensed*. If readers don't know what the word means, they can find a synonym later in the sentence: *illegal*. By following "downloads are unlicensed" with a semicolon and a restatement of the idea—"they are illegal"—the writer helps readers figure out the unfamiliar word's meaning.

BE CAREFUL!

Synonyms are not always set off by commas:

> *Some companies offer users a one-time fee so that people can download music without fear of litigation or lawsuits.*

Here, the synonym for *litigation* is *lawsuits*, which is not set off by commas. If you are unsure of a word's meaning, use an Internet dictionary. Synonyms are also listed in these online dictionaries.

Practice

Write the highlighted word and its synonym in the first two boxes. Using the synonym context clues, write another meaning of the word in the third box.

Mario is a fantastic singer and songwriter. Everyone enjoys his music because it expresses his individuality or personality. Many of his lyrics are complex; they are as complicated as the issues his teenage fans face. Mario has uploaded several of his songs to the Internet, and he hopes to acquire, or amass, a large fan base. I think Mario is a great businessperson, and with his online success, he will continue to be a successful entrepreneur.

WORD	SYNONYM	WORD MEANING
individuality	personality	a person's unique characteristics
complex	complicated	having more than one meaning or part; not simple
acquire	amass	to gather or collect
entrepreneur	businessperson	a person who runs a business

CCSS Vocabulary: 4.a.; Reading (Informational Text): 4. (See pp. T16–17.)

Practice for Tests

Fill in the bubble next to the answer that best completes the sentence or answers the question.

1. Read this sentence.

   Our library is going to *levy* a stiff fine on all overdue books and videos.

   Levy means:

   ○ **A** check out
   ○ **B** sell
   ● **C** impose
   ○ **D** print

2. When you *usurp* someone else's freedoms, you:

   ○ **A** support them
   ○ **B** question them
   ○ **C** disagree with them
   ● **D** take them

3. With *deregulation* of the energy industry, the energy companies:

   ● **A** have more freedom
   ○ **B** have less freedom
   ○ **C** have the same freedom
   ○ **D** lose a lot of money

4. A hurricane is *imminent*. That means the hurricane is NOT:

   ○ **A** nearby
   ● **B** far away
   ○ **C** approaching
   ○ **D** dangerous

5. Merchandise that is *disposable* is most likely to be:

   ○ **A** used again
   ○ **B** free to customers
   ● **C** thrown away
   ○ **D** expensive and overpriced

6. If you *winnow* topics for a research paper, you:

   ● **A** select a few good ones
   ○ **B** list as many as you can think of
   ○ **C** search the Internet for them
   ○ **D** gather information from multiple sources

7. Read this sentence.

   The *unlicensed* broadcaster was taken off the air.

   In this sentence, *unlicensed* means:

   ○ **A** wicked
   ○ **B** wrongful
   ○ **C** forbidden
   ● **D** unauthorized

8. The Chamber of *Commerce* is a group that:

   ● **A** encourages business
   ○ **B** conducts driver training
   ○ **C** promotes health and safety
   ○ **D** lobbies for higher taxes

9. One reason an author obtains a *copyright* on a written work is so he or she can:

   ○ **A** become famous
   ○ **B** decide who can and cannot read the work
   ● **C** maintain exclusive rights to the work
   ○ **D** be considered for literary awards

10. If an *eminent* guest speaker attends an event, he or she is most likely:

    ○ **A** intense
    ○ **B** mysterious
    ○ **C** intimidating
    ● **D** distinguished

If students answered B, C, or D for Item 3, remind them that deregulation involves fewer rules, less oversight, and therefore more freedom.

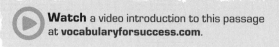
Watch a video introduction to this passage at **vocabularyforsuccess.com**.

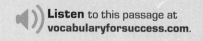
Listen to this passage at **vocabularyforsuccess.com**.

C CCSS Vocabulary: 4; Reading (Informational Text): 4, 6. (See pp. T16–17.)

Has Online Commerce Destroyed the Brick-and-Mortar Store?

<compare-and-contrast essay>

Who would have suspected that the closing of several brick-and-mortar bookstores last year would elicit extreme reactions from the public? Some customers felt depressed and began moaning and crying. How were they going to purchase a book if they couldn't browse the aisles, flip through the crisp pages of a new novel, and smell the fresh scent of paper and ink? Other consumers, though, didn't blink an eye. They sat right down in front of a computer and happily ordered their books with the click of a mouse. The manner and location of the purchase are different, but is online shopping really that much different from shopping at the mall? Truth be told, online commerce has more in common with brick-and-mortar stores than most people realize.

Both traditional and virtual stores have one main objective—to sell merchandise. Whether a business sells something ordinary, such as pet supplies, or has a specialization, such as providing organic shampoos for allergic pets, the goal is to earn a profit. To make that profit, both physical and online stores must spend money. They both have to buy inventory and warehouse space and pay employees. If the online company is small, it may require a funder to provide these start-up costs. The company spends money on advertising, marketing, and even payroll. (Yes, online commerce requires real flesh-and-blood people to fill and ship the orders!) On the other hand, large chain stores, including franchises, have the financial resources of their parent companies behind them. A giant corporate chain can even purchase or create a subsidiary to make the products or provide the services it needs.

There are big differences between shopping online and shopping in a physical store. First, there is the experience itself. Most shoppers want to check out the product they are buying. They want to feel the quality of material, look at the color in "real life," and try on the outfit. The online world can't provide a hands-on experience. The click of a mouse can facilitate purchasing, but the "virtual" nature of online buying can hinder full shopping satisfaction. When the product finally arrives, it may not fit. Or the customer simply may not like it. The purchaser ends up returning the item. That means there's no sale.

Physical stores—with their sales clerks, customer service, special sale offers, and attractive interior décor—have traditionally offered shoppers a sense of security and legitimacy. Customers are loyal to stores that provide consistent shopping experiences and quality merchandise. Online shopping sites can seem anonymous and impersonal, and they lack the social interactions that are a key to commercial relationships.

Another major difference lies in the fact that the fiduciary relationship that exists between a consumer and a retail store is not easily formed with an Internet site. Consumers simply find

Add to cart

46

Explain to students that a compare-and-contrast essay is an expository form of writing that examines similarities and differences between two subjects.

it easier to trust in a store with a physical location. Shoppers may have to make a leap of faith that an online business is legitimate; no one wants to take the chance of disclosing credit card information to an illicit business. To alleviate this problem, online commerce has taken many steps to institutionalize online security.

To "click it" or "brick it" is a matter of personal choice. People still need goods, regardless of where they shop. Online commerce is here to stay, but most people agree that brick-and-mortar stores are not going anywhere just yet. Buying online is convenient, but going to an actual store can be an entertaining, social, and fun experience.

VOCABULARY

elicit	payroll	anonymous
depressed	franchise	fiduciary
specialization	subsidiary	illicit
funder	facilitate	institutionalize

TALK ABOUT IT

With a partner, answer the questions below. Use as many of the highlighted words in the selection as you can.

1. Why do some Internet sites— for shopping, for researching, or for social networking— often seem *anonymous*?

2. Why do you think people would feel *depressed* about a physical store closing its doors?

People continue to shop at brick-and-mortar stores despite the ease of online shopping.

Word Meanings

For each highlighted word on pages 46–47, the meaning or meanings are given below.

For practice with synonyms, see page 66.

1. **anonymous** (uh-NON-uh-muhss) **adj.** unnamed; impersonal; lacking individuality or personality. A building can be so *anonymous* and drab that you don't even notice it as you walk by. **SYNONYMS:** indistinct, bland, unremarkable; **adj.** unidentified; nameless. People who want to remain *anonymous* do not give their names when they call the police.

2. **depressed** (di-PREST) **adj.** feeling gloomy or sad. People who are *depressed* feel unhappy and often lack the energy to get out of bed or interact with other people. **SYNONYMS:** miserable, glum, disheartened; **adj.** characterized by slow economic growth and high unemployment. In a *depressed* economy, jobs are in short supply, and consumers tend to be cautious about spending money. **SYNONYMS:** weak, flat

3. **elicit** (i-LISS-it) **v.** to draw out a reaction or an emotion. Certain events *elicit* strong reactions from people. **SYNONYMS:** evoke, extract

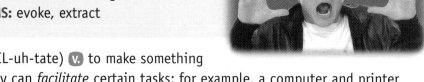

4. **facilitate** (fuh-SIL-uh-tate) **v.** to make something easier. Technology can *facilitate* certain tasks; for example, a computer and printer facilitate writing papers. **SYNONYMS:** ease, simplify, assist

5. **fiduciary** (fi-DOO-shee-air-ee) **adj.** related to the trust in a relationship based on money. Banks have a *fiduciary* responsibility to protect their account holders' money. **n.** a person who manages someone else's money. Some people use a *fiduciary* to make their investments. **SYNONYMS:** trustee, guardian

6. **franchise** (FRAN-chize) **n.** a business that has permission to use a well-known company's name and sell its goods. If you want to operate a popular food or clothing *franchise*, you must pay the company a fee to use its name and sell its products. **SYNONYMS:** dealership, business; **n.** the right to vote. The U.S. government granted the *franchise* to women for the first time in 1920. **SYNONYMS:** suffrage, voice

7. **funder** (FUHN-dur) **n.** a person who gives some or all of the money needed for a business or an organization to run. A nonprofit organization must find a suitable *funder* to help pay the operating costs. **SYNONYMS:** financier, investor, sponsor

8. **illicit** (i-LISS-it) **adj.** against the law. It is a crime to run an *illicit* business. **SYNONYMS:** illegal, illegitimate, unauthorized

C CCSS Vocabulary: 4.c., 4.d. (See pp. T16–17.)

▶ **Watch** a video introduction for each word at **vocabularyforsuccess.com**.

🔊 **Listen** to iWords at **vocabularyforsuccess.com**.

📖 **Refer** to the online dictionary at **vocabularyforsuccess.com**.

9. **institutionalize** (in-stuh-TOO-shuhn-uhl-ize) **v.** to make into a custom or a formal practice. When companies *institutionalize* free shipping, they offer it on a regular basis. SYNONYMS: standardize, establish

10. **payroll** (PAY-rohl) **n.** the money required to pay employees for their work. Even a small company with few employees needs to manage its *payroll*. SYNONYMS: wages, salaries; **n.** the list of a business's employees and their rates of pay. When workers are laid off or fired from a job, they are removed from the *payroll*.

11. **specialization** (SPESH-uh-luh-ZAY-shuhn) **n.** supplying a product made for a certain purpose or to meet the needs of certain shoppers. If a beauty business wants to reach shoppers who like organic products, its *specialization* would include shampoos made from organic plants. SYNONYMS: focus, concentration

12. **subsidiary** (suhb-SID-ee-er-ee) **n.** a company controlled by another company. A major corporation may open a *subsidiary* to provide a related product or service. SYNONYMS: division, extension; **adj.** providing additional support or backing. A *subsidiary* theme in a novel strengthens the main theme. SYNONYMS: auxiliary, supplementary, ancillary

More on Meanings: Confusing Word Pairs

There are many confusing word pairs in the English language. A common mistake is to confuse *elicit* with *illicit*, because of their similar spellings. Compare these two sentences:

The author wanted to **elicit** an emotional response from his readers.

The criminal was involved in **illicit** activities.

Notice that *elicit* is a verb and *illicit* is an adjective. Now consider these sentences:

Many passages in Tolkien's *Lord of the Rings* trilogy **allude** to ancient Anglo-Saxon and Norse myths and legends.

In stories and movies about Sherlock Holmes, criminals think they can **elude** the great detective, but they never succeed.

Both of these words are verbs, but *allude* means "to make an indirect reference" and *elude* means "to escape or evade."

Challenge Choose one word pair below. Use both words correctly in the same sentence. Check a dictionary if you need help.

forward, foreword   *personal, personnel*
precede, proceed

If students confuse *elicit* and *illicit*, provide them with a memory aid using alliteration: *Elicit* means "to <u>e</u>voke or <u>e</u>ntice." *Illicit* means "<u>i</u>llegal."

🄲 CCSS Vocabulary: 4.a., 5. (See pp. T16–17.)

vocabularyforsuccess.com ▶   **49**

Word Talk

Each lesson word has been placed in a category. With a partner, discuss and list items that belong in each category. Compare your results with those of another pair of students.

C CCSS Vocabulary: 6. (See pp. T16–17.)

Examples of *Specialization* for the Teen Market

young adult novels, posters of celebrities, skateboard gear

Reasons People Get *Depressed*

a bad grade on a test, a disappointment, a rejection

Professions Involving *Fiduciary* Duties

banking, investing, law, commerce

Places That Can Seem *Anonymous*

gas stations, hospital rooms, industrial buildings, bus depots

How to *Institutionalize* a Change

make a new law or rule, advertise, get everybody to do it

Reasons to Run a Food *Franchise*

customers already know and like the food, people like to eat out

Reasons a Company Starts a *Subsidiary*

to grow, to make new products, to hire more people

Examples of *Illicit* Activities Involving Money

bank robbery, tax fraud, selling stolen products

Organizations a Good-Hearted *Funder* Might Invest In

animal shelters, nonprofit arts organizations, children's charities

Types of Businesses with a High *Payroll*

professional sports teams, law firms, hospitals, software-development companies

Ways to *Facilitate* Getting to School

take the bus, ride your bike, let someone drive you

Things That *Elicit* a Happy Response

a good report card, winning a contest, making the team

Check for Understanding

Choose the lesson word that completes each sentence. Write the word on the line provided. Some words will be used twice.

anonymous	facilitate	funder	payroll
depressed	fiduciary	illicit	specialization
elicit	franchise	institutionalize	subsidiary

1. People who focus on the positive are less likely to feel ___depressed___.

2. A/an ___fiduciary___ duty of a literary agent is to make sure publishers pay writers the amounts agreed to in their contracts.

3. A food store that has a/an ___specialization___ offers items you won't find in an ordinary grocery store.

4. If you don't have a lot of cash to open a business, consider finding a/an ___funder___.

5. The photographer has won awards for her images of featureless, ___anonymous___ places such as abandoned mini-malls and factories.

6. The office will ___institutionalize___ casual Fridays so workers can wear jeans to work.

7. Hannah's parents knew that the letter of acceptance to the exclusive music camp would ___elicit___ a joyous response from their daughter.

8. The shop owner calculated the monthly ___payroll___ for his employees.

9. After Terence failed to make the science-quiz team, he felt quite ___depressed___.

10. My brother wants to manage a/an ___franchise___ of a well-known sandwich chain.

11. People should be wary of phone scammers who run ___illicit___ businesses.

12. This website has information that could ___facilitate___ your application process.

13. Grubbie Kids is a/an ___subsidiary___ of the global company, Grubbies Incorporated.

14. The school district decided to ___institutionalize___ mandatory summer school.

If students answer *illicit* for Item 7 or *elicit* for Item 11, have them review the More on Meanings: Confusing Word Pairs feature on page 49.

Word Associations

Use what you know about the lesson word in italics to answer each question. Circle the letter next to the phrase that best answers the question. Be prepared to explain your answers.

1. What happens if the police catch a person engaging in an *illicit* activity?

   a. The person will probably be arrested.
   b. The person might receive a medal.
   c. The person will get to start a business.

2. Why do some donors to charities prefer to remain *anonymous*?

   a. They like keeping secrets.
   b. They value their privacy.
   c. They enjoy the recognition.

3. Where would you shop if you were looking for *specialization*?

   a. a chain grocery store
   b. a department store
   c. an organic cotton clothing store

4. Which is a sign of a *depressed* economy?

   a. home sales
   b. business failures
   c. power outages

5. Which of the following might require a *funder*?

   a. a start-up company
   b. a successful company
   c. an established company

6. Who would be on the *payroll* at a hair salon?

   a. a nurse
   b. a stylist
   c. a painter

7. If a company wants to *facilitate* the return of merchandise, what will it do?

   a. It will use three-day shipping.
   b. It will offer items at half price.
   c. It will provide shipping labels and free postage.

8. Which is a *fiduciary* task?

   a. to challenge other businesses
   b. to keep records of money spent
   c. to share the financial data of clients

9. Which response might a half-price sale at a popular electronics superstore *elicit*?

   a. extreme shock
   b. mild curiosity
   c. frenzied excitement

10. What is an example of a *subsidiary*?

    a. a shoe manufacturer owned by a large clothing company
    b. a family-owned restaurant
    c. a local hot dog stand

11. Which of the following is the benefit of running a *franchise*?

    a. You get to name the business.
    b. You get to make an original product.
    c. You get to run a business that people already know and like.

12. What will happen if a restaurant decides to *institutionalize* free refills?

    a. Customers will need coupons for refills.
    b. Customers will receive free refills all the time.
    c. Customers will get free refills only at the grand opening.

CCSS Vocabulary: 4.a. (See pp. T16–17.)

Check Again

Use what you know about the lesson word in italics to complete each sentence. Be sure your sentences make sense.

1. A *franchise* is a business that ___ has the right to use a known company's name and sell its products. ___

2. To remain *anonymous* means that you ___ remain unknown. ___

3. Sometimes people get *depressed* when ___ the weather is cloudy or cold and rainy for many weeks. ___

4. A store that offers *specialization* to its customers is ___ intended for a specific set of shoppers. ___

5. In order to prepare the *payroll*, a small-business owner has to ___ be sure there is enough money to ___ cover paychecks for all employees. ___

6. If you *facilitate* something, you ___ try to make it easier. ___

7. People involved in *illicit* business practices are ___ committing a crime. ___

8. A person assuming a *fiduciary* responsibility should ___ be trustworthy. ___

9. Some people require a *funder* in order to open a business because ___ they do not have a lot of money. ___

10. A *subsidiary* is a company that ___ is owned by a larger company. ___

11. Someone yelling "fire" in a crowded shopping mall would *elicit* ___ chaos and panic. ___

12. If you want to *institutionalize* an idea at your school, you must ___ create regular rules or practices. ___

Write Your Own

1. **Write a nine-word sentence using the word *depressed*.**

   The depressed economy kept many teenagers from finding jobs.

2. **Write a thirteen-word sentence using the word *franchise* as a noun in the fifth position.**

   To be granted the franchise would be the greatest gift to unliberated people.

Word-Solving Strategies:
Context Clues

Antonyms

Writers often use antonyms to help readers determine the meaning of an unknown word. Reread this sentence from "Has Online Commerce Destroyed the Brick-and-Mortar Store?":

The click of a mouse can facilitate purchasing, but the "virtual" nature of online buying can hinder full shopping satisfaction.

The word *hinder* is the opposite of *facilitate*. The word *but* is a clue that the sentence might contain an antonym. The reader should understand that although clicking a mouse can facilitate shopping, it also hinders, or gets in the way of, the shopping experience, because the consumer might be dissatisfied and simply send back the item.

BE CAREFUL!

Antonyms are not always indicated by contrast-clue words.

Shoppers may have to make a leap of faith that an online business is legitimate; no one wants to take the chance of disclosing credit card information to an illicit business.

The words *legitimate* and *illicit* are antonyms, but the sentence does not provide a contrast-clue word. If you are unsure about a word's meaning, work with a peer to figure it out.

Practice

Write six sentences using each of the highlighted words from the paragraph below. Use antonyms as context clues.

What if you can't make an online purchase because your debit account has been suspended and cannot be reinstated? The cause may simply be a temporary deficit of funds in your account, and you will need to create a surplus. But what if you discover that your credit limit is exceeded because of fraudulent use of your financial information? Although you have done everything legal, you're a victim of identity theft, a violation of your privacy without your permission that can be difficult to clear up.

1. _____ My pass to the gym was suspended for a week, but I got it reactivated. _____

2. _____ If I have a deficit of concepts for my comic strip, I look in my notebook for a surplus of ideas. _____

3. _____ Fraudulent practices are not innocent but punishable by law. _____

4. _____ It a violation of privacy, not a respectful act, to enter this property without our permission. _____

5. _____ Now that the drought is over, there's an abundance instead of a deficit of Texas peaches. _____

6. _____ The contract turned out not to be fraudulent after all; it was completely legal. _____

Practice for Tests

For a quiz and additional practice for this lesson, go to **vocabularyforsuccess.com**.

Fill in the bubble next to the answer that best completes the sentence or answers the question.

1. Read this sentence.

   A *fiduciary* must represent the best interests of the people who hire him or her.

   Fiduciary means:

   ○ **A** guard
   ● **B** trustee
   ○ **C** loyalty
   ○ **D** supporter

2. An economy that is *depressed* is NOT:

   ● **A** growing
   ○ **B** gloomy
   ○ **C** necessary
   ○ **D** decreasing

3. If you are preparing a *payroll*, you are:

   ○ **A** writing job descriptions
   ○ **B** providing evaluations
   ● **C** calculating salaries
   ○ **D** paying taxes

4. An advantage of having a *funder* when opening a new business is that:

   ○ **A** you both share the work
   ● **B** you have financial support
   ○ **C** one of you takes all the risk
   ○ **D** one of you assumes all the power

5. A company with a *specialization* is one that provides:

   ○ **A** online goods
   ○ **B** a variety of goods
   ○ **C** inexpensive goods
   ● **D** specific goods

6. Which action would *elicit* a positive response from friends?

   ○ **A** asking them to clean your room
   ● **B** inviting them out for dinner
   ○ **C** borrowing money from them
   ○ **D** telling them you don't want to spend time with them

7. Read this sentence.

   The city council wanted to *institutionalize* a new process for public hearings.

   Institutionalize means:

   ○ **A** to create funds
   ● **B** to establish a practice
   ○ **C** to become famous
   ○ **D** to hire employees

8. A company might create a *subsidiary* because:

   ○ **A** it is losing money
   ○ **B** it wants a new name
   ● **C** it wants to grow
   ○ **D** it needs better management

9. An *illicit* business is one that:

   ● **A** operates outside the law
   ○ **B** protects its customers
   ○ **C** manages operations online
   ○ **D** requests customer feedback

10. If an online site wants to *facilitate* your shopping experience, it will:

    ○ **A** ignore you
    ○ **B** overcharge you
    ● **C** try to help you
    ○ **D** encourage you to buy more

If students answer B, C, or D for Item 2, remind them that they need to choose the word that has the opposite meaning of *depressed*.

C CCSS Vocabulary: 4.a., 6. (See pp. T16–17.)

vocabularyforsuccess.com   55

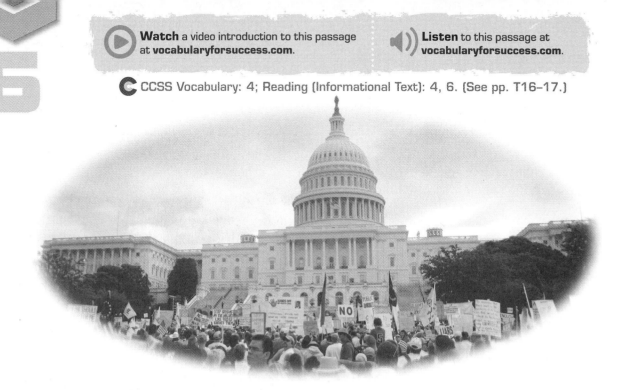

▶ **Watch** a video introduction to this passage at **vocabularyforsuccess.com**.

◀)) **Listen** to this passage at **vocabularyforsuccess.com**.

C CCSS Vocabulary: 4; Reading (Informational Text): 4, 6. (See pp. T16–17.)

Protect Your Privacy When Buying Online

\<persuasive essay\>

If you're like me, you probably shop online because it's convenient. You may believe that your transactions are private and secure. But let the buyer beware! Shopping online can leave us open to fraud, and our privacy may be invaded without our even knowing it.

The number of counterfeit stores is rising. These sites pose as legitimate stores and "sell" merchandise, all in the hope of collecting credit card information. Sometimes it's difficult to discern which online shops are fake. Although most savvy shoppers know the tips to follow to avoid online scams, there is still another systemic problem with online shopping—invasion of privacy. Don't make the mistake of thinking that this problem is limited to sham online businesses; established, supposedly trustworthy businesses can endanger our privacy as well.

Legitimate online businesses invade consumers' privacy in a more subtle way than illegitimate businesses do. Every time you visit a website, your privacy is secretly compromised. Internet businesses track your shopping record and use this information to their advantage. Your shopping habits provide businesses with a wealth of data, including what products you buy, your age, your interests, your income level, what books you like, your medical conditions, and your political affiliation. The list is endless. What do they do with this information? They sell it to advertisers!

Although many computer browsers have a private mode that limits tracking during browsing, very few of us use this feature. Think about the last time you ordered a pair of shoes online. Did you start to notice more and more shoe ads during your other online searches? Did shoe catalogs inexplicably arrive in the mail? Although you didn't order these catalogs, your online persona did! Businesses and advertisers claim that this tracking is harmless; I disagree.

VOCABULARY

It's easy to assign blame to the businesses, but we online shoppers need to assert our rights. We can't expect professional organizations for advertisers to pass a bylaw that would end the practice. It's time for us to demand a consumer bill of rights. We need to establish clear rules that protect consumers and that businesses must abide by. With more of us shopping online for the best deals and quickest purchases, it's more important now than ever to make sure that our right to privacy is protected. A law should state that consumers have a right to secure handling of their personal information. A clause within the legislation should clearly define how information about us can be used, and we should be able to opt out of providing that information.

You may be familiar with the quote, "Big Brother is watching you." It's a reference to George Orwell's novel *Nineteen Eighty-Four*, about a terrifying future in which the government sees all and knows all and personal freedom and privacy no longer exist. In a way, Orwell's vision has come true. But today's Big Brother is not the government; it's the Internet. The Internet enables private companies to spy on us and take advantage of our desire to shop conveniently. They're tracking our shopping habits and collecting all kinds of personal data. The implementation of a consumer bill of rights would deter this intrusion. I call for shoppers to congregate at the Capitol this month. By gathering together we can find strength in numbers and stand up for our right to online privacy! It's better to have our rights protected than to suffer the slings and arrows of outrageous online spies and scammers!

Online shopping is easy, but it can leave consumers open to fraud and identity theft.

TALK ABOUT IT

With a partner, answer the questions below. Use as many of the highlighted words in the selection as you can.

1. How do *counterfeit* businesses ruin the reputation of online shopping?

2. If you were responsible for the *implementation* of rules for protecting online privacy, what steps would you take to get the job done?

Word Meanings

For each highlighted word on pages 56–57, the meaning or meanings are given below.

For practice with synonyms, see page 66.

1. **assign** (uh-SINE) **v.** to give someone a responsibility. If you *assign* someone a task, you tell that person to do something. **SYNONYMS:** allocate, dispense, appoint

2. **bylaw** (BYE-law) **n.** a rule made by a group to govern the group. An organization adopts a *bylaw* to address a problem or situation within it. **SYNONYMS:** regulation, ruling, law

3. **clause** (KLAWZ) **n.** a particular section of a legal document. Sometimes a *clause* is added to clarify a key point in a legal contract. **SYNONYMS:** provision, paragraph, amendment; **n.** a grammatical structure; a part of a sentence. A dependent *clause* contains a noun and a verb but does not express a complete thought.

4. **congregate** (KON-gri-gate) **v.** to gather together. When the principal asks the whole school to *congregate* in the gym, everyone will meet there. **SYNONYMS:** assemble, convene; (KON-gri-guht) **adj.** gathered together; referring to group services. *Congregate* day care centers help parents in a community. **SYNONYMS:** collective, communal, shared

5. **counterfeit** (KOUN-tur-fit) **adj.** copied illegally; fake, phony. People who make *counterfeit* money are breaking the law; only governments can print genuine currency. **SYNONYM:** fraudulent; **v.** to copy something illegally and pass it off as genuine. To *counterfeit* credit cards is illegal; only banks can issue them. **SYNONYM:** copy

6. **fraud** (FRAWD) **n.** a dishonest act carried out on purpose. *Fraud* is a crime that occurs when someone cheats or tricks someone else in a business deal. **SYNONYMS:** deception, scam; **n.** a swindler. A person who cheats you or pretends to be someone else is a *fraud*. **SYNONYMS:** con artist, scam artist

7. **implementation** (im-pluh-men-TAY-shuhn) **n.** the act of carrying out a process. The *implementation* of a plan can be much more difficult than the conception of it. **SYNONYMS:** execution, achievement, accomplishment

8. **mode** (MOHD) **n.** an option on a device. You can switch to a different *mode* on an electronic device to make it function in a new way. **SYNONYMS:** operation, feature; **n.** a particular type or form. E-mail is one *mode* of communication. **SYNONYM:** means; **n.** a way of acting. An on-duty police officer should operate in a professional *mode*. **SYNONYMS:** characteristic, manner, procedure

C CCSS Vocabulary: 4.c., 4.d. (See pp. T16–17.)

Watch a video introduction for each word at **vocabularyforsuccess.com**.

Listen to iWords at **vocabularyforsuccess.com**.

Refer to the online dictionary at **vocabularyforsuccess.com**.

9. **persona** (pur-SOH-nuh) **n.** an element of one's character; a role. You might have a different *persona* on the basketball team than you have in your regular classes. SYNONYMS: character, personality, facade

10. **pose** (POHZ) **v.** to present oneself in a deceptive manner. If you decide to *pose* as a police officer in order to get out of a speeding ticket, you could get into serious trouble. SYNONYMS: model, impersonate; **v.** to ask or put forward. A teacher will *pose* a question for the class to consider. SYNONYMS: ask, present, suggest; **n.** a way of standing or holding one's body. A photographer may ask his or her subject to assume a *pose*. SYNONYM: position

11. **quote** (KWOTE) **n.** a saying, short for *quotation*. When using a *quote* in a speech, be sure to repeat it accurately. SYNONYM: line; **v.** to repeat someone's words. To *quote* a source means to use the words exactly. SYNONYM: recite

12. **systemic** (siss-TEM-ik) **adj.** affecting an entire system. If no one speaks against injustice, the problem can become *systemic*. SYNONYMS: universal, widespread

More on Meanings: Multiple-Meaning Words

Many words have more than one meaning. In some cases, the word may be used as the same part of speech but have different meanings. Compare these two sentences:

She suspected that the critic was a **fraud**.

The jury found the artist guilty of **fraud**.

Now compare these sentences.

"Why did you **pose** as the movie's director?" the reporters asked the actor.

"You **pose** a good question," she replied.

Then, she stopped to **pose** for the cameras.

How long can she keep up that **pose**?

All four meanings of *pose* are different. The first three sentences show different verb meanings. The fourth uses *pose as* a noun.

Challenge

1. Choose two of the multiple-meaning words below. For each, write two sentences that illustrate different meanings of the word.

   chime   *baste*   *clink*   *shank*

2. Use the multiple-meaning words below to write a short paragraph.

   cram   *ebb*   *redeem*

If students confuse the meanings of *fraud*, explain that both meanings deal with deceptive activities; one refers to the act itself, but the other refers to the person who commits it.

Word Talk

Each lesson word has been placed in a category. With a partner, discuss and list items that belong in each category. Compare your results with those of another pair of students.

C CCSS Vocabulary: 6. [See pp. T16–17.]

Homework Your Teachers Might *Assign*

read a story, complete a worksheet, write an essay, conduct an interview

Where You Might Read a *Clause*

product warranty, a legal document, the Constitution

Situations in Which You Might Use a *Quote*

a research paper, a speech, a job interview

Examples of a *Bylaw* of a School Sport or Club

An adult must be present during meetings; players cannot be paid; teams cannot discriminate.

Examples of Goods That Might Be *Counterfeit*

designer purses, sport shoes, electronic components, medication

Reasons You Might *Pose* as Someone Else

to spy on someone, to go undercover, to expose a cover-up

People with a Public *Persona*

celebrities, politicians, sports stars

Examples of *Fraud*

hacking a computer, using an alias, falsely claiming an insurance loss

Places Where People *Congregate*

the mall, free concerts, political meetings

Questions to Consider Before the *Implementation* of a Written Plan

Is the plan realistic? How will the plan meet my goals? Who can help me?

Examples of Different *Modes* on Electronic Devices

silent or airplane mode on a cell phone, widescreen mode on a television remote control, sleep mode on a computer

Systemic Problems in Our Society

poverty, hunger, violence, injustice

Check for Understanding

Choose the lesson word that completes each sentence. Write the word on the line provided. Some words will be used twice.

assign	congregate	implementation	pose
bylaw	counterfeit	mode	quote
clause	fraud	persona	systemic

1. The computers crashed because of a/an _____systemic_____ problem, not an individual user's error.

2. When Jimmy signed the contract, he made sure the lawyer added a/an _____clause_____ allowing him to bring his dog backstage.

3. When you go to the theater, put your phone on mute _____mode_____.

4. The police set up a sting operation to curtail recent incidents of _____fraud_____.

5. Our neighborhood association added a new _____bylaw_____ that states the local pool is open to all residents and their guests.

6. Some professional speakers begin every speech with a/an _____quote_____ to grab the audience's attention.

7. The street fair vendors were caught selling _____counterfeit_____ goods.

8. When Marianne writes poems, she often assumes a masculine _____persona_____.

9. The novel's main character likes to _____pose_____ in public as a successful businessman, even though he is an unemployed actor.

10. The science teacher will _____assign_____ each student a new partner.

11. Citizens are urged to _____congregate_____ outside of the city hall to protest the new law.

12. The lawyers evaluated the impact of the _____implementation_____ of the new privacy rules.

13. My favorite _____quote_____ is "When one door closes, another opens."

14. Before you sign the agreement, read each _____clause_____ carefully.

If students answer clause *for Item 5, review the difference between a clause and a bylaw.*

Word Associations

Use what you know about the lesson word in italics to answer each question. Circle the letter next to the phrase that best answers the question. Be prepared to explain your answers.

1. Which *mode* of transportation would be fastest for an overseas trip?

   a. a private jet
   b. a cruise ship
   c. a commercial airliner

2. Why is *counterfeit* money illegal?

   a. It is handmade.
   b. It is fake.
   c. It is attractive.

3. What is the first step in the *implementation* of a plan?

   a. executing the plan
   b. explaining the plan
   c. thinking up the plan

4. Which of the following would most likely be included in an organization's *bylaws*?

   a. names of directors
   b. a community calendar
   c. responsibilities of officers

5. How might a musician establish a *persona*?

   a. change his or her name
   b. buy a new guitar
   c. rewrite lyrics to earlier songs

6. Which of the following would be considered an act of *fraud*?

   a. lying to yourself
   b. cheating on a test
   c. using someone else's car

7. How might a parent *assign* a task to a child?

   a. write it on a chore chart
   b. determine if it has been done
   c. make sure someone else does it

8. If you *quote* a line from Shakespeare, what do you do?

   a. look up the line
   b. repeat the line
   c. invent the line

9. Which of the following makes up a *clause*?

   a. a verb and its object
   b. an adjective and a noun
   c. a noun and a verb

10. In which situation might you strike a *pose*?

    a. while running a race
    b. while in a photo booth
    c. while writing an essay

11. What is an example of a *congregate* activity?

    a. taking a walk with your best friend
    b. camping in a tent by yourself
    c. eating lunch in a school cafeteria

12. What kind of disease is *systemic*?

    a. one that affects an individual organ
    b. one that affects the entire body
    c. one that affects the skin

CCSS Vocabulary: 4.a. (See pp. T16–17.)

Check Again

Use what you know about the lesson word in italics to complete each sentence. Be sure your sentences make sense.

1. One reason people *congregate* at sports events is to _____ cheer their favorite team.

2. Baseball coaches *assign* positions to players in order to _____ make sure all areas of the field are defended.

3. It's difficult to successfully *counterfeit* a great work of art because _____ artistic styles are unique and not easily imitated.

4. If you suddenly go into a "panic *mode*," then you are _____ excitedly reacting to something with fear.

5. A person with a distinct public *persona* might behave differently when _____ he or she is at an intimate dinner.

6. An example of a famous *quote* is _____ "To be, or not to be; that is the question."

7. If you wanted to make a *systemic* change at your school, you would have to _____ get everyone to agree to it.

8. If you do not understand a *clause* in a document, you _____ should ask for clarification.

9. Some people dislike having to *pose* for photos because _____ they feel silly in a fake position.

10. If you were starting a new club or organization, you might create *bylaws* _____ to establish rules and guidelines.

11. A person convicted of *fraud* is someone who _____ is a liar and has deceived others.

12. People who want to stop the *implementation* of a law might _____ protest or write a letter to their state representative.

Write Your Own

Reread the passage on pages 56–57. Then, on a separate sheet of paper, write a one-paragraph response to the question, "How can online shoppers best protect their money and privacy?" Use at least two words from the lesson word list and support your answer by referring to the text of the passage.

Word-Solving Strategies: Context Clues

Inferences

Sometimes context clues are not explicit. Then you have to make inferences, or educated guesses, about a word's meaning. Reread this sentence from "Protect Your Privacy When Buying Online":

> These sites pose as legitimate stores and "sell" merchandise, all in the hope of collecting credit card information. Sometimes, it's difficult to discern which online shops are fake.

The word *sell* is in quotation marks, implying that the sale is not real. The writer also states that it is difficult to know which shops are fake. These clues lead you to infer that *pose* means "to represent oneself in a false way."

BE CAREFUL!

Sometimes the information you need is in a different sentence.

I call for shoppers to congregate at the Capitol this month. By gathering together we can find strength in numbers and stand up for our right to online privacy!

The second sentence provides the clue— "gathering"— to the meaning of *congregate*. If you are unsure about a word's meaning, consult a thesaurus.

Practice

Write the highlighted word and the clues that helped you infer the meaning in the first two boxes. Then write the word's meaning in the third box.

Early online businesses envisioned changing the way people shopped. Their dreams of success were delayed, however, because of potential customers' distrust. Some dishonest businesses misused customers' personal information, and shoppers' computers started to fill up with copious amounts of unwanted spam. Reactionaries laughed; they never believed the newfangled online shopping was safe. Eventually, new laws forced online businesses to change their ways and to conduct business conscientiously, and soon customers returned to online stores.

WORD	INFERENCE CLUES	WORD MEANING
envisioned	dreams	imagined; visualized
copious	computers started to fill up	numerous; abundant
reactionaries	never believed, newfangled	people who have conservative views or are cautious about change
conscientiously	new laws forced, change their ways, customers returned	ethically and honestly; with care

CCSS Vocabulary: 4.a.; Reading (Informational Text): 4. (See pp. T16–17.)

Practice for Tests

For a quiz and additional practice for this lesson, go to **vocabularyforsuccess.com**.

Fill in the bubble next to the answer that best completes the sentence or answers the question.

1. Read this sentence.

   Doctors did their best to save the patient, but her wounds caused a *systemic* shutdown.

   Systemic means:

   ○ **A** gaping
   ○ **B** secretive
   ● **C** complete
   ○ **D** impressive

2. A *fraud* is a person who:

   ○ **A** opposes justice
   ○ **B** wears disguises
   ○ **C** lives honestly
   ● **D** deceives others

3. If you *assign* all the roles in a play, you:

   ○ **A** share them
   ● **B** distribute them
   ○ **C** explain them
   ○ **D** discard them

4. You might want to pay attention to the wording of a *clause* when you:

   ○ **A** read a bestselling novel
   ○ **B** receive your new class schedule
   ● **C** agree to the terms of a computer software program
   ○ **D** write an essay

5. Which of the following is NOT a characteristic of someone who is in a professional *mode*?

   ○ **A** punctual
   ○ **B** disciplined
   ○ **C** polite
   ● **D** enraged

   If students answered D for Item 4, remind them that the clause in question most likely appears in a formal or legal document; it is not the grammatical term.

6. A *counterfeit* watch is one that is:

   ● **A** phony
   ○ **B** concealed
   ○ **C** guaranteed
   ○ **D** dependable

7. When you *quote* a source in an essay, you:

   ○ **A** summarize the main idea
   ● **B** cite its exact words
   ○ **C** claim the words as your own
   ○ **D** rewrite the idea in your own words

8. Read this sentence.

   The interviewer will likely *pose* the following questions.

   Pose means:

   ○ **A** to establish a fact
   ○ **B** to stand in a certain position
   ○ **C** to represent oneself in a false way
   ● **D** to ask

9. You would be most likely to find *congregate* care for the elderly in:

   ● **A** an assisted-living facility
   ○ **B** a hospital room
   ○ **C** a doctor's office
   ○ **D** an emergency room

10. When an actor assumes a *persona* onstage, he or she:

    ○ **A** is wearing a mask
    ○ **B** performs unnaturally
    ○ **C** memorizes the dialogue
    ● **D** becomes immersed in the role

Synonyms and Antonyms

In the following Word Bank, you will find synonyms and antonyms for some of the words in Lessons 4–6. (Remember: Some words have both synonyms and antonyms.) Study these words; then complete the exercises below.

hinder	authorized	distant	flock	sad	impostor
appeal	control	uncertified	authentic	forged	justice

A. For each sentence, fill in the blank with a SYNONYM for the word in boldface.

1. If you are an **unlicensed** driver, you are _____uncertified_____ and shouldn't be driving.

2. Imagine the collector's outrage when he realized that his stolen masterpiece was **counterfeit**, and he could not collect insurance on a/an _____forged_____ work of art.

3. The players felt **depressed** when the team lost the semifinal game, and the seniors on the team grew _____sad_____ as they realized they would never play the game again.

4. The detective was able to determine that the con artist was a **fraud** who had posed as a/an _____impostor_____ to get money from innocent people.

5. Geese tend to **congregate** in large numbers; they _____flock_____ together for safety.

B. For each sentence, fill in the blank with an ANTONYM for the word in boldface.

6. When **deregulation** of U.S. banks led to a financial crisis, voters appealed to Congress for new laws that would give the government more _____control_____ of the industry.

7. A shuttle bus will **facilitate** the transportation of fans to the stadium because if too many people drive their cars, they will _____hinder_____ the flow of traffic.

8. Saving only when retirement is **imminent** is not a sound fiscal strategy. Unfortunately, for young adults, retirement is so _____distant_____ that they do not save money.

9. When he began as an apprentice plumber, he was **unlicensed**, but after working hard for several years, he was finally _____authorized_____ to run his own plumbing business.

10. One must always be alert for **fraud** when looking for bargains in the fashion market, because some people are tempted to copy _____authentic_____ designs and sell them for less.

Word Study: Idioms

If your friend tells you that she is "on pins and needles" while waiting for the results of her math test, she does not literally mean that she is sitting on sharp objects. Your friend means that she feels anxious or nervous. The expression "on pins and needles" is an idiom, a short phrase that is meant figuratively. The words that make up an idiom have a different meaning from the literal meanings of the individual words.

Some of the words in Lessons 4–6 have meanings that can also be expressed as idioms. If you wanted to comment on how some people tend to **congregate** (Lesson 6) based on common interests, you might say "birds of a feather flock together."

Practice

Read each sentence. Use context clues to figure out the meaning of each idiom in bold print. Then write the letter of the definition for the idiom in the sentence.

_d_ **1.** Lana's account of her vacation was **short and sweet**.

_b_ **2.** When the inspector discovered we did not have a building permit, she **pulled the plug** on the project.

_e_ **3.** The new employee has been a **thorn in my side** since he started.

_c_ **4.** Alicia wants to plan all the activities for our vacation, but I would rather **play it by ear**.

_f_ **5.** I thought the cabdriver had sent us on a **wild goose chase** as we tried to locate a vegan restaurant.

_a_ **6.** I **bit my tongue** when my best friend asked what I thought about her singing.

a. avoided saying what I really think

b. ended all support

c. decide as we go along

d. brief but to the point

e. a nuisance or irritation

f. a lengthy but useless pursuit

g. listen closely

Apply

Work with a partner to find out the meaning of each idiom. (Use an online or print dictionary.) Then work together to write a sentence for each idiom.

1. walking on eggshells

2. dial it back

3. a drop in the ocean

4. make ends meet

5. call it a day

6. a nest egg

7. run a tight ship

8. a fish out of water

Vocabulary for Comprehension

Read the following passage, in which some of the words you have studied in Lessons 4–6 appear in boldface type. Then answer questions 1–6.

Tips for Online Shopping

Online **commerce** can **facilitate** your getting the merchandise you want quickly and at a good price. However, it is important for consumers to be vigilant. E-commerce is not always safe. How
5 can consumers be more savvy? Here are a few tips for the online shopper:

1. If you shop at a reputable **franchise**, you will decrease the possibility of a **counterfeit** transaction. Use your computer as a research
10 tool and search for lists of **unlicensed** businesses. Then avoid them.

2. Make sure the site has a trusted symbol that indicates your information is protected. Some networks **assign** different levels of security to
15 online businesses.

3. Read the privacy terms the site provides. The site may have a **clause** stating that it can share your data with other business.

Shopping online can seem like an **anonymous**
20 experience, but online consumerism continues to grow. With that growth comes the possibility of **fraud**. So, when you shop online, look for signs of **illicit** activities. Don't be a victim of "phishing"—an attempt to get you to provide
25 private information to a hidden third party. Avoid leaving cookies—data stored in your browser that companies can use to construct a history of your online activity.

So, follow these tips and be a mindful online
30 shopper.

---

1. In sentence 1, **commerce** refers to
- ○ **A** money
- ● **B** business
- ○ **C** computers
- ○ **D** advertisements

2. A **franchise** (line 7) is a
- ○ **A** specialized tax
- ○ **B** shopping permit
- ● **C** business with a license to sell a brand
- ○ **D** fast food restaurant

3. When networks **assign** (line 14) a security rating, they
- ● **A** award it
- ○ **B** vote on it
- ○ **C** register it
- ○ **D** pay for it

4. A **clause** (line 17) is something that
- ○ **A** improves services
- ○ **B** protects a business
- ○ **C** offers special deals
- ● **D** defines an agreement

5. An **anonymous** (line 19) experience is NOT
- ○ **A** faceless
- ○ **B** obscure
- ● **C** memorable
- ○ **D** secretive

6. In line 22, **fraud** means
- ○ **A** a funny prank
- ● **B** a dishonest scheme
- ○ **C** an obvious imposter
- ○ **D** an awful imitation

If students answer A for Item 1, remind them that commerce involves money but means "the buying or selling of goods," so B is the correct answer.

Biotechnology Gives New Hope

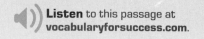 **Watch** a video introduction to this passage at **vocabularyforsuccess.com**.

Listen to this passage at **vocabularyforsuccess.com**.

CCSS Vocabulary: 4; Reading (Informational Text): 4, 6. (See pp. T16–17.)

The Biotechnology of Restoring the Senses

<scientific essay>

At the height of his career, Theodore Hersh began to lose his vision. He had retinitis pigmentosa, an eye disease affecting the retina's photoreceptor cells, which process light signals. The disease damages these cells, leading to a steady loss in visual acuity and, eventually, blindness. An energetic medical doctor and researcher, he soon had to give up both jobs. Hersh began seeking a diversion for his love of medicine. He decided to take part in an experimental research study. This time, however, the researcher would be the research subject.

Hersh found a study involving encapsulated cell technology, or ECT. The therapy involves inserting a tiny "factory" inside the body. A porous capsule $\frac{1}{4}$ inch long and as wide as a pencil lead is inserted into the eye. Inside the capsule, genetically modified retinal cells churn out proteins that signal cells to grow or survive. This kind of protein is called a growth factor, and making growth factors in the lab has become a hallmark of biotechnology. The ECT researchers believed that the growth factor could slow, stop, or even reverse the damage to Hersh's photoreceptor cells.

In 2004, after a brief operation, Hersh became one of the first humans to receive the implant. Within a few months his sight had improved. The therapy is now being studied in patients with macular degeneration, the leading cause of blindness in older people.

ECT is biotechnology at its most versatile, because it can be used to treat a wide range of diseases by switching the type of biological material within the capsule. It also represents a change in the paradigm of biotechnology since the late twentieth century.

The design for a living cell does not belong to anyone. At least that was the conventional wisdom until a few decades ago. But a 1980 Supreme Court ruling would invert that notion when it ruled that a genetically altered cell could be patented. The ruling was the articulation of the dream of many an entrepreneurial scientist. It paved the way for new biotech firms already energized by advances in genetic engineering. With the protection of a patent, a biotech firm could invest in and profit from research and development. In just few decades, biotechnology underwent a complete metamorphosis.

THE ANATOMICAL STRUCTURE OF THE HUMAN EYE

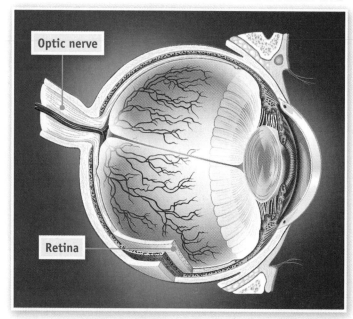

Optic nerve

Retina

A scientific essay is a piece of expository writing that examines a single scientific topic.

Suddenly, medical researchers could use a host of biological materials modified in the laboratory to solve a variety of problems.

Restoring Hearing

A technological wonder, the tiny cochlear implant restores some hearing to many people with profound hearing loss. But even when it works, the device can have serious side effects. Because the device and the process for inserting it involve contact with more than one delicate ear channel, infections are common.

Biological materials may be the future of hearing restoration. They are easier to implant and less prone to infection than devices. Just as biotech treatments for vision impairment are being tested on humans, similar treatments for hearing loss are being tested on animals. Researchers around the world are conducting experiments with brain derived neurotrophic factor (BDNF). BDNF signals nerve cells, such as those in the ear, to grow or protect themselves. BDNF's name would seem to belie its location, because it can be found anywhere in the body, and it can be made in the laboratory. One recent study suggested that BDNF could avert hearing loss in infants infected with bacterial meningitis, a leading cause of deafness in children.

TALK ABOUT IT

With a partner, answer the questions below. Use as many of the highlighted words in the selection as you can.

1. If you were a scientist conducting research on the *restoration* of one of the five senses, on which sense would you focus? Why?

2. The essay mentions animal testing. If scientists can help future generations *avert* hearing or vision loss through animal testing, do you think they should? Why or why not?

Models of BDNFs (brain derived neurotrophic factors)

Word Meanings

For each highlighted word on pages 70–71, the meaning or meanings are given below.

For practice with synonyms, see page 100.

1. **acuity** (uh-KYOO-uh-tee) **n.** clarity or sharpness of perception. A debater with great mental *acuity* can quickly identify the logical flaws in an opponent's argument. **SYNONYMS:** keenness, perceptiveness

2. **articulation** (ar-tik-yuh-LAY-shuhn) **n.** the expression in words of an idea or thought. *Articulation* of your desires means telling other people exactly what you want. **SYNONYMS:** expression, formulation; **n.** having movable joints, as between bones or cartilage. A toy action figure with many movable joints has a wide range of *articulation*.

3. **avert** (uh-VURT) **v.** to keep from happening. To *avert* something, such as an accident or disaster, is to prevent it from happening. **SYNONYMS:** prevent, head off; **v.** to turn away. You may want to *avert* your eyes from a gory or disturbing scene in a movie.

4. **belie** (bi-LYE) **v.** to give a misleading impression of. A person's attractive outer appearance can *belie* an unattractive personality. **SYNONYMS:** disguise, misrepresent; **v.** to prove false. If you act guilty when denying a wrongdoing, your behavior can *belie* your claim of innocence. **SYNONYM:** discredit

5. **biotechnology** (bye-oh-tek-NOL-uh-jee) **n.** the engineering or use of organisms and cells to produce products for human use. *Biotechnology* has been used to produce everything from food to new medicine.

6. **channel** (CHAN-uhl) **n.** a round or tube-shaped passage. You might think of your veins and arteries as a series of *channels*, or small pipes, through which your blood moves. **SYNONYMS:** tube, conduit; **v.** To direct through a certain path. You *channel* your energy when you direct it toward a specific goal. **SYNONYMS:** conduct, direct

7. **diversion** (duh-VUR-zhuhn) **n.** a turning away from one path or activity and toward another. When you seek a *diversion* from something, you look for something different to do. **SYNONYMS:** deviation, distraction; **n.** something that amuses or entertains. After passing a test that you studied hard for, you may feel ready for the *diversion* of a movie. **SYNONYM:** pastime

8. **invert** (in-VURT) **v.** to reverse in position or order. If you *invert* something, you turn it upside down. **SYNONYMS:** flip, reverse

CCSS Vocabulary: 4.c., 4.d. (See pp. T16–17.)

Watch a video introduction for each word at **vocabularyforsuccess.com**.

Listen to iWords at **vocabularyforsuccess.com**.

Refer to the online dictionary at **vocabularyforsuccess.com**.

9. **metamorphosis** (met-uh-MOR-fuh-siss) **n.** a dramatic change in appearance or character. A *metamorphosis* is a complete change in someone or something. **SYNONYM:** transformation; **n.** a thorough and rapid change in the form of some animals between the immature stage and the adult stage. A caterpillar undergoes a *metamorphosis* when it changes into a butterfly.

10. **paradigm** (PA-ruh-dime) **n.** a theory about how something should be done or thought about. A model classroom can test the merits of a new educational *paradigm*. **SYNONYM:** framework; **n.** an outstanding example. A hero may be held up as a *paradigm,* or an example to follow. **SYNONYMS:** model, archetype

11. **restoration** (ress-tuh-RAY-shuhn) **n.** the act of bringing back to an earlier and generally better condition. An old house that has been painted and repaired is an example of a *restoration*. **SYNONYMS:** repair, regeneration, return

12. **versatile** (VUR-suh-tuhl) **adj.** having many applications; turning easily from one thing to another. If you are a *versatile* person, you can adapt to a variety of situations. **SYNONYMS:** adaptable, all-around, universal

More on Meanings: Confusing Word Pairs

Many words in English can be traced back to a single Latin root. These families of words can be similar in meaning and structure. The words *invert* and *avert* both contain the Latin root *vert,* which means "to turn." Each word's prefix changes its meaning. Compare these sentences:

To **avert** an argument, Julie suggested that the siblings share the new toy.

If you **invert** the letter *M,* it looks like a *W.*

Avert is a verb meaning "to prevent or avoid." *Invert* is a verb meaning "to turn over."

Words in a confusing word pair are not always the same part of speech. For example:

As a **finale**, the band played "The End."

The concert was **finally** over, and we headed home.

Finale and *finally* both share the Latin root *finis,* which means "end." *Finale* is a noun that means "the last piece of music played," while *finally* is an adverb meaning "after a long time."

Challenge Choose two word pairs below. Use each of the words in a sentence.

preposition, proposition   a lot, allot
afflict, inflict

Point out to students that *preposition* and *proposition* share a common root, *ponere,* "to place." The words *afflict* and *inflict* also share a common root, *fligere,* "to strike."

C CCSS Vocabulary: 4.a., 5. (See pp. T16–17.)

vocabularyforsuccess.com

73

Word Talk

Each lesson word has been placed in a category. With a partner, discuss and list items that belong in each category. Compare your results with those of another pair of students.
C CCSS Vocabulary: 6. (See pp. T16–17.)

Senses or Abilities Whose *Acuity* Can Be Measured

sight, hearing, intelligence

Versatile Tools

hammer, screwdriver, adjustable wrench

Ways That People *Belie* Their Boredom During a Conversation

nodding, smiling, saying "uh-huh"

Things in Need of *Restoration*

historic buildings in disrepair, peace in various war zones, civility in daily interactions

Examples of a *Channel* in Your House

water pipes, garden hose, sink drain

Things Designed to *Avert* Injury in Accidents

seatbelts, airbags, helmets, kneepads

Fields Where *Biotechnology* Is Used Today

medicine, pharmaceuticals, agriculture, food industry, environmental science

Inventions That Have Led to a New *Paradigm* in Entertainment

telephone, television, cell phone, portable electronic devices

Things That Can Bring About a *Metamorphosis* in One's Appearance

new and dramatic haircut, makeup, or style of clothing

Best Genres for the *Articulation* of Romantic Feelings

poetry, ballads, Valentine's card

More Appropriate *Diversion* of a Graffiti Artist's Energies

painting on canvas, drawing on paper, creating murals

Things You Should Not *Invert*

glasses or other open containers full of liquid, automobiles

Check for Understanding

Choose the lesson word that completes each sentence. Write the word on the line provided. Some words will be used twice.

acuity	belie	diversion	paradigm
articulation	biotechnology	invert	restoration
avert	channel	metamorphosis	versatile

1. With his new, deep voice and three added inches of height, Drew appeared to have undergone a complete __metamorphosis__ over the summer.

2. He has lost some __acuity__ in his vision, but Grandfather's mind is still sharp.

3. To __avert__ the growth of mildew in the shower, wipe it down after use.

4. With its outdoor classroom, recycling program, and student garden, the new school is following a nature-centered __paradigm__ of education.

5. A/an __versatile__ athlete, Janine was on the volleyball and track teams.

6. The company used __biotechnology__ to develop a protein to combat blindness.

7. Special theme days like "crazy hat" day __invert__ the usual dress code at school.

8. War-weary citizens eagerly awaited the __restoration__ of peace.

9. This pipe is the __channel__ for the building's water.

10. The book is a/an __articulation__ of the candidate's ideas about government.

11. Stage actors' heavy makeup can __belie__ their true appearance.

12. Alarmed by the crayon marks on the wall, the babysitter sought a/an __diversion__ for the toddler's artistic impulses.

13. Advances in 3-D technology have created a new __paradigm__ for filmmaking.

14. The debaters received points for the clear __articulation__ of their arguments.

If students answer *diversion* for Item 9, explain that a diversion involves moving something away from one course and toward another; the water is not being moved off course but directed via a channel along its proper course.

Word Associations

Use what you know about the lesson word in italics to answer each question. Circle the letter next to the phrase that best answers the question. Be prepared to explain your answers.

1. Which of the following activities involves *biotechnology*?

   a. resetting a broken limb and casting it
   b. processing minerals to make cosmetics
   c. changing the genetic material in a cell

2. What happens if you *invert* a milk jug?

   a. The milk spills.
   b. The milk boils.
   c. The milk turns yellow.

3. How can you *avert* a lecture on responsibility?

   a. by forgetting your chores
   b. by listening quietly to the lecture
   c. by doing chores without being nagged

4. Which of the following would signal a change in a *paradigm*?

   a. Public libraries begin selling books instead of lending them.
   b. A local restaurant stops serving water during a drought.
   c. You are sent to your room for misbehavior.

5. You best perceive the *articulation* in your fingers when you

   a. straighten them
   b. clean them well
   c. curl them

6. If evidence *belies* the testimony of a witness, then the jury will likely

   a. think the witness was not reliable
   b. believe the witness's testimony
   c. know the witness committed the crime

7. Which of the following demonstrates how *versatile* a scarf is?

   a. Its fine silk fibers make it shimmer.
   b. It can be worn around the head, neck, or waist.
   c. It you don't like it, you can return it with a receipt.

8. Which of these is a *diversion*?

   a. a comedic play
   b. a traffic jam
   c. a confession

9. Which of the following might be a good way to *channel* excess energy?

   a. watching educational films
   b. practicing martial arts
   c. stifling feelings of anger

10. Which is an example of *acuity* in creative writing?

    a. sharply drawn characters
    b. vague descriptions
    c. dull dialogue

11. Which is the most likely candidate for *restoration*?

    a. a new government building
    b. an old shack
    c. an historical building

12. To which of the following could the word *metamorphosis* apply?

    a. a tadpole turning into a frog
    b. the hatching of a chicken's egg
    c. a moth flitting around a light bulb

CCSS Vocabulary: 4.a. (See pp. T16–17.)

Check Again

Use what you know about the lesson word in italics to complete each sentence. Be sure your sentences make sense.

1. When you *invert* a pan to remove the cake, you _____ turn the pan upside down.

2. Insect-resistant plants are examples of *biotechnology* because they are _____ biological materials that have been engineered for human use.

3. Fishing is just a *diversion* for some people, but for others _____ it's necessary for survival.

4. Smart phones have created a new communication *paradigm* because _____ they have changed the way people live their daily lives.

5. Businesses seek *versatile* employees because _____ they can do a wide variety of tasks.

6. If you don't *avert* your eyes from the sun, _____ you might harm your vision.

7. High school can be a time of *metamorphosis* because _____ most teens undergo dramatic physical and mental changes.

8. *Articulation* of your likes and dislikes is helpful when _____ you first get to know someone.

9. Active young people often *channel* their energies into activities such as _____ swimming and Glee Club.

10. You might *belie* your own cheerful personality by _____ acting grumpy or unkind.

11. If an animal has visual *acuity*, it can _____ see small prey from far away.

12. The *restoration* of an old hotel would involve _____ repairing it and making it like new again.

Write Your Own

Reread the passage on pages 70–71. Then, on a separate sheet of paper, write a one-paragraph response to the question, "How is biotechnology helping people with vision or hearing loss?" Use at least two words from the lesson word list and support your answer by referring to the text of the passage.

Word-Solving Strategies:
Latin and Greek Roots

Latin Root **vers, vert**: "to turn"

If you know the meaning of Latin and Greek roots, you can figure out the meanings of many unfamiliar words. One root that is useful to know is *vers* (or *vert*), which comes from the Latin word *vertere* and means "to turn." Four lesson words contain the root: *avert*, *diversion*, *invert*, and *versatile*.

Let's examine the word *avert*. You know that *vert* means "to turn." The prefix *a-* is usually short for *ab-* ("away from") or *ad-* ("toward"). These word parts, together with the context in which the word appears, can help you determine that *avert* means "to turn away." That brings you fairly close to the definition you learned—"to prevent or avoid."

Now let's look at the word *diversion*. The prefix *di-* can mean "apart or opposite," and the suffix *-ion* can mean "the act, condition, or result of." When you put these meanings together with the the root, you see that *diversion* means "a turning away from one path or activity and toward another."

More Examples Look at the words *invert* and *versatile*. You can use the root and the prefix or suffix to figure out the meaning.

in- → to, toward

vers → turn

-ile → like, suitable for

To *invert* means "to turn inward, over, or upside down." Something that is *versatile* can be used for many purposes.

BE CAREFUL!

Many prefixes have multiple meanings. The prefix *a-* has another meaning in words from Old English (*awake*, *asleep*), and yet another in words from ancient Greek (*atypical*). By using the root word and context, you can figure out which prefix meaning fits.

Practice

Read each sentence below. Then use what you know about the Latin root *vers/vert* to write the meaning of the word in italics. Check your answers in a dictionary.

1. Comic books were once considered a *subversive* form of reading.

   seeking to undermine authority
   _____

2. Freya is often warm and friendly but deep down she is quite *introverted*.

   tending to direct one's attention inward
   _____

3. Since my sister became a vegetarian, she's been trying to *convert* me.

   to change from one course

   or way of life to another

4. A *perversion* of the leash law resulted in the parks not allowing dogs at all.

   a turning away from the intended

   meaning or use; distortion

CCSS Vocabulary: 4.c. (See pp. T16–17.)

Practice for Tests

For a quiz and additional practice for this lesson, go to **vocabularyforsuccess.com**.

Fill in the bubble next to the answer that best completes the sentence or answers the question.

1. Read this sentence.

   When I get my braces off, my personal *metamorphosis* will be complete!

   Metamorphosis means:

   ○ **A** condition
   ○ **B** alteration
   ○ **C** hygiene
   ● **D** transformation

2. When you fail to *avert* an injury, you do NOT:

   ○ **A** invite it
   ● **B** prevent it
   ○ **C** fear it
   ○ **D** ignore it

3. *Biotechnology* involves the manipulation of:

   ● **A** living organisms or their parts
   ○ **B** minerals found on Earth's surface
   ○ **C** microorganisms found in the oceans
   ○ **D** the use of robots to do humans' work

4. If you *invert* a bowl on your head, you:

   ○ **A** balance it on your head
   ● **B** turn it over on your head
   ○ **C** break it over your head
   ○ **D** spin it on your head

5. A loss of *acuity* in a person's sense of smell means that it:

   ○ **A** is gone
   ● **B** is less sharp
   ○ **C** is better than most
   ○ **D** is unable to distinguish among smells

6. If your facial expression *belies* your feelings, it:

   ○ **A** influences them
   ○ **B** affects them
   ○ **C** exaggerates them
   ● **D** disguises them

7. Read this sentence.

   A stent is a small, cylindrical device used to improve air or blood flow within a *channel* of the human body.

   Channel means:

   ● **A** a tubular passage
   ○ **B** a heart valve
   ○ **C** an artery or vein
   ○ **D** a vital organ

8. In sports, a *versatile* athlete is one who:

   ○ **A** always gets the job done
   ● **B** can play different sports or positions
   ○ **C** has had many injuries
   ○ **D** will be replaced by another player

9. If you need a *diversion* during a long weekend, you might:

   ○ **A** pay attention to the time
   ● **B** read a fan magazine
   ○ **C** study for a test
   ○ **D** observe bicycle safety laws

10. If a prisoner demands the *restoration* of his rights, he wants them

    ○ **A** legalized
    ● **B** returned to him
    ○ **C** thoroughly reviewed
    ○ **D** made comparable to those of other prisoners

If students answer B or C for Item 7, point out that the sentence mentions air or blood flow, so the channel must be a generic tube or passage, not an artery or vein.

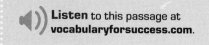

Watch a video introduction to this passage at **vocabularyforsuccess.com**.

Listen to this passage at **vocabularyforsuccess.com**.

CCSS Vocabulary: 4; Reading (Informational Text): 4, 6. (See pp. T16–17.)

The Biotechnology of Restoring Mobility

\<timeline\>

Recent breakthroughs in treating people with impaired mobility involve a branch of biotechnology known as biomedical engineering. This field brings engineering tools to the practice of medicine. Here's a look at some developments from the past decade.

2004 Researchers at the University of Pittsburgh and Carnegie-Mellon teach Pearce, a monkey, to operate a mechanical arm with his mind. They implant a tiny electronic grid over the part of Pearce's brain that controls arm movement. The grid connects to a computer. The researchers then tape Pearce's arm to his side and mount a mechanical arm to his left shoulder. Pearce learns to use the arm as an integral part of his body.

Functional electrical stimulation (FES) had been used in humans to activate paralyzed muscles. But never before had the stimulation been controlled by brain signals. The goal of the research is to implant an electronic grid into the brains of patients with spinal cord injuries so they may reactivate paralyzed limbs with the power of their thoughts.

2006 Biomedical engineers develop the first "bionic" assistive device for people with missing limbs. Tiny sensors in the new prosthetic hand read nerve and muscle impulses through the skin at the stump. Learning to use this prosthetic is an intuitive process for patients working to rehabilitate their bodies. "Every day that I have the hand, it surprises me," said Iraq veteran Juan Arredondo. "Now I can pick up a paper cup without crushing it." Also available are individual prosthetic fingers to supplement a partially amputated hand.

2009 Wearing a cap with sensors, the rider of a motorized wheelchair sends brain signals to a

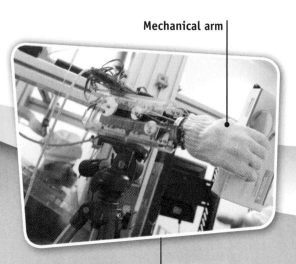

Mechanical arm

"Bionic" prosthetic hand

2002   2003   **2004**   2005   **2006**   2007   200

computer to operate the chair. The new system shows a refinement that the researchers in Pittsburgh had hoped for: The computer filters out stray brain signals, using only those relating to the relevant locomotion.

2010 Cartilage—connective tissue in our joints—wears away as we age. Once we reach adulthood, the loss is irreversible because cartilage can't regrow itself. But researchers at Northwestern University created a "bioactive nanogel" that when injected into a joint stimulates the bone marrow stem cells to produce cartilage. Eventually, new cartilage replaces the gel. This type of therapy is called regenerative medicine.

2012 Dutch researchers work on an implant to help people with scoliosis, a curvature of the spine. The implant has elasticity to allow mobility but also rigidity to prevent the spine from curving further. The preliminary model eventually fuses with the vertebrae and must be replaced. Researchers are working to develop a material that won't bind to the spine.

Many biomedical engineers are driven by a sheer sense of wonder. As one practitioner put it,

VOCABULARY

integral	refinement	elasticity
reactivate	locomotion	rigidity
rehabilitate	irreversible	preliminary
supplement	regenerative	practitioner

"We all quote these humanitarian reasons for why we're doing this work, but at the end of the day we just enjoy it. Being at the interface of biology and engineering is fun."

TALK ABOUT IT

With a partner, answer the questions below. Use as many of the highlighted words in the selection as you can.

1. What is one benefit of *regenerative* medicine?

2. How can research on the brain be an *integral* part of helping people with mobility issues?

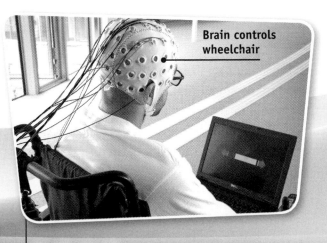

Brain controls wheelchair

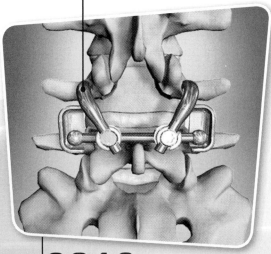

Spine implant

2009   2010   2011   2012   2013   2014

Word Meanings

For each highlighted word on pages 80–81, the meaning or meanings are given below.

For practice with synonyms, see page 100.

1. **elasticity** (i-lass-TISS-uh-tee) **n.** the ability to spring back to original condition after being stretched or squeezed. Something that can stretch enough to fit around a larger item has *elasticity*. **SYNONYMS:** springiness, flexibility, resilience

2. **integral** (IN-tuh-gruhl) **adj.** necessary for completeness or wholeness. A balanced diet is *integral* to good health. **SYNONYM:** fundamental; **adj.** made of parts that form a whole. In an *integral* system, all of the parts are present. **SYNONYMS:** unified, complete, whole

3. **irreversible** (ihr-uh-VER-suh-buhl) **adj.** impossible to undo or repair. Some actions, such as taking a person's life, are *irreversible* because they can never be undone. **SYNONYMS:** irreparable, irrevocable, permanent

4. **locomotion** (loh-kuh-MOH-shuhn) **n.** movement. Flying, swimming, hopping, walking, and jumping are means of *locomotion* used by different animals. **SYNONYMS:** mobility, motion

5. **practitioner** (prak-TISH-uh-nur) **n.** a person who works at or actively engages in a profession, art, or other skilled activity. A *practitioner* is anyone who uses a particular set of knowledge and skills to do something.

6. **preliminary** (pri-LIM-uh-ner-ee) **adj.** coming before or leading up to something. *Preliminary* work, such as researching sources and taking good notes, makes report writing go more smoothly. **SYNONYMS:** early, initial, introductory, opening

7. **reactivate** (ree-AK-tuh-vayt) **v.** to make active again; to restart. You can sometimes *reactivate* an online account just by starting to use it again. **SYNONYMS:** reenergize, reinstate

8. **refinement** (ri-FINE-muhnt) **n.** the act or result of making something more precise or polished. *Refinement* is the process of improving something, such as a piece of writing. **SYNONYM:** improvement; **n.** the process of removing impurities from a substance. Substances such as sugar and gold undergo *refinement* to make them pure and clean of other substances. **n.** highly developed manners, elegance, or taste. You can show *refinement* by exhibiting politeness and good manners. **SYNONYMS:** cultivation, sophistication

ⓒ CCSS Vocabulary: 4.c., 4.d. (See pp. T16–17.)

Watch a video introduction for each word at **vocabularyforsuccess.com**.

Listen to iWords at **vocabularyforsuccess.com**.

Refer to the online dictionary at **vocabularyforsuccess.com**.

9. **regenerative** (ri-JEN-uh-ruh-tiv) **adj.** able to grow anew, restore, or be reborn. Some creatures, such as starfish, have a *regenerative* capacity and can regrow lost limbs. **SYNONYMS:** revitalizing, restorative

10. **rehabilitate** (ree-uh-BIL-uh-tate) **v.** to bring someone or something back to wellness through treatment and therapy. To *rehabilitate* someone means to make his or her health, behavior, or life better.

11. **rigidity** (ri-JID-uh-tee) **n.** inability to bend. The *rigidity* of a metal pole makes it almost impossible to bend. **SYNONYMS:** firmness, hardness, inelasticity, immobility; **n.** inability to adapt. In a person, *rigidity* is the inability to change behavior or make compromises. **SYNONYM:** inflexibility

12. **supplement** (SUHP-luh-muhnt) **v.** to add something to make up for something missing or lacking. You can *supplement* your allowance by working at a part-time job. **SYNONYMS:** boost, complement, increase; **n.** something added to make up for a lack. People take multivitamins as a *supplement* to their diet. **SYNONYMS:** addition, accessory

More on Meanings: Multiple-Meaning Words

Many words have more than one meaning. Often, the differences are obvious. Read these sentences:

There have been many **refinements** in the printing process since Gutenberg's day.

The **refinement** of copper involves melting and remelting it.

My aunt is a lady of great **refinement**.

The first sentence reflects the general meaning of *refinement*: "improvement." In the second sentence, the word means "the removal of impurities." In the third, *refinement* refers to the sophistication of a person's manners.

Sometimes words have similar meanings but are different parts of speech. Read these sentences:

I **supplement** my packed lunch with something from the snack bar.

Read *The Diary of Anne Frank* as a **supplement** to your Holocaust study.

Supplement always carries the meaning of "something additional." In the first sentence, however, *supplement* acts as a verb. In the second, it's a noun.

Challenge Choose two of the multiple-meaning words below. For each, write two sentences that illustrate different meanings of the word.

relic   grave   rift   tributary   vault

Remind students that multiple-meaning words may be the same or different parts of speech. Have them consult a dictionary to find the different meanings of the challenge words, if necessary.

CCSS Vocabulary: 4.a., 5. (See pp. T16–17.)

vocabularyforsuccess.com   83

Word Talk

Each lesson word has been placed in a category. With a partner, discuss and list items that belong in each category. Compare your results with those of another pair of students.

CCSS Vocabulary: 6. [See pp. T16–17.]

Ways to *Supplement* Your Study of Your State's History

a trip to the Capitol, talking to long-time state residents, reading a historical novel

Activities *Preliminary* to Exercising

dressing, stretching, drinking water

***Regenerative* Activities After Exercising**

drinking water, showering, napping, eating

Things That Can Do *Irreversible* Damage to Your Body

smoking, staring at the sun, not using sunscreen

Construction Materials Valued for Their *Rigidity*

steel, wood, glass, titanium, brick, stone

Everyday Items That Have *Elasticity*

rubber bands, balloons, stretchy fabric, coil springs

***Integral* Parts of a Pizza**

crust, sauce, cheese

***Refinements* to Twentieth Century Inventions**

Cell phones got smarter, PCs got faster, TV images got sharper.

Possible Ways to *Rehabilitate* a Criminal

community service, education, counseling

Things You Might Need to *Reactivate* When School Starts

lunch money account, transit pass, study plan

Reasons to Visit a Medical *Practitioner*

flu, infection, sprained ankle, annual checkup

Different Methods of *Locomotion*

walking, running, riding in a car or bus, riding a bike, flying in an airplane

Check for Understanding

Choose the lesson word that completes each sentence. Write the word on the line provided. Some words will be used twice.

elasticity	locomotion	reactivate	rehabilitate
integral	practitioner	refinement	rigidity
irreversible	preliminary	regenerative	supplement

1. Once you get _____preliminary_____ approval for your topic, you can start your research.

2. Sam lost access to his account for a month, but he was able to _____reactivate_____ it.

3. This rubber band lacked _____elasticity_____; it broke after one use.

4. I _____supplement_____ my study of Spanish by watching the Spanish TV station.

5. Avoid the risk of _____irreversible_____ brain damage by wearing a bike helmet.

6. This safety glass combines _____rigidity_____ and strength, making it extremely difficult to bend or break.

7. Marisol is a physical therapist who helps _____rehabilitate_____ injured veterans.

8. My mother has become a daily _____practitioner_____ of yoga.

9. Regular practice is a/an _____integral_____ part of learning to play the violin.

10. My history project needs some _____refinement_____ before I can hand it in for a grade.

11. After a tough day, nothing beats the _____regenerative_____ power of sleep.

12. Though it may be hard to imagine being unable to walk, restoring _____locomotion_____ is not the first concern of many people paralyzed by spinal cord injuries.

13. The new therapies for eye disease are promising, but they need _____refinement_____.

14. These digital slides are _____integral_____ to my oral report on severe weather.

If students answer *reactivate* for Item 7, explain that common usage dictates that *rehabilitate* is the word to use in this context. The word conveys the specific meaning of helping others become able again.

Word Associations

Use what you know about the lesson word in italics to answer each question. Circle the letter next to the phrase that best answers the question. Be prepared to explain your answers.

1. In which of the following do you expect *elasticity*?

   a. leather boots
   b. an old hair band
   c. new socks

2. If you remove something from an *integral* system, what generally happens?

   a. The system doesn't work well.
   b. The system works better.
   c. The system functions normally.

3. How can you *rehabilitate* an old bike?

   a. sell it online
   b. donate it to charity
   c. put new tires on it

4. Which of the following is considered a dietary *supplement*?

   a. peanut butter
   b. vitamin C tablets
   c. artificial sweetener

5. *Rigidity* in a person means that he or she

   a. can be changed easily
   b. is resistant to change
   c. needs to be praised often

6. Which of the following is a sign of *refinement*?

   a. knowledge of art history
   b. natural athletic ability
   c. red hair with freckles

7. Which of the following is designed for *locomotion*?

   a. a globe spinning on an axis
   b. a water pump
   c. a scooter

8. What happens when you *reactivate* a library card?

   a. You can check out books again.
   b. You return it to the nearest library.
   c. You put a "hold" on your account.

9. Which of the following is a medical *practitioner*?

   a. a patient
   b. a physician
   c. a receptionist

10. Which of the following actions is *irreversible*?

    a. unrolling a spool of thread
    b. sewing a seam
    c. cutting fabric

11. Which of the following is a target of *regenerative* medicine?

    a. the common cold
    b. a damaged spinal cord
    c. a vaccination

12. When do you write a *preliminary* draft of an essay?

    a. early in the writing process
    b. near the end of the writing process
    c. when you are ready to publish your essay

CCSS Vocabulary: 4.a. (See pp. T16–17.)

Check Again

Use what you know about the lesson word in italics to complete each sentence. Be sure your sentences make sense.

1. The *elasticity* of synthetic fabrics makes them good for _____ wearing while running or swimming.

2. When the loss of a leg makes *locomotion* impossible, a person can _____ use a wheelchair or be fitted for a prosthetic limb.

3. After a trip, you can *reactivate* your newspaper or mail by _____ calling the delivery service or the post office.

4. After an oil spill, volunteers help *rehabilitate* wildlife by _____ washing the oil off the animals or removing them to safer places.

5. You might *supplement* your allowance during the summer by _____ getting a part-time job.

6. A joystick is an *integral* part of most _____ video game systems.

7. You might need to see a dental *practitioner* if _____ you have tooth pain or a cavity.

8. A bad haircut is not *irreversible* because _____ hair grows back.

9. A rough draft might need *refinement* because _____ the ideas are not clearly expressed.

10. Some *preliminary* steps to take when buying a new bike might be _____ to research the best bikes and compare prices.

11. A school dress code that lacks *rigidity* will likely result in _____ students wearing whatever they want.

12. An animal has *regenerative* abilities if it _____ can regrow damaged or missing body parts.

Write Your Own

1. Write a ten-word sentence using the word *supplement* as a noun.

The newspaper included a weekly supplement with TV program listings.

2. Write a ten-word sentence using the word *refinement* in the seventh position.

"I consider myself a man of refinement," said the critic.

Word-Solving Strategies:
Prefixes

The Prefix re-: "back," "again"

A root can form the base of many words. Prefixes are word parts at the beginning of a word that change its meaning. The prefix *re-* is from Latin and means "back" or "again." Now let's look at the word *reactivate*. Using what you know about the prefix *re-*, you can figure out that *reactivate* means "to activate again."

Other words from the lesson have parts that may not be as easy to recognize. Take *rehabilitate*. It's a combination of the prefix *re-* and the Latin verb *habilitare*, "to make fit, or enable." Combined, they make a word that means "to make fit again."

Look at the words *refinement* and *regenerative*. Use the meaning of each word's parts to help determine its meaning.

re- → again

fin → finish

-ment → a result

A *refinement* is a process of finishing to make something better—whether it be a metal, an invention, or a person's manners.

re- → again

gen → give birth, produce

-ative → denoting a characteristic

A medical treatment that helps tissue grow back is *regenerative*, as is any experience that helps people feel young or awake again.

BE CAREFUL!

Some words contain several word parts. For example, *irreversible* contains *re-*, *ir-* (which means "not"), and *vers* (which means "turn"). By analyzing the word parts, you can figure out that *irreversible* means "not able to be changed back."

Practice

Use what you've learned about the prefix *re-* to write a definition of each of these words. Include the words "back" or "again" in your definitions. You may use a dictionary.

1. irretrievable

not able to be brought back

2. recuperate

to get back something lost

3. reform

to change something back to a better form

4. reimburse

to pay back

5. reinspect

to inspect, or examine, again

6. recede

to go back or withdraw

7. renegotiate

to negotiate, or make arrangements, again

8. review

to look at again

9. retract

to draw back

10. unremitting

not easing back

CCSS Vocabulary: 4.c. (See pp. T16–17.)

Practice for Tests

For a quiz and additional practice for this lesson, go to **vocabularyforsuccess.com**.

Fill in the bubble next to the answer that best completes the sentence or answers the question.

1. Read this sentence.

    The city council gave *preliminary* approval for the new water treatment plant.

    Preliminary means:

    ○ **A** premature
    ○ **B** final
    ○ **C** overall
    ● **D** initial

2. When surgeons *reactivate* a heart, they:

    ○ **A** massage it
    ● **B** restart it
    ○ **C** transplant it
    ○ **D** donate it

3. *Elasticity* is NOT a desirable trait in:

    ○ **A** a shoe sole
    ● **B** a skyscraper
    ○ **C** clothing
    ○ **D** a trampoline

4. A *regenerative* sleep leaves you:

    ○ **A** feeling exhausted
    ● **B** feeling well rested
    ○ **C** with additional brain cells
    ○ **D** with vivid memory of dreams

5. *Rigidity* can best be seen in:

    ○ **A** a jump rope
    ● **B** a flag pole
    ○ **C** a piece of paper
    ○ **D** a necklace

6. If you *supplement* your normal diet, you:

    ○ **A** analyze it
    ○ **B** reduce it to lose weight
    ○ **C** replace it with something else
    ● **D** add something to it

7. A surgery to improve a patient's *locomotion* would improve the ability to:

    ● **A** move from place to place
    ○ **B** control one's arms and fingers
    ○ **C** wiggle one's fingers and toes
    ○ **D** calm upsetting thoughts

8. To *rehabilitate* a patient is to:

    ○ **A** ask him or her to pay the medical bills
    ● **B** help him or her return to health and activity
    ○ **C** operate on his or her legs with the aim of restoring mobility
    ○ **D** attempt to reform his or her character

9. Read this sentence.

    The Inca developed a unique method for the *refinement* of gold.

    Refinement means:

    ○ **A** mining
    ○ **B** melting
    ○ **C** combining with other metals
    ● **D** purification

10. A part that is *integral* to something:

    ○ **A** is not needed
    ● **B** is necessary
    ○ **C** is an added bonus
    ○ **D** can be discarded

If students choose B or C for Item 7, emphasize that *locomotion* has to do with movement to a different location, not the movement of body parts.

 Watch a video introduction to this passage at **vocabularyforsuccess.com**.

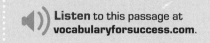 **Listen** to this passage at **vocabularyforsuccess.com**.

C CCSS Vocabulary: 4; Reading (Informational Text): 4, 6. (See pp. T16–17.)

Biotechnology and Traumatic Brain Injury

\<magazine article\>

Dr. Ning Zhang

What is the aftermath of being in a car crash? For people with traumatic brain injury (TBI), the event causing the damage can be painful and frightening. Unfortunately, the brain's response to the injury can be even more deleterious than the injury itself.

The neuron, or nerve cell, is the basic unit of your body's central nervous system. When part of the brain is injured, the neurons in that area break apart. They are unable to connect with other neurons, so they release toxic levels of neurotransmitters. A neurotransmitter is a chemical that normally helps brain cells communicate. The toxins can cause neurons to die, usually within a day or so after the injury.

Some neurons, however, can heal themselves and resume normal connections with other nearby neurons. But a number of things can go wrong. For example, low cerebral blood flow often disrupts the brain's natural healing process in TBI patients. That's where biotechnology plays a role.

Dr. Ning Zhang of Clemson University in South Carolina has developed an injectable gel that helps in two ways. The gel delivers adult stem cells to the injured part of the brain to replace dead or damaged neurons. It also delivers chemicals that cause stimulation of blood flow in the damaged area so that the new cells can

thrive. So far the gel has been tested only on rats, but the animals showed dramatic improvement. Zhang plans to test volunteer TBI patients soon.

Children generally heal more quickly than adults. But when a child has severe TBI, the outcome can be grim. A recent study in Houston offers new hope. Ten children received intravenous stem cells from their own bone marrow. The study was conducted to test the safety of the procedure rather than its effectiveness. However, six months after the procedure, all ten children had improved; seven had little or no disability.

The two studies seem to provide incontrovertible proof that adult stem cells—not to be confused with embryonic stem cells—can be used effectively to treat patients with TBI. They are illustrative of how biotechnology is giving new hope to TBI patients everywhere.

Not all cutting-edge technology helping TBI patients is microscopic. Some of the screening tools that neurologists use can fill up a room. Medical imaging technology, such as CAT and MRI, has improved neurologists' understanding of how the brain works and how best to heal it. For example, SPECT provides 3-D images of the brain. Such images aren't only used to screen patients for brain injury or disease. They can also help train doctors. Using the 3-D brains as brain atlases, doctors can deconstruct the brain (something they obviously can't do with an actual, living brain) in a simulation of actual brain surgery.

Another technology helping TBI patients is so discreet you'd never know it was an assistive device, because it looks just like a cell phone. In fact, it is a cell phone outfitted with special software that helps TBI patients complete daily routines, make plans, track time, multitask, and remember details. In short, it helps with executive function, one of the brain functions impaired by TBI.

VOCABULARY

traumatic	cerebral	screen
deleterious	stimulation	deconstruct
neuron	incontrovertible	simulation
chemical	illustrative	discreet

TALK ABOUT IT

With a partner, answer the questions below. Use as many of the highlighted words in the selection as you can.

Left: A human brain in X-ray view

1. Do you think some of the features of the cell phone software used by patients with *traumatic* brain injury might be helpful to you? Why or why not?

2. Doctors and researchers are finding out more and more about the brain. Do you think you would be interested in doing research on *cerebral* functions?

Below left: SPECT imaging machine

Below: SPECT images of a healthy brain, left, and an injured brain

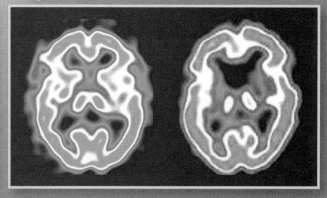

Word Meanings

For each highlighted word on pages 90–91, the meaning or meanings are given below.

For practice with synonyms, see page 100.

1. **cerebral** (suh-REE-bruhl) **adj.** having to do with the brain. A *cerebral* injury can cause loss of balance. **adj.** intellectual or logical. *Cerebral* activities, such as chess, involve thinking rather than physical action. **SYNONYMS:** rational, bookish, brainy

2. **chemical** (KEM-uh-kuhl) **n.** substance used to produce a change in another substance or that results when substances react. A *chemical* is a substance that causes or results from a reaction. **adj.** relating to the interaction of substances; relating to chemistry. Studying how *chemical* substances interact is part of what happens in a chemistry lab.

3. **deconstruct** (dee-kuhn-STRUHKT) **v.** to analyze or take apart, usually to find weaknesses. When you *deconstruct* something, you examine its parts to find problems or figure out how it works. **SYNONYMS:** analyze, dismantle, dissect

4. **deleterious** (del-uh-TIR-ee-uhs) **adj.** harmful to one's health or safety. Not getting enough sleep is *deleterious* to your health. **SYNONYMS:** damaging, injurious

5. **discreet** (diss-KREET) **adj.** hardly noticeable; not likely to attract attention. A *discreet* action, such as entering a room silently, is unlikely to be noticed. **SYNONYMS:** unobtrusive; modest; **adj.** careful in speech and action, especially about sensitive information. You're being *discreet* when you choose not to spread gossip. **SYNONYMS:** careful, cautious, diplomatic, guarded, tactful

6. **illustrative** (i-LUHSS-truh-tiv) **adj.** serving as an example. If you were explaining a complicated process, you might include an *illustrative* comparison to make the explanation clearer. **SYNONYMS:** indicative, symbolic, typical

7. **incontrovertible** (in-kon-truh-VURT-uh-buhl) **adj.** impossible to debate or dispute. The idea that the sun comes up every morning is an *incontrovertible* truth. **SYNONYMS:** certain, conclusive, definitive, undeniable

8. **neuron** (NOO-ron) **n.** the nervous system's basic unit, which conducts impulses. A *neuron* sends messages through the body and makes up much of the brain. **SYNONYM:** nerve cell

C CCSS Vocabulary: 4.c., 4.d. (See pp. T16–17.)

Watch a video introduction for each word at **vocabularyforsuccess.com**.

Listen to iWords at **vocabularyforsuccess.com**.

Refer to the online dictionary at **vocabularyforsuccess.com**.

9. **screen** (SKREEN) **v.** to test in order to find something specific. If you have a symptom, a doctor may *screen* you for an illness or condition. **SYNONYMS:** check, examine, test; **v.** to hide or shelter. Parents will *screen* their children from television content that kids are too young to understand. **SYNONYMS:** protect, safeguard

10. **simulation** (sim-yoo-LAY-shuhn) **n.** the use of a model to calculate and predict the effects of an actual process. Computers are used to create an accurate *simulation* of dangerous weather patterns. **n.** the act of pretending. A movie might contain a scene with the *simulation* of violence, not actual violence. **SYNONYMS:** appearance, pretense, sham

11. **stimulation** (stim-yuh-LAY-shuhn) **n.** the effect of something outside on an internal process. *Stimulation* occurs when an external agent causes a physical reaction, as when a bright light causes the pupils of the eye to contract. **n.** an act that activates or invigorates. You might find *stimulation* by trying a new activity that really interests you. **SYNONYMS:** spark, impetus, revitalization

12. **traumatic** (traw-MAT-ik) **adj.** severe. A car collision can result in a serious or *traumatic* injury. **adj.** shocking, upsetting. Something that is emotionally painful, such as witnessing violence, can be *traumatic*. **SYNONYMS:** devastating, distressing

More on Meanings: Confusing Word Pairs

Some word pairs are confusing because their spellings are similar. Compare these sentences:

The computer **simulation** showed that the virus could spread worldwide.

One treatment for paralysis involves the **stimulation** of muscles with electrodes.

Simulation means "model to study a topic." *Stimulation* means "the effect of an outside force." Some confusing word pairs consist of words that are pronounced the same and share an origin but don't mean the same thing.

Compare these sentences:

He made **discreet** inquiries about her.

Each house is a **discrete** section of the neighborhood.

Discreet means "unlikely to attract attention." *Discrete* means "separate and distinct."

Challenge Choose two word pairs below. Use each of the words in a sentence.

beach, beech   formally, formerly
envelop, envelope

Point out to students that the meanings of *envelop* and *envelope* are related, but the words are used very differently.

CCSS Vocabulary: 4.a., 5. (See pp. T16–17.)

vocabularyforsuccess.com   93

Word Talk

Each lesson word has been placed in a category. With a partner, discuss and list items that belong in each category. Compare your results with those of another pair of students.

C CCSS Vocabulary: 6. (See pp. T16–17.)

Causes of *Traumatic* Brain Injury

motorcycle accidents, football injuries, war-related injuries

Conditions Your School Nurse May *Screen* You For

vision problems, hearing problems, tuberculosis

Actions That Should Be *Discreet* in Public

blowing your nose; talking on a cell phone; indicating a third person (without pointing)

Things You Can *Deconstruct*

bicycle, bookcase, camping tent, portable table

Stimulation for Involuntary Reflexes

tickling, tapping on ankle or knee, shining a light into the eye's pupil

Places in Your Body Where You Can Find a *Neuron*

throughout the human body, the brain

Things *Illustrative* of an Ideal School

windows, open courtyard, one-on-one instruction, happy students and teachers

Computer *Simulation* You Can Use or See in Everyday Life

arcade games, driver training programs, online science experiments

Things That Are *Incontrovertible*

If you drop something, it will fall down; water is wet; tomorrow is another day.

Evidence That One *Chemical* Has Reacted to Another

smoke, explosion, fire, rust

Things *Deleterious* to Your Eyes

too much sun, excessive computer use, air pollution

Things That Help *Cerebral* Development

learning games, sleep, crossword puzzles

Check for Understanding

Choose the lesson word that completes each sentence. Write the word on the line provided. Some words will be used twice.

cerebral	deleterious	incontrovertible	simulation
chemical	discreet	neuron	stimulation
deconstruct	illustrative	screen	traumatic

1. If you're not certain how one _____chemical_____ interacts with another, you should not mix them, or you might have an explosion.

2. Rebecca's stunning multimedia presentation is _____illustrative_____ of the school's strong media literacy program.

3. "My client's fingerprints at the house are _____incontrovertible_____ proof that he was there," admitted the lawyer.

4. Scratching my dog's ribs results in the _____stimulation_____ of an involuntary kicking reflex.

5. The surgeon will first _____deconstruct_____ the hip and then replace parts of the worn ball-and-socket joint with new, artificial ones.

6. The most _____deleterious_____ effects of sunbathing may not show up until middle age.

7. If you damage a/an _____neuron_____ in your brain, it ordinarily won't grow back.

8. A fire drill is a/an _____simulation_____ so that people learn how to react during fire.

9. Go to the emergency room if you have a/an _____traumatic_____ injury.

10. He studied the _____cerebral_____ cortex in biology.

11. The nurse came to the school to _____screen_____ children for vision problems.

12. Puzzles and word games provide mental _____stimulation_____ during a long trip.

13. Ahmed offered to _____deconstruct_____ my watch to find out why it stopped running.

14. He has diabetes, so he wears a/an _____discreet_____ insulin pump that is barely noticeable under his shirt.

If students answer *chemical* for Item 14, explain that the sentence contains the context clue "barely noticeable" that indicates the answer is *discreet*.

Word Associations

Use what you know about the lesson word in italics to answer each question. Circle the letter next to the phrase that best answers the question. Be prepared to explain your answers.

1. Which of the following is *deleterious* to your health?

   a. eating an apple
   b. exercising
   c. smoking

2. If your friends consider you *discreet*, how are they likely to treat you?

   a. as a trusted listener
   b. with great caution
   c. as an outsider

3. Why might people show a *simulation* of enthusiasm about a birthday party?

   a. They really want to go to the party.
   b. They like the person giving the party.
   c. They are not interested but don't want to seem rude.

4. If you think you need *stimulation,* what do you need?

   a. peace and quiet
   b. excitement
   c. sleep

5. Which of the following is a sign that seeing a certain movie was a *traumatic* experience?

   a. deciding to take up filmmaking afterward
   b. having recurring nightmares about it
   c. giggling during the movie

6. Something *illustrative* of bad manners is

   a. chewing with your mouth open
   b. never being reprimanded or corrected
   c. being invited to a party

7. Which of the following is a *cerebral* activity?

   a. cooing over a baby
   b. lifting weights
   c. studying physics

8. From what should you *screen* small children?

   a. bad language
   b. growing older
   c. vision and hearing tests

9. Where will you find a *neuron*?

   a. in outer space
   b. in the nervous system
   c. inside a blood cell

10. Which of the following is a *chemical* reaction?

    a. a wink
    b. uncontrolled anger
    c. an explosion

11. Why might you *deconstruct* an advertisement?

    a. to stop getting unwanted emails about it
    b. to understand how it works on your emotions
    c. to learn more about the product

12. Which of the following is *incontrovertible*?

    a. The earth is round.
    b. A lead weight floats in water.
    c. Cancer will be cured in the next century.

CCSS Vocabulary: 4.a. (See pp. T16–17.)

Check Again

Use what you know about the lesson word in italics to complete each sentence. Be sure your sentences make sense.

1. You can experience a *simulation* of flying a plane or driving by _____ playing a video game. _____

2. You can create a *chemical* reaction by _____ mixing vinegar and baking soda. _____

3. A writer looking for a personal assistant might *screen* applicants who _____ have no computer experience. _____
_____

4. An avid reader might *deconstruct* a novel to _____ figure out why it was enjoyable. _____
_____

5. A person behaving in a *deleterious* way should feel bad because _____ he or she is harming his or
her health or safety or the safety of others. _____

6. A *cerebral* activity is one that involves _____ thinking rather than acting. _____

7. After a long week of being sick in bed, you might long for the *stimulation* of _____ going out with
your friends. _____

8. You might be wasting *neurons* if you spend a lot of time _____ watching television. _____

9. The popularity of films about comic book heroes is *illustrative* of _____ people's need for escapism. _____

10. When arriving late to a performance, it is important to be *discreet* because _____ you don't want to disturb
other people or cause a commotion. _____

11. You would have *incontrovertible* proof that a surprise party was being planned for you if _____ you found
presents hidden in closets or under beds. _____

12. If you experience a *traumatic* injury, you need _____ immediate emergency treatment. _____

Write Your Own

Reread the passage on pages 90–91. Then, on a separate sheet of paper, write a one-paragraph response to the question, "How are the new treatments for traumatic brain injury improving patients' lives?" Use at least two words from the lesson in your response.

Word-Solving Strategies: Context Clues

Synonyms and Restatement

A synonym is a word with the same or nearly the same meaning as another word. A restatement is a phrase or sentence that defines a word. Sometimes synonyms or restatements can be found near the unfamiliar word. Read this example from "Biotechnology and Traumatic Brain Injury":

The neuron, or nerve cell, is the basic unit of your body's central nervous system.

Notice in the example that *nerve cell*, the synonym for *neuron*, is in a phrase set off by commas near the unfamiliar word.

BE CAREFUL!

Synonym and restatement context clues are not always near the word they define or set off by commas. Read this sentence:

For example, low cerebral blood flow often disrupts the brain's natural healing process in TBI patients.

The synonym for *cerebral* is *brain's* (that is, "of the brain"). This synonym is not set off by commas, or even near *cerebral*.

Practice

Write a highlighted word from the paragraph below, and the context clue that helps define it, in the first two boxes. Then write the meaning of the word in the third box.

Many TBI patients suffer from mental problems such as depression. One way to deal with the frustration of TBI and expedite or speed up the progress of recovery is to track symptoms. For example, when a TBI patient suffers from paranoia, a serious illness that causes the patient to falsely believe that people are trying to harm him or her, keeping tabs on that irrational or unreasonable feeling of persecution may help a patient overcome it.

WORD	SYNONYM OR RESTATEMENT	MEANING
expedite	speed up	to cause something to happen faster
paranoia	a serious illness that causes the patient to falsely believe that people are trying to harm him or her	feelings of suspicion and distrustfulness that are not based in reality
irrational	unreasonable	not using reason or good judgment
persecution	people are trying to harm him or her	cruel, unfair treatment

CCSS Vocabulary: 4.a.; Reading (Informational Text): 4. (See pp. T16–17.)

Practice for Tests

For a quiz and additional practice for this lesson, go to **vocabularyforsuccess.com**.

Fill in the bubble next to the answer that best completes the sentence or answers the question.

1. Read this sentence.

    A *discreet* signal to the waiter failed to get his attention.

    Discreet means:

    ○ **A** cautious
    ○ **B** angry
    ○ **C** unusual
    ● **D** subtle

2. When a film critic *deconstructs* a movie, he or she:

    ○ **A** directs it
    ● **B** analyzes it
    ○ **C** produces it
    ○ **D** recommends it

3. A *chemical* reaction is the result of the interaction of two or more:

    ● **A** substances
    ○ **B** feelings
    ○ **C** muscles
    ○ **D** thoughts

4. A *deleterious* side effect of a medication is:

    ○ **A** harmless
    ○ **B** minor
    ● **C** damaging
    ○ **D** new

5. Someone who craves *stimulation* is probably NOT:

    ● **A** exhausted
    ○ **B** bored
    ○ **C** outgoing
    ○ **D** excitable

6. If you *screen* patients for tuberculosis, you:

    ○ **A** treat them for it
    ○ **B** vaccinate them against it
    ○ **C** seek them out for a study
    ● **D** test them to see if they have it

7. Read this sentence.

    The patient had a *traumatic* wound to her leg.

    Here, *traumatic* means:

    ● **A** serious
    ○ **B** superficial
    ○ **C** infected
    ○ **D** unsettling

8. A *cerebral* discussion is:

    ○ **A** a violent one
    ○ **B** a humorous one
    ○ **C** an emotional one
    ● **D** an intellectual one

9. A *simulation* of fear is:

    ○ **A** a ritual of it
    ○ **B** a pure act of it
    ● **C** a pretense of it
    ○ **D** an overwhelming display of it

10. A *neuron* is a:

    ● **A** nerve cell
    ○ **B** chemical that sends signals in the brain
    ○ **C** protein that promotes the growth of nerve cells
    ○ **D** threadlike structure that extends from one nerve cell to another

If students answer B or D for Item 7, remind students that a traumatic event is serious (not superficial) and often shocking (not just unsettling).

Synonyms and Antonyms

In the following Word Bank, you will find synonyms and antonyms for some of the words in Lessons 7–9. (Remember: Some words have both synonyms and antonyms.) Study these words; then complete the exercises below.

essential	doubtful	careless	improvement	unnoticeable	flexibility
overturn	emotional	confirm	amusement	representative	dullness

A. For each sentence, fill in the blank with a SYNONYM for the word in boldface.

1. If you are looking for a **diversion** this summer, you might find _____amusement_____ at the new youth center.

2. The Green Club has become an **integral** part of the school, providing _____essential_____ services such as recycling paper and plastic.

3. My friend's assistive hearing device is so **discreet** that it's almost _____unnoticeable_____.

4. The onset of World War II would **invert** restrictions about women working outside the home and _____overturn_____ fashion taboos as well.

5. Computer learning games for toddlers are **illustrative** of our digital era and also _____representative_____ of parents' obsession with early academic learning.

B. For each sentence, fill in the blank with an ANTONYM for the word in boldface.

6. The sparkle in Rita's eyes seemed to **belie** her bored expression and _____confirm_____ my suspicion that she was planning a surprise.

7. Fortunately for their marriage, the **rigidity** of my father's personality was matched by my mother's _____flexibility_____.

8. Myrna begged Rupert to be **discreet** about the secret, but the young man instead became _____careless_____ and told many people.

9. Unless you can provide **incontrovertible** proof, your claim that this oil painting is by Leonardo da Vinci seems _____doubtful_____.

10. The man's ragged clothing and slow gait suggested a general _____dullness_____ about him, but when he spoke we were riveted by the **acuity** of his words.

Word Study: Proverbs

A proverb is a popular saying that expresses a widely held idea. This proverb gives an opinion about inherited traits: "The apple doesn't fall far from the tree." Use proverbs in your writing to add interest to your work.

Some of the words in Lessons 7–9 can be used to help explain the meanings of proverbs. For example, the proverb "A rumor goes in one ear and out many mouths" means that you will have trouble with gossip unless you can be *discreet* (Lesson 9) and keep it to yourself.

Practice

Read each sentence. Use context clues to figure out the meaning of each proverb in boldface. Then write the letter of the explanation of the proverb.

___b___ **1.** By refusing to pay a small fee to advertise his yard sale, Mr. Potter was being **penny wise and pound foolish.**

___f___ **2.** When Bobby wrecked his own snow fort to keep his sister from playing in it, he was **cutting off his nose to spite his face.**

___g___ **3.** I never thought Mikki would say she misses her old school, but I guess **absence makes the heart grow fonder.**

___a___ **4.** "**Beggars can't be choosers**," Shania's uncle said when Shania asked if the laptop he gave her was new or used.

___c___ **5.** "Some of you are wondering whether you can complete the 5-mile run," said Coach Moreno. "Well, **say 'I can' or say 'I can't,' and you're right either way.**"

___e___ **6.** "Be careful what you say around the children," said Grandma. "**Little pitchers have big ears.**"

a. Don't be critical of a gift or of good fortune.

b. You might save money in the short term but lose more in the long term.

c. Your attitude often determines your chances of success.

d. Listen carefully before you say something.

e. Children often overhear things that aren't meant for them.

f. Spiteful revenge can result in one's own hurt or loss.

g. The lack of something increases the desire for it.

Apply

Work with a partner to figure out the meaning of each proverb. (Use an online or print dictionary.) Then work together to write a sentence for each proverb.

1. Loose lips sink ships.

2. Fight fire with fire.

3. Look before you leap.

4. Failing to plan is planning to fail.

5. Familiarity breeds contempt.

6. Many a true word is said in jest.

7. Slow and steady wins the race.

8. Take the bitter with the sweet.

Vocabulary for Comprehension

Read the following passage, in which some of the words you have studied in Lessons 7–9 appear in boldface type. Then answer questions 1–6.

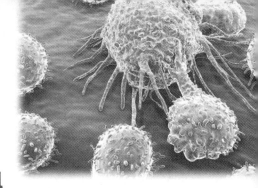

The Promising T-Cell

Not all cancer tumors are equal. Scientists have made headway in treating some cancerous tumors. But the growth of solid tumors, like those found in lung and colon
5 cancer, is frequently **irreversible**. Advances in **biotechnology**, however, offer hope. The key may lie not in chemotherapy—which floods the body with often **deleterious** levels of **chemicals**—but in the **stimulation** of the
10 body's immune system.

New therapies work with the body's own T-cells. T-cells are white blood cells that work to destroy microbe-infected cells. Scientists are looking for ways to make T-cells fight cancer
15 cells just as they fight microbial infections. Steven Rosenberg, who is a cancer surgeon at the National Cancer Institute, has developed a therapy called "adoptive cell transfer."

Rosenberg took T-cells from the tumor of a
20 patient with melanoma, a deadly type of skin cancer. He inserted into them a stimulant that caused them to replicate. When these T-cells were injected into the patient's heart, the patient developed a high fever. The **supplement** of
25 fortified T-cells seemed to **reactivate** his immune system, and the melanoma disappeared.

In a **refinement** of adoptive cell transfer, Rosenberg now engineers a patient's T-cells by inserting a gene that fights a particular protein
30 identified with a third of common cancers. The **preliminary** results are promising. They point to a future of cancer treatment that lies in the **restoration** of the body's own defense system.

If students answer A, B, or D for Item 5, review the different meanings of *refinement*.

1. In sentence 3, an **irreversible** cancer will
   - ● **A** continue to spread
   - ○ **B** become harmless
   - ○ **C** stop growing
   - ○ **D** become contagious

2. Something that is **deleterious** (line 8) causes
   - ○ **A** healing
   - ● **B** harm
   - ○ **C** infection
   - ○ **D** removal

3. A substance that causes **stimulation** (line 9) will
   - ○ **A** create something
   - ○ **B** imitate something
   - ○ **C** shrink something
   - ● **D** spark something

4. A **supplement** (line 24) is something that you
   - ○ **A** take away
   - ● **B** add
   - ○ **C** test
   - ○ **D** substitute

5. In line 27, **refinement** means
   - ○ **A** elegance
   - ○ **B** purification
   - ● **C** improvement
   - ○ **D** sophistication

6. In line 31, **preliminary** means
   - ○ **A** regular
   - ● **B** introductory
   - ○ **C** unexamined
   - ○ **D** premature

CCSS Vocabulary: 4.a., 6; Reading (Informational Text): 4. (See pp. T16–17.)

The Cultural Mosaic in the 21st Century

LESSON 10

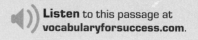

▶ **Watch** a video introduction to this passage at **vocabularyforsuccess.com**.

◀)) **Listen** to this passage at **vocabularyforsuccess.com**.

C CCSS Vocabulary: 4; Reading (Informational Text): 4, 6. (See pp. T16–17.)

The Lost Boys of Sudan Grow Up

\<profile\>

Mabior Deng is a refugee living in Philadelphia, a so-called Lost Boy of Sudan. He has traveled very far, both in miles and in time, to come to this place. He recently joined a gathering of other Lost Boys to commemorate both their past experiences and their achievements in the United States. No longer boys, these young men have much to celebrate and be proud of and also much to mourn.

Mabior was only seven years old when his village was attacked. It was 1983, and the place was Sudan, the largest country in Africa. A fierce civil war raged between the mainly Arab Muslim north of the country and the south, where most of the people were Christians. Friction between the groups erupted into civil war because of cultural differences and competition for the rich oil fields in the south. The peaceful lives of Mabior and the other residents were shattered as soldiers stormed into their village. Boys who were away from the village tending cattle were able to escape the horror by taking refuge in the forest.

When the boys were finally able to creep back to their village, they discovered the devastation— the village destroyed and their mothers, fathers, sisters, and grandparents either dead or gone. With no homes to return to, the boys embarked on a journey by foot to find a safe place.

In contrast to the life of comfort and joy they took for granted in their village, conditions were wretched on the road. The northern forces would kill any boys they found, or force them to become child soldiers, taking up arms against their own people. The boys needed to stay on the move. They had little food or water and became sick. Some boys, too weak to walk, were picked up by their friends and carried. Others collapsed on the road, dying of hunger, thirst, exhaustion, or disease. Only a boy with a strong body and resilient spirit, or psyche, would manage to survive.

After walking 1,000 miles through the desert, Mabior and his friends ended up at a refugee camp in the neighboring country of Ethiopia. Though they were safe from the militias, their days there were hardly happy. They had no families and little to do. Hence, they spent their days in boredom and anxiety, with the life they once knew wiped out and their future uncertain.

As the world slowly began to take note of the boys' plight, world leaders were presented with an ethical dilemma: who was responsible for the boys? In 2002, the United States government decided to liberate thousands of Lost Boys from the camps and resettle them in American cities. Mabior was one of those young men. Some of the boys, as they've grown into manhood, exhibit signs of their trauma, but many, like Mabior, have settled into their new lives—going to school, finding jobs, and making new friends—with no signs of psychological problems.

A profile is a nonfiction piece that describes aspects of a person's life.

Mabior wishes he could forget the days when he had to cower in the forest. But now he and his friends have new lives as future U.S. citizens. Some have managed to reunite with their families in the newly created country of South Sudan, turning a story of tragedy into one of hope.

Displaced by Sudan's civil war, young boys walk hundreds of miles in search of safety.

TALK ABOUT IT

With a partner, answer the questions below. Use as many of the highlighted words in the selection as you can.

1. Where do you take *refuge* in daily life and why?

2. Describe a time when you have had to *exhibit* courage and resourcefulness to meet a challenge.

Word Meanings

For each highlighted word on pages 104–105, the meaning or meanings are given below.

For practice with synonyms, see page 134.

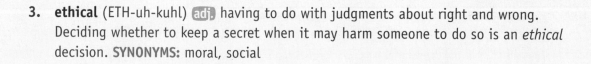

1. **commemorate** (kuh-MEM-uh-rate) **v.** to remember by holding a ceremony. People *commemorate* important events to give them meaning and to avoid forgetting them. **SYNONYMS:** observe, honor

2. **cower** (KOU-er) **v.** to crouch down in fear. Sometimes pet dogs and cats *cower* under a table or bed at the sound of thunder or fireworks. **SYNONYMS:** cringe, recoil

3. **ethical** (ETH-uh-kuhl) **adj.** having to do with judgments about right and wrong. Deciding whether to keep a secret when it may harm someone to do so is an *ethical* decision. **SYNONYMS:** moral, social

4. **exhibit** (eg-ZIB-it) **v.** to show or present something. As people get older, they *exhibit* signs of aging, such as wrinkled skin and gray hair. **SYNONYMS:** reveal, express; **n.** a presentation. You can see an *exhibit* of artifacts at a history museum. **SYNONYMS:** collection, showing

5. **friction** (FRIK-shuhn) **n.** bad feelings caused by conflicting desires or goals. When *friction* between people gets extreme, a fight may break out. **SYNONYMS:** discord, strife, conflict, tension, hostility; **n.** the resistance when one surface moves over another. *Friction* between the road and a car's tires is what enables vehicles to move. **SYNONYMS:** abrasion, rubbing, drag

6. **hence** (HENSS) **adv.** for this reason, as a result of. Herbal tea has relaxing compounds in it; *hence* some people drink it at bedtime. **SYNONYMS:** so, consequently, therefore

7. **liberate** (LIB-uh-rate) **v.** to set someone or something free. Summer vacation will *liberate* people from their winter routines. **SYNONYMS:** free, emancipate

8. **psyche** (SYE-kee) **n.** a person's mind, soul, or consciousness. The word *psyche* comes from the ancient Greek word for "soul," and it refers to a person's self or personality. **SYNONYMS:** ego, being

9. **psychological** (sye-kuh-LOJ-uh-kuhl) **adj.** relating to a person's state of mind or typical emotional characteristics. Various *psychological* problems can result from a person's experiencing extreme and long-term stress. **SYNONYM:** mental

C CCSS Vocabulary: 4.c., 4.d. (See pp. T16–17.)

Watch a video introduction for each word at **vocabularyforsuccess.com**.

Listen to iWords at **vocabularyforsuccess.com**.

Refer to the online dictionary at **vocabularyforsuccess.com**.

10. **refuge** (REF-yooj) **n.** a place that provides safety from danger. National parks in Africa provide *refuge* for large mammals that otherwise might be killed by hunters. **SYNONYMS:** sanctuary, shelter, haven

11. **refugee** (ref-yuh-JEE) **n.** a person who has fled his or her country as a result of war, natural disaster, or other danger. Sometimes, in order to stay in a new country, a *refugee* must prove he will be harmed if he goes back to his home country. **SYNONYMS:** exile, displaced person

12. **wretched** (RECH-id) **adj.** extremely bad. *Wretched* living conditions might include filth, vermin, crowded conditions, and lack of heat. **SYNONYMS:** harsh, miserable, pitiful; **adj.** feeling very unhappy or unfortunate. People might feel *wretched* after a personal failure or setback. **SYNONYMS:** sorrowful, distressed, despairing

More on Meanings: Confusing Word Pairs

The English language includes many pairs of words that can be confused because they look and sound alike and also have related meanings. Compare these sentences:

The flood victims took **refuge** at the shelter.

The war **refugee** found a new home in the United States.

In the first sentence, *refuge* is a noun meaning "a place that provides safety from danger." In the second sentence, *refugee* is a noun meaning "a person who has fled home as a result of war, natural disaster, or other danger." Both words are related to needing or finding shelter.

Confusing words pairs can sound exactly the same and be the same part of speech. Look at these sentences:

Take a **bite** of this delicious stew.

It would be a good idea to add another **byte** of memory to this computer.

Take care that wild animal doesn't **bite** you.

In the first two sentences, *bite* and *byte* are nouns. However, *bite* means "the act of cutting with one's teeth," and *byte* means "a unit of data in computing." *Bite* is also a verb meaning "to cut with the teeth."

Sometimes a confusing word pair consists of words that are used infrequently. As a result, even though they have completely different meanings, they are often mixed up. Compare these sentences:

During the Middle Ages, while a lord was off at war, the **vassals** took care of the estate.

During the operation, the surgeon carefully repaired the damaged blood **vessels**.

Challenge Choose one word pair below. Use both words correctly in the same sentence.

they'll, there'll   *impart, in part*
knight, night

Review with students the use of contractions, noting that *they'll* is the contraction for *they will* and *there'll* is the contraction for *there will*.

CCSS Vocabulary: 4.a., 5. (See pp. T16–17.)

vocabularyforsuccess.com   **107**

Word Talk

Each lesson word has been placed in a category. With a partner, discuss and list items that belong in each category. Compare your results with those of another pair of students.

C CCSS Vocabulary: 6. (See pp. T16–17.)

Ceremonies That *Commemorate* Significant Events

weddings, funerals, quinceañeras, graduations

Things a *Refugee* Might Need Help With

learning a new language, getting a job, getting proper identification

Ways to Describe the *Psyche* of an Artist

creative, imaginative, observant, visionary, inspired

Places That Might Be Described as *Wretched*

a slum, a shantytown, a dump

Things That Could Make Someone *Cower*

a tornado, a scary movie, a grizzly bear

Examples of *Ethical* Decisions

whether to do something wrong based on peer pressure, whether to keep found money, whether to tell on a classmate

Things a Child Might *Liberate*

a butterfly from a jar, a bird from a cage, a balloon from a string

Phrases You Can Replace with the Word *Hence*

as a result, because of that, that being so, for this reason

Places Where You Might Find *Refuge*

in a storm shelter, at a library, in your bedroom

How You Might *Exhibit* Artistic Talent

drawing a picture, singing a song, playing in a band, dancing

Activities That Benefit People in a *Psychological* Way

exercising, taking responsibility, sharing feelings, volunteering, meditating

Situations in Which People Experience *Friction*

in heavy traffic, in a crowded store, waiting in line

Check for Understanding

Choose the lesson word that completes each sentence. Write the word on the line provided. Some words will be used twice.

commemorate	exhibit	liberate	refuge
cower	friction	psyche	refugee
ethical	hence	psychological	wretched

1. Gabby used all her carnival tickets; _____hence_____ she never rode the ferris wheel.

2. Malek made his friends _____cower_____ when he wore his Bigfoot costume.

3. Wildlife rehabilitators _____liberate_____ the animals back into their natural habitats.

4. The two friends' disagreements caused constant _____friction_____ between them.

5. Chess requires not only logical skill but also _____psychological_____ understanding, because you have to get into the mind of your opponent.

6. We saw zebras, elephants, and rhinos at the wildlife _____refuge_____.

7. To make a/an _____ethical_____ decision, think about what's right and honorable.

8. After Amber heard a Mozart concerto, her _____psyche_____ was forever changed; she knew she would be a violinist.

9. The prison was shut down because of its _____wretched_____ conditions.

10. On Cinco de Mayo, we _____commemorate_____ an important victory in Mexico's history.

11. Whenever I _____exhibit_____ signs of illness, my mother keeps me home from school.

12. Our class is sponsoring a/an _____refugee_____ from Mali to help her get settled in the United States.

13. My doctor will _____liberate_____ my foot from this cast; then I won't need crutches.

14. The grimy linens and the flies at the _____wretched_____ youth hostel appalled Monica.

If students choose *exhibit* for item 3, explain that the point of rehabilitating wildlife usually is to release animals back into their habitats, not to put them in a zoo.

Word Associations

Use what you know about the lesson word in italics to answer each question. Circle the letter next to the phrase that best answers the question. Be prepared to explain your answers.

1. Which thing would a *refugee* most likely be leaving behind?

   a. a good job
   b. war
   c. an election

2. How might a city *commemorate* the home team's winning a tournament?

   a. by building a new stadium
   b. by closing the post office
   c. by hosting a parade

3. Which is an example of a *psychological* issue?

   a. poverty
   b. hunger
   c. depression

4. Hearing which of these statements might make you *cower*?

   a. "Pizza's ready!"
   b. "Look out—wasps!"
   c. "Please take your seat!"

5. Which action is the most *ethical*?

   a. looking at someone else's test paper
   b. turning a wallet in to Lost and Found
   c. ordering the most expensive item at a restaurant

6. What can you use to reduce *friction* with your computer mouse?

   a. a keyboard
   b. a mouse pad
   c. a monitor

7. Which might be a *refuge* for a mouse?

   a. under the floorboards
   b. on the kitchen counter
   c. near the cat's food bowl

8. I sat on my own foot for a half hour; *hence*

   a. my foot fell asleep.
   b. there wasn't room for me to stretch.
   c. I stood up.

9. Which of these words describes a person's *psyche*?

   a. tidy
   b. husky
   c. imaginative

10. Where would you most likely find an *exhibit*?

    a. at a gas station
    b. at the mall
    c. at a museum

11. Which situation might make you feel *wretched*?

    a. Your pet guinea pig died.
    b. You won a scholarship.
    c. You got eight hours of sleep.

12. Which of these would be most difficult to *liberate*?

    a. a doll from a box
    b. a bear from a trap
    c. a dog from a leash

C CCSS Vocabulary: 4.a. (See pp. T16–17.)

Check Again

Use what you know about the lesson word in italics to complete each sentence. Be sure your sentences make sense.

1. One way to soothe your *psyche* is _____ to listen to quiet music.

2. You might see a *refugee* on TV if you were watching a program about _____ an earthquake.

_____

3. An appropriate day to *commemorate* war heroes would be _____ Memorial Day or Veterans Day.

4. A person who acts in an *ethical* manner is also likely to be _____ someone you can trust.

_____

5. A person might need *refuge* because _____ the person has lost his or her home.

6. If a doctor said your headaches had a *psychological* cause, you might try to cure them by _____ figuring out why you feel stressed.

7. When people *cower*, they are trying to _____ protect themselves from harm.

8. If you feel *wretched* about a misunderstanding with your best friend, then you probably feel _____ upset and distressed.

9. If you wanted to impress someone, three traits you would try to *exhibit* might be _____ trustworthiness, patience, and ambition.

10. On the news, you might see rescuers coming to *liberate* people _____ from a mine collapse.

11. Neil failed to notice the "check engine" light was on in his car; *hence* _____ his car broke down, and he had to walk home from band practice.

12. There is little or no *friction* when you walk on ice, so it is _____ very slippery.

Write Your Own

Reread the passage on pages 104–105. Then, on a separate sheet of paper, write a one-paragraph response to the question, "How would you feel if you had to flee your home and settle in an unfamiliar land?" Use at least two words from the lesson word list and support your answer by referring to the text of the passage.

Word-Solving Strategies: Context Clues

Antonyms

Antonyms are a kind of context clue that suggests an unfamiliar word's meaning by presenting a word or a series of words with the opposite meaning. Reread this sentence from "The Lost Boys of Sudan Grow Up":

> In contrast to the life of comfort and joy they took for granted in their village, conditions were wretched on the road.

The sentence says that wretched conditions are in contrast to comfort and joy. It suggests that *wretched* conditions are the opposite—discomfort and sadness. To signal a contrast or the use of antonyms, a writer might use the following clue words or phrases: *in contrast, instead, on the other hand, as opposed to, but, no,* or *not.*

BE CAREFUL!

The clue words or phrases do not always indicate the presence of an antonym. Look at this excerpt from the passage about the Lost Boys:

> . . . *many, like Mabior, have settled into their new lives—going to school, finding jobs, and making new friends— with no signs of psychological problems.*

Here, the word *no* is not a clue word. There is no antonym in the sentence to directly explain what *psychological* means.

Practice

Write a highlighted word and the antonym that helps define it in the first two boxes. Then write the meaning of the word in the third box.

When Radovan left the army, the economy was oscillating, and there were few jobs and no stability. He felt it was crucial to go where the job market was expanding, and everything else was unimportant. He applied for a visa to the United States. At first, his application was denied as deficient, but finally everything was found to be adequate and approved. For several years, he felt tentative about whether moving was a good decision, but as he began to thrive, he became certain that immigrating was the right thing to do.

WORD	ANTONYM	WORD MEANING
oscillating	stability	going back and forth
crucial	unimportant	of great importance
deficient	adequate	lacking
tentative	certain	uncertain, hesitant

CCSS Vocabulary: 4.a.; Reading (Informational Text): 4. (See pp. T16–17.)

Practice for Tests

For a quiz and additional practice for this lesson, go to **vocabularyforsuccess.com**.

Fill in the bubble next to the answer that best completes the sentence or answers the question.

1. When you *commemorate* an event, you:
   - ○ **A** read about it on the Internet
   - ○ **B** learn about it at school
   - ● **C** do something to remember it
   - ○ **D** write a letter to the editor about it

2. Read this sentence.

   It was raining on the day Jonah promised to take his brother to the zoo—*hence* they went bowling.

   Hence means:

   - ○ **A** but
   - ○ **B** anyway
   - ● **C** therefore
   - ○ **D** incidentally

3. You are in search of *refuge*. That means that you:
   - ● **A** need a place to stay
   - ○ **B** make enemies easily
   - ○ **C** are feeling confident
   - ○ **D** have enough money

4. If you *cower* during a scary movie, you are probably NOT:
   - ● **A** bored
   - ○ **B** feeling afraid
   - ○ **C** worried
   - ○ **D** nervous

5. If you are a *refugee*, then you are:
   - ○ **A** living comfortably at home
   - ● **B** escaping a bad situation
   - ○ **C** chasing after an enemy
   - ○ **D** feeling hopeful

   If students choose D for Item 5, have them review the definition of the word *refugee* on page 107. Remind students that a refugee's primary goal is to flee from danger. A refugee may or may not be hopeful.

6. An example of an *ethical* act is:
   - ○ **A** ignoring someone's cry for help
   - ○ **B** letting someone else take the blame for you
   - ○ **C** sharing someone else's secrets
   - ● **D** confessing to making a mistake

7. If you want to *liberate* your feet from your shoes, you want:
   - ○ **A** to separate them
   - ● **B** to free them
   - ○ **C** to soak them
   - ○ **D** to measure them

8. Read this sentence.

   Tony wanted to *exhibit* toughness, smarts, and confidence at the debate.

   Exhibit means:

   - ○ **A** to remember
   - ○ **B** to enhance
   - ● **C** to display
   - ○ **D** to discover

9. If you like movies with a *psychological* theme, you would most likely enjoy watching a movie about:
   - ○ **A** world champion surfers
   - ○ **B** gorillas in the rain forest
   - ○ **C** the invention of the airplane
   - ● **D** lonely teens who become friends

10. A good way to avoid *friction* when working with others is to:
   - ○ **A** try to make sure you get your way
   - ● **B** be polite during disagreements
   - ○ **C** work only in small groups
   - ○ **D** do projects one step at a time

 Watch a video introduction to this passage at **vocabularyforsuccess.com**.

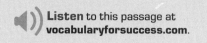 **Listen** to this passage at **vocabularyforsuccess.com**.

C **CCSS Vocabulary:** 4; Reading (Informational Text): 4, 6. (See pp. T16–17.)

Muslim Imam Puts Down Roots in Tiny Spoonerville

<newspaper article>

Spoonerville, Arkansas, May 31, 2012

A small, converted shed behind the local gas station in the tiny town of Spoonerville, Arkansas, population 291, might seem like an unlikely place to hold Muslim religious services. But this neat, white-painted building, which also serves as an Internet café and a mailing center, rings out with prayers five times a day. For a small Muslim community in central Arkansas, it is their mosque. The imam, Mehmed Sulejmanovic, also runs the business, an unusual yet effective symbiotic creation. There, he can perform outreach services to other Bosnian refugees, care for the spiritual needs of the dozen or so other Muslims in the area, and make a modest living.

The tiny community Sulejmanovic leads is one of a growing number of Muslim groups throughout the South. Since 1988, over 200,000 Muslim refugees have settled in the United States. They came to escape a variety of hardships in their home countries, including war, famine, and persecution. Sulejmanovic, his wife, Raifa, and his three children are refugees from Bosnia who escaped to the United States in 1999 following the Serbian campaign of ethnic cleansing, in which thousands of Muslims of the Bosnian ethnicity were murdered.

The U.S. Muslim population is growing—that much is clear. No one knows exactly how many Muslims live in the country today, but the number is significant. Estimates put the population from 2.3 million to as many as 7 million. Though Muslims share a religious faith, their diversity makes overgeneralization about their needs, habits, and ability to assimilate into this country impossible. The overall community is hardly homogeneous: Muslim immigrants come from some seventy-seven different countries, speak dozens of languages, and represent a range of lifestyles, from educated urbanites to farmers who cannot read or write.

Explain that a newspaper article is a
piece of informational writing published
in a newspaper.

VOCABULARY

symbiotic	assimilate	acculturate
ethnicity	homogeneous	quandary
significant	inaccuracy	ideology
overgeneralization	nuance	vacillate

Sulejmanovic was a highly educated teacher at a religious school, though it would be an inaccuracy to say that this background has given him an advantage in a tough job market. He spoke a little English before he came here, and today his English is quite competent. But as he admits with a warm smile, he sometimes misses the nuance of his new tongue. "My children often have to explain the more subtle meanings of words to me. But I continue to work hard to acculturate myself into this country because this is now my home."

His children include his daughter, Fadila, and sons Samir and Kamal. Fadila is comfortable in the traditional hijab, or headscarf, but when she first arrived, she was in a quandary. The school left it up to her whether she would wear it, as did her father, who wanted her to fit in. She was tempted to give it up as well, but in the end, ideology won out and she chose to keep her head covered. His sons, on the other hand, vacillate between much less weighty options. "They cannot decide whether they want to become baseball stars or basketball stars," he laughs.

In this new home, Mehmed Sulejmanovic has carved out a peaceful oasis for himself and his family. He is, he says with assurance, "here to stay."

TALK ABOUT IT

With a partner, answer the questions below. Use as many of the highlighted words in the selection as you can.

1. The article describes how a Muslim family has had to *assimilate* into unfamiliar surroundings. How do you think you would deal with moving to a totally different culture?

2. What do you think is the most *significant* change for the family in the article?

Muslims have found new homes in the United States and enjoy the freedom to live and worship.

Word Meanings

For each highlighted word on pages 114–115, the meaning or meanings are given below.

For practice with synonyms, see page 134.

1. **acculturate** (uh-KUHL-chur-ate) **v.** to change one's habits, beliefs, and practices to become part of a new culture. People *acculturate* to varying degrees when they move to a new country. **SYNONYMS:** fit in, assimilate

2. **assimilate** (uh-SIM-uh-late) **v.** to adopt the ways of another culture and fully become part of a different society. It often takes a generation for new immigrants to *assimilate* into their new home countries. **SYNONYMS:** integrate, acculturate; **v.** to take in and use. The bodies of living things *assimilate* nutrients for energy. **SYNONYMS:** integrate, digest, ingest, learn, master

3. **ethnicity** (eth-NIH-si-tee) **n.** a particular group with a shared racial, tribal, or national background. A person's *ethnicity* often determines his or her religion, language, and other cultural practices. **SYNONYMS:** nationality, race

4. **homogeneous** (hoh-muh-JEE-nee-uhs) **adj.** made up of parts that are all similar. A *homogeneous* society is made up of people of the same culture, religion, and racial background. **SYNONYMS:** unvaried, similar

5. **ideology** (eye-dee-OL-uh-jee) **n.** a way of thinking or set of ideas that is characteristic of a particular group of people. Teenagers often share an *ideology* that is different from that of their parents. **SYNONYMS:** beliefs, philosophy

6. **inaccuracy** (in-AK-yuh-ruh-see) **n.** a mistake or error. An *inaccuracy* refers to a mistake that is factual, rather than a mistake in judgment or behavior. **SYNONYMS:** error, oversight, misstep

7. **nuance** (NOO-ahnss) **n.** a difference or variation that is difficult to perceive. An example of *nuance* is the difference between light blue and sky blue. **SYNONYM:** shade, subtlety

8. **overgeneralization** (OH-vur-JEN-ruh-luh-ZAY-shuhn) **n.** a broad conclusion that is not completely supported by the evidence. It would be an *overgeneralization* to say that all dogs are brown based on seeing a group of brown dogs. **SYNONYM:** conclusion

9. **quandary** (KWAHN-duh-ree) **n.** confusion or doubt about how to deal with a challenge. You might experience a *quandary* if two friends ask you to the same dance. **SYNONYMS:** predicament, bind

Watch a video introduction for each word at **vocabularyforsuccess.com**.

Listen to iWords at **vocabularyforsuccess.com**.

Refer to the online dictionary at **vocabularyforsuccess.com**.

10. **significant** (sig-NIF-uh-kuhnt) **adj.** large or important enough to attract attention. A strong windstorm can cause *significant* physical damage to houses and trees. **SYNONYMS:** noteworthy, remarkable, momentous; **adj.** having a particular meaning that is not stated outright. A *significant* glance may be enough to tell you someone is irritated with you. **SYNONYMS:** meaningful, expressive, suggestive

11. **symbiotic** (sim-bee-OT-ik) **adj.** mutually beneficial, or beneficial to all parties. A *symbiotic* relationship is one in which everyone involved receives some kind of benefit. **SYNONYM:** interdependent

12. **vacillate** (VASS-uh-late) **v.** to go back and forth between options; to hesitate when trying to decide something. If you love all flavors of frozen yogurt, you may *vacillate* as you decide on the one you want to order. **SYNONYMS:** waver, alternate, be indecisive

More on Meanings: Denotation and Connotation

Most words not only have literal meanings, or denotations, but also have shades of implied meaning, or *connotations*. Connotations, as you know, can be positive, negative, or neutral. For example, compare these sentences:

Shari found an **inaccuracy** in her test.

Shari found an **error** in her test.

Shari found a **mistake** in her test.

The word *inaccuracy* has a neutral connotation, with no particular feeling associated with it. The words *mistake* and *error* are more straightforward and have negative connotations, implying something that is undeniably wrong.

In working with words, you will often find synonyms that have the same denotation, but different connotations. Here's an example:

Rodney was in a **quandary** about how to break the news to his family.

Rodney was in a **pickle** about how to break the news to his family.

Both *quandary* and *pickle* mean "a state of confusion," but the different connotations of the words affect the tone of the two sentences. *Quandary* has a neutral connotation and doesn't say much about Rodney's situation. *Pickle*, however, suggests that Rodney's situation is somewhat humorous.

Challenge Choose two of the words below. For each, suggest two synonyms, one with a positive connotation, one with a negative connotation. Then use each synonym in a sentence that demonstrates the feeling associated with it.

interact	*apologize*	*depart*
request	*rule*	*bend*

If students have difficulty identifying synonyms with different connotations, allow them to use a thesaurus to generate a pool of synonyms and identify their connotations as neutral, positive, or negative.

CCSS Vocabulary: 5.b. (See pp. T16–17.)

vocabularyforsuccess.com

117

Word Talk

Each lesson word has been placed in a category. With a partner, discuss and list items that belong in each category. Compare your results with those of another pair of students.

C CCSS Vocabulary: 6. (See pp. T16–17.)

Animals That Live in *Homogeneous* Groups

ants in colonies, cows in herds, wolves in packs, birds in flocks

Times When a Person May *Vacillate*

when shopping, when choosing an elective in high school, when making a decision

Things or People in a *Symbiotic* Relationship

a police detective and an informant, a reporter and a source, an insect and a flower

Ways That Immigrants Can *Acculturate*

learn the language of the country, go to school, watch television, become a citizen

Things That Show *Nuance*

hair color, flavors, similar emotions (like, love, adoration)

Examples of an *Ideology*

political parties, religion, views on nature, views on treatment of animals

Categories of *Ethnicity*

African American, Chinese, Hispanic, Japanese, Korean, Russian, Thai, Vietnamese

Significant Events in a Person's Life

graduating from high school, finding a job, getting married, having a child, running a marathon, winning a scholarship

Things People Might Make an *Overgeneralization* About

the climate or weather in a place, the skill of a sports team

Situations That Might Cause a *Quandary*

having little money and a long shopping list, not having enough time to do everything one needs to do in a day, having several obligations on the same day

Places Where People Might Want to *Assimilate*

a new school, a foreign country, a new neighborhood

Places Where You Have Seen an *Inaccuracy*

on a test, in a math problem, in a news article

Check for Understanding

Choose the lesson word that completes each sentence. Write the word on the line provided. Some words will be used twice.

acculturate	homogeneous	nuance	significant
assimilate	ideology	overgeneralization	symbiotic
ethnicity	inaccuracy	quandary	vacillate

1. Learning a new language from an early age often makes it easier for the children of immigrants to _____acculturate_____ than the parents.

2. _____Inaccuracy_____ is undesirable in a research paper, which requires facts.

3. Natasha realized that she had made a/an _____overgeneralization_____ when she discovered that her bus pass didn't work on the trains as well.

4. Our team's bake sale raised a/an _____significant_____ amount of money.

5. The plant life in the northern forest is not varied, but is actually _____homogeneous_____.

6. Alexei wanted to _____assimilate_____ into his new school, so he practiced speaking with an American accent.

7. Manny's _____ideology_____ about the environment was shaped by his growing up near a national park.

8. In speech class, we pay careful attention to the _____nuances_____ of words' meanings.

9. The newspaper published a small notice correcting the _____inaccuracy_____ in its spelling of Mayor Christofilakis's last name.

10. Jodie was in a/an _____quandary_____ about what to wear for the nature walk.

11. During the monsoon season, _____significant_____ amounts of rain fall in areas of India.

12. Jahalla studied the menu carefully in order not to _____vacillate_____ when ordering.

13. Terri's report examined the _____symbiotic_____ relationship between ants and aphids.

14. For the question about _____ethnicity_____, Deon checked the box marked "other."

If students answer *assimilate* for Item 1 and *acculturate* for Item 6, review the words' meanings. Note that the preposition *into* is a clue for the answer *assimilate* in Item 6.

Word Associations

Use what you know about the lesson word in italics to answer each question. Circle the letter next to the phrase that best answers the question. Be prepared to explain your answers.

1. Which of the following is an expression of a person's *ideology*?

   a. "Broccoli is tasty and nutritious."
   b. "The window washers come every other Tuesday."
   c. "Treat others as you would like to be treated."

2. What would you do during a *significant* drought?

   a. begin to conserve water
   b. seek shelter inside
   c. water your lawn every day

3. Which emotion would one most likely experience when in a *quandary*?

   a. joy
   b. anxiety
   c. confidence

4. Which of the following would you most want to be *homogeneous*?

   a. a box of cookies to serve at a party
   b. a box of adhesive bandages
   c. a box of staples for your stapler

5. What is the best thing you can do to *acculturate* yourself to a new country?

   a. Avoid meeting new people.
   b. Learn the country's language.
   c. Read books about it before you go.

6. Which of the following statements contains an *inaccuracy*?

   a. The United States has fifty states.
   b. Mexico is north of the United States.
   c. The United States is a democracy.

7. Which of these might give a clue to a person's *ethnicity*?

   a. his or her e-mail address
   b. his or her clothing
   c. his or her last name

8. Which action is an example of *nuance*?

   a. a hearty handshake
   b. a slight shrug of the shoulders
   c. a loud laugh

9. Which of these is an example of *overgeneralization*?

   a. bringing three dishes to a potluck
   b. wearing sunscreen today to make up for a sunburn the day before
   c. biting into a sour peach and concluding all peaches are sour

10. How might you *assimilate* what you read?

    a. Skim it briefly and then move on.
    b. Verify it in a reliable online reference.
    c. Review the material every day.

11. Which of these can *vacillate*?

    a. a tree in the fall
    b. a tall building on a windy day
    c. a person's mood

12. If two species of fish have a *symbiotic* relationship, what might happen?

    a. Species A eats parasites off the body of species B.
    b. Species A has protective coloration to prevent species B from eating it.
    c. Species A lays its eggs in the same place as species B.

CCSS Vocabulary: 4.a. (See pp. T16–17.)

Check Again

Use what you know about the lesson word in italics to complete each sentence. Be sure your sentences make sense.

1. Cheryl didn't want her party to be totally *homogeneous*, so she __invited kids from the glee club__ and the soccer team.

2. There is a great deal of *nuance* in paint colors, so __there are many different shades to pick from.__

3. Someone made a *significant* donation to the school, so __the school could buy more books.__

4. Josh's grandfather had a very different political *ideology* from his dad's, and as a result __they often__ had arguments about the role of government.

5. In Ralph and Julio's *symbiotic* studying relationship, Ralph tutored Julio in math, while _____ Julio tutored Ralph in American history.

6. Teddy tended to *vacillate* when making any decision, __so he always asked his friends' advice.__

7. The *inaccuracy* of the bill for the meal meant that __the customer had to pay more than required.__

8. If you want to *assimilate* as an exchange student, __follow the country's traditions and cultural ways.__

9. Ken helped resolve the yearly family *quandary* over who would host Thanksgiving dinner by _____ suggesting that everyone eat at a restaurant.

10. Delia showed pride in her *ethnicity* by __serving traditional dishes from her family's culture.__

11. If your job is boring, it would be an *overgeneralization* to conclude that __all jobs are boring.__

12. Today, immigrant children in the United States have programs to help them *acculturate*, such as __ instruction in the English language.

Write Your Own

1. **Write a fourteen-word sentence using the word *significant* in the eighth position.**

   I plan to study hard and make significant gains on my college entrance exams.

2. **Write a thirteen-word sentence using the word *inaccuracy* to describe a step you take to make sure that your homework is correct.**

   I always double-check each answer to make sure it doesn't contain an inaccuracy.

Word-Solving Strategies: Context Clues

Inferences

Sometimes a word or phrase is not defined within the sentence or clarified by examples, synonyms, or antonyms. Relationships between words that are not obvious are implied, and the reader must make an inference. Reread this sentence from the passage:

But this neat, white-painted building, which also serves as an Internet café and a mailing center, rings out with prayers five times a day. For a small Muslim community in central Arkansas, it is their mosque. The imam, Mehmed Sulejmanovic, also runs the business, an unusual yet effective symbiotic creation.

Readers can see that both the community and the owner/imam benefit from the business and the religious leadership and therefore infer that *symbiotic* means "beneficial to all parties."

Inference clues can appear anywhere in a paragraph. Read this example:

She was tempted to give it up as well, but in the end, ideology won out and she chose to keep her head covered.

To find the meaning of the word *ideology*, readers must go back to the beginning of the paragraph and infer that *ideology* refers to a religious tradition requiring head coverings.

BE CAREFUL!

Practice

Write sentences for the four highlighted words in the paragraph below. Include inferences as context clues in the sentences. Use two words twice.

After much exertion, Jamila found a job, but the search was easier than succeeding at the job once she had it. Her supervisor was unresponsive, and her requests for help went unanswered. Though she wanted to make friends with her coworkers, they would misinterpret her quiet personality as lack of interest. Once she learned that she needed to be more friendly and outgoing, her coworkers found her to be amiable and welcomed her warmly.

1. The exertion required to find a new job was not as great as the everyday effort in doing the job.

2. The patient was unresponsive to the treatment and did not show any progress.

3. If you run across unfamliar words, it's easy to misinterpret their true meaning.

4. His amiable nature made it pleasant to be around him, as he was easy to talk to.

5. A triathlon requires much exertion to run, bike, and swim long distances.

6. Since text messages are so short, it is easy to misinterpret what they are really saying.

CCSS Vocabulary: 4.a.; Reading (Informational Text): 4. (See pp. T16–17.)

Practice for Tests

For a quiz and additional practice for this lesson, go to **vocabularyforsuccess.com**.

Fill in the bubble next to the answer that best completes the sentence or answers the question.

1. A questionnaire asks you about your *ethnicity*. That means you should identify:

   ○ **A** your favorite school subjects
   ○ **B** your gender
   ○ **C** your age
   ● **D** your race

2. An example of an *overgeneralization* is:

   ○ **A** Petra prefers corn tortillas to flour.
   ○ **B** Bill has more money than Joe because he is thrifty.
   ○ **C** Plums grow on trees, while grapes grow on vines.
   ● **D** American cars get the worst gas mileage.

3. Read this sentence.

   This book on U.S. politics suggests that the *ideology* of older people is different from that of younger people.

   Ideology means:

   ● **A** philosophy
   ○ **B** policy
   ○ **C** common sense
   ○ **D** commitment

4. The fabric samples appeared *homogeneous* because they were all:

   ● **A** the same color
   ○ **B** on sale
   ○ **C** of different quality
   ○ **D** located in the same store

5. If you speak with *nuance*, your words express:

   ○ **A** irony
   ● **B** shades of meaning
   ○ **C** facts and figures
   ○ **D** emotion

6. Read this sentence.

   Sophia was in a *quandary* over whether to buy a cheap bike now or wait until she could save up for a better one.

   Quandary means a state of:

   ○ **A** excitement
   ○ **B** poverty
   ● **C** uncertainty
   ○ **D** impatience

7. If you *vacillate* when you make choices, you are NOT:

   ○ **A** conflicted
   ○ **B** hesitant
   ○ **C** doubtful
   ● **D** decisive

8. If human cells *assimilate* water to do their jobs, they:

   ○ **A** pass through it
   ● **B** absorb it
   ○ **C** drown in it
   ○ **D** warm it up

9. To avoid *inaccuracy* in a research paper, a student should:

   ○ **A** write the first draft quickly
   ○ **B** pick a complicated topic
   ● **C** use trustworthy sources
   ○ **D** type it on a computer

10. One way new immigrants to the United States can *acculturate* successfully is to:

    ○ **A** settle in isolated communities
    ● **B** become active in their communities
    ○ **C** send money back home
    ○ **D** avoid watching television

If students choose A for Item 8, have them review the meaning of *assimilate* on page 116 and note that the word is used here to mean "to take in."

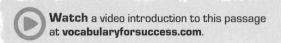

Watch a video introduction to this passage at **vocabularyforsuccess.com**.

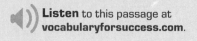

Listen to this passage at **vocabularyforsuccess.com**.

C CCSS Vocabulary: 4; Reading (Informational Text): 4, 6. (See pp. T16–17.)

The Military as a Path to Citizenship

<speech>

Thank you for attending this recruiting event. I'm here to tell you how you can speed up the process of becoming a citizen while starting a great career in the military.

To begin, I'd like to acknowledge that there are ways of becoming a citizen other than military service. And it may not seem self-evident that military service is the best path to citizenship, but let me outline a couple of points. First, let's compare the typical pathway to citizenship to getting citizenship within the armed forces. Under normal circumstances, a noncitizen has to be a legal permanent resident of the United States for a minimum of five years before applying for citizenship. In the past, military personnel had to serve only three years before applying for citizenship.

Then in 2001, the 9/11 attacks happened, and the country perceived a need for military buildup. The following year, President George W. Bush signed an executive order to greatly speed up the path to citizenship for anyone serving in the armed forces of the United States. Now the Army and the Navy both have programs in which basic

training and preparations for citizenship can be concurrent. That's right; you can do them both at the same time, and when you graduate from basic training, you will also be a U.S. citizen.

There is more than one parameter that holds true whether you are seeking citizenship through the military or in the civilian mode. You'll need to demonstrate proficiency in writing, speaking, and reading English. You will need to pass a civics exam, which means you'll have to know basic facts about U.S. history and how the government works. And you will have to prove that you are of good moral character. These requirements are no different from those of civilians. But by serving in the armed forces, you will be a citizen in as little as ten weeks, not five years.

I'm confident that you're all here because you're interested not only in citizenship but also in exploring the possibility of military service. You may be on the threshold of signing up, or you may only have a desire to learn more. Wherever you stand in the process, I hope this talk will motivate you to take action. For some of you, citizenship is the most important goal.

A speech is an expression of thoughts about a topic; it may include an anecdote, or short personal story, and is usually written and then presented before an audience.

For others, it is subordinate to other aims, such as learning a skill, developing problem-solving acumen that comes only with real-life experience, supporting a cause you believe in, or even taking part in an adventure. I promise you that the military experience has the potential to be any or all of these things.

I will append my remarks by pointing out some of the advantages of citizenship. One of the most important ones is that it will enfranchise you. Living in the U.S. without being able to vote can feel like standing at the perimeter of the basketball court and not being able to play the game. There is nothing like voting to make you feel that your voice is heard. As a citizen, you are entitled to all the rights and protections afforded by the U.S. government. You will be part of a great nation, perhaps the greatest nation in the world. If I sound vehement, it is only because this is something I am passionate about. I want to be emphatic that this could be the best decision you will make in your entire life.

VOCABULARY

acknowledge	threshold	append
self-evident	motivate	enfranchise
concurrent	subordinate	perimeter
parameter	acumen	vehement

TALK ABOUT IT

With a partner, answer the questions below. Use as many of the highlighted words in the selection as you can.

1. What do you think this talk could *motivate* someone to do? Explain your answer.

2. In the passage, the speaker says he is vehement about this topic. What issue or cause do you feel *vehement* about? Why?

New armed forces recruits proclaim their allegiance to their country as they take the oath of enlistment.

Word Meanings

For each highlighted word on pages 124–125, the meaning or meanings are given below.

For practice with synonyms, see page 134.

1. **acknowledge** (ak-NOL-ij) **v.** to accept that something exists or is true. You must *acknowledge* something to be true if someone provides clear evidence. **SYNONYM:** recognize; **v.** to show that one has noticed someone else's presence. You might *acknowledge* someone by making eye contact. **SYNONYMS:** greet, salute

2. **acumen** (AK-yoo-muhn) **n.** the ability to figure out a situation quickly and make good decisions. Someone with sports *acumen* understands the game and plays well. **SYNONYMS:** astuteness, sharpness, perception, savvy

3. **append** (uh-PEND) **v.** to add or attach something. To *append* a note to a document means to add additional information to the document, usually at the end. **SYNONYM:** supplement

4. **concurrent** (kuhn-KUR-uhnt) **adj.** existing or happening at the same time. Two TV shows that both start at 9:00 are *concurrent*. **SYNONYMS:** simultaneous, coincident

5. **enfranchise** (en-FRAN-chize) **v.** to give someone the right to vote. The government passed the 19th Amendment in 1920 to *enfranchise* women. **SYNONYM:** authorize

6. **motivate** (MOH-tuh-vate) **v.** to provide someone with the desire or ability to get something done. To *motivate* oneself is often the first step to completing a difficult task. **SYNONYMS:** prompt, inspire, stimulate

7. **parameter** (puh-RAM-uh-tur) **n.** a limiting factor that affects the outcome. The size of the theater is a *parameter* that affects the number of people who can see the show. **SYNONYMS:** determinant, limit

8. **perimeter** (puh-RIM-uh-tur) **n.** the boundary around a shape or an area. One way to mark the *perimeter* of a property is with a fence. **SYNONYMS:** circumference, border, boundary, edge

9. **self-evident** (self-EV-uh-duhnt) **adj.** obvious, not needing an explanation. Something that is *self-evident* is the observation that the sky is blue. **SYNONYMS:** plain, clear

▶ **Watch** a video introduction for each word at **vocabularyforsuccess.com**.

🔊 **Listen** to iWords 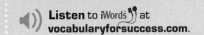 at **vocabularyforsuccess.com**.

📖 **Refer** to the online dictionary at **vocabularyforsuccess.com**.

10. **subordinate** (suh-BORD-uhn-it) **adj.** of a lower rank or position. *Subordinate* officers have to take orders from higher-ups. **SYNONYMS:** junior, lower; **n.** someone who has less power or authority than someone else. In the military, a captain is the *subordinate* of a general. **SYNONYMS:** assistant, aide

11. **threshold** (THRESH-ohld) **n.** the entry point or beginning of something. A baseball team might be on the *threshold* of victory in the ninth inning. **SYNONYMS:** verge, cusp, brink; **n.** the wood, metal, or stone base of a doorway. You step over the *threshold* when you enter a building. **SYNONYM:** entry

12. **vehement** (VEE-uh-muhnt) **adj.** showing passion, strong feeling, or intensity. When people speak in a *vehement* manner, it means they strongly want to make a point. **SYNONYMS:** forceful, ardent, spirited, fervent, emphatic

More on Meanings: Confusing Word Pairs

It's easy to confuse words that look or sound alike but have different meanings. The words *parameter* and *perimeter* are easy to confuse. Compare these sentences:

The yellow flags mark the **perimeter** of the property.

The temperature is the **parameter** that will determine whether we get rain or snow.

Both *perimeter* and *parameter* are nouns, and their spellings are very close. A perimeter is a boundary line. A parameter is a limiting factor that affects the outcome of an event.

The two words in a confusing word pair can be the same or different parts of speech.

My keycard gives us **access** to the top floor.

Can you **access** your phone messages from your computer?

Use a towel to soak up the **excess** moisture.

Our garden produced an **excess** of corn.

In these sentences, *access* is a noun meaning "a way in" and a verb meaning "to get"; *excess* is an adjective meaning "too much" and a noun meaning "an abundance."

Sometimes a confusing word pair consists of words with meanings that are closely related.

She showed only **minimal** interest in books.

I took the **minimum** dose of the medicine.

Both *minimal* and *minimum* are adjectives that refer to size. In the first sentence, *minimal* describes the smallest degree of interest. In the second sentence, *minimum* describes the smallest possible amount of medicine.

Challenge Choose one word pair below. Use both words correctly in the same sentence.

command, commend   *defective, deficient*
respectively, respectfully

Point out that in addition to *respectively* ("in the order indicated") and *respectfully* ("in a respectful manner"), *respectably* ("in a respectable manner") might be confusing.

ⓒ CCSS Vocabulary: 4.a., 5. (See pp. T16–17.)

vocabularyforsuccess.com ▶   **127**

Word Talk

Each lesson word has been placed in a category. With a partner, discuss and list items that belong in each category. Compare your results with those of another pair of students.

C CCSS Vocabulary: 6. (See pp. T16–17.)

Reasons to *Enfranchise* People

to promote democracy, to give people a voice in elections, to ensure equality

Things That Are *Concurrent*

different classes, movies at a multiplex theater, riding in a car and listening to music, singing and playing guitar

Parameters of Cooking

temperature, ingredients, recipe, flavors, the cook's skill

Characteristics of a *Vehement* Manner

loud, intense, passionate

Things That Are *Self-Evident*

The sun rises every day; water is wet; Friday follows Thursday.

Ways to *Motivate* Yourself to Study

imagining getting a good grade, meeting with a study group, determining daily study goals

How Others Might *Acknowledge* Your Worth

buy a gift, hire for a job, ask for advice

Milestones at the *Threshold* of Adulthood

getting a first job, graduating from school, buying a car, opening a checking account

Things That Have a *Perimeter*

a circle, a field, a crime scene

Activities That Require Business *Acumen*

running a store, selling merchandise online, buying stock

Times When Playing Games Is *Subordinate*

when studying, when there's a job to do, when chores must get done

Things You Might *Append* to a Research Paper

charts, graphs, lists of sources, places to get additional information, illustrations

Check for Understanding

Choose the lesson word that completes each sentence. Write the word on the line provided. Some words will be used twice.

acknowledge	concurrent	parameter	subordinate
acumen	enfranchise	perimeter	threshold
append	motivate	self-evident	vehement

1. Because of Bernard's political _____acumen_____, he ran several successful campaigns.

2. To _____motivate_____ others, inspire them with reasons to work hard and to achieve.

3. Elizabeth's mother was _____vehement_____ in her refusal to host a sleepover.

4. The prisoner will serve three five-year prison sentences, but they are _____concurrent_____, so he will be out in exactly five years.

5. After losing three straight games to Juanita, Durrell had to _____acknowledge_____ that his sister was the better chess player.

6. One _____parameter_____ of the speed of a go-cart is the size of the wheels.

7. It is _____self-evident_____ that a grade of A is better than a grade of B.

8. Mr. Henderson asked his lawyer to _____append_____ a document to his will.

9. For Jillian, everything was _____subordinate_____ to her getting a part in the school musical, so she rehearsed three hours a day.

10. Gavin planned to build a stone path around the _____perimeter_____ of his garden.

11. When you _____enfranchise_____ new citizens, they truly become part of their new nation.

12. _____Concurrent_____ activities at the party will be storytelling, pantomining, and eating popcorn and cake.

13. Dr. Annan, on the _____threshold_____ of a breakthrough, was awarded a research grant.

14. I'm a night owl, and although I try, I can't _____motivate_____ myself to get up early.

If students choose *perimeter* for Item 6, explain that the sentence addresses a factor that affects the speed, a parameter. It doesn't ask for the size of the wheels.

Word Associations

Use what you know about the lesson word in italics to answer each question. Circle the letter next to the phrase that best answers the question. Be prepared to explain your answers.

1. Which statement sounds the most *vehement*?

   a. A majority of citizens have expressed concerns about the plan.
   b. The city council must stop this disastrous plan immediately.
   c. This new plan will impact traffic.

2. How might you *motivate* your classmates to vote for you in a class election?

   a. Don't tell them you're running.
   b. Tell them about your ideas for improving the school.
   c. Go visit other schools to see how they run elections.

3. Which might improve your math *acumen*?

   a. practicing solving equations
   b. buying a calculator
   c. sharing your math homework with a classmate

4. Which of these has a *perimeter*?

   a. a gust of wind
   b. the sky
   c. a lake

5. When you're on the *threshold* of a building, where are you?

   a. on the doorstep
   b. in the parking garage
   c. in the hallway

6. How might a government *enfranchise* a group of people?

   a. by passing a law
   b. by collecting a tax
   c. by closing borders

7. Why might you *append* a letter that you write?

   a. You do not know the correct address where you should mail the document.
   b. You remembered some information you left out of the original document.
   c. You changed your mind about sending a document to someone.

8. How should a military officer who is a *subordinate* behave toward a senior officer?

   a. give him or her orders
   b. follow his or her orders
   c. act as his or her equal

9. Which of these would be a *parameter* of a science experiment?

   a. the materials tested
   b. the grade received
   c. the science textbook

10. Which pair describes *concurrent* events?

    a. a parade and a marching band
    b. day and night
    c. sleeping and awakening

11. How might you *acknowledge* friends' birthdays?

    a. say hello when you see them
    b. send them cards and gifts
    c. hope they throw a party

12. Which statement is *self-evident*?

    a. All my time is spent studying.
    b. One can never eat enough fruit.
    c. Cats have legs.

C CCSS Vocabulary: 4.a. (See pp. T16–17.)

Check Again

Use what you know about the lesson word in italics to complete each sentence. Be sure your sentences make sense.

1. Gregor wanted his studying and his laundry to be *concurrent* so that ___he could finish both at the___ same time.

2. The main *parameter* of the debate was ___the amount of time that debaters were given to speak.___

3. When the government decides to *enfranchise* a group of people, it ___allows them to vote in elections.___

4. Jerome has a high *threshold* for physical labor, so he is the perfect person to ___help build the___ stone wall.

5. You may *append* your comments at the end of the meeting if ___you think of something more to say.___

6. Alex was *vehement* about protecting the environment because ___it was a cause he deeply believed in.___

7. Manny decided his desire to go surfing should be *subordinate* to his need to go to work because ___he was saving money for college.___

8. If you want Mr. Wright to *acknowledge* your hard work on the project, ___make sure he knows how___ much you contributed.

9. People who believe population growth is *self-evident* point to ___the number of new homes being built.___

10. All the family members will *motivate* themselves to read more books by ___attending a___ book discussion group.

11. Billy had so much fishing *acumen* that he could ___tell where the fish were just by looking at the___ surface of the water.

12. Walk around the *perimeter* of the park rather than across it if ___the ground is too muddy.___

Write Your Own

Reread the passage on pages 124–125. Then, on a separate sheet of paper, write a one-paragraph response to the question, "What does it mean to you to be a U.S. citizen?" Use at least two words from the lesson word list and support your answer by referring to the text of the passage.

Word-Solving Strategies: Context Clues

Synonyms

A synonym is a kind of context clue that can help you figure out the meaning of an unfamiliar word. Synonyms can be a single word, or sometimes they can be phrases. Read this excerpt:

> Now the army and the navy both have programs in which basic training and preparations for citizenship can be concurrent. That's right; you can do them both at the same time, and when you graduate from basic training, you will also be a U.S. citizen.

If a reader is puzzling over the word *concurrent*, the writer provides a clue in the next sentence. He or she uses the phrase to explain that concurrent events can be done "at the same time." The phrase "at the same time" is a synonym for *concurrent*.

There may be times when you are presented with a pair of synonyms and you do not know the meaning of either of them. Use a dictionary if you need to find the words' meanings.

New recruits are often so ravenous after a session of basic training that they have to eat a lot of food to make themselves feel less famished.

In this sentence, if you don't know what either *ravenous* or *famished* means, refer to a dictionary.

BE CAREFUL!

Practice

Write each highlighted word and the synonym that helps define it in the first two boxes. Then write the meaning of the word in the third box.

Several reputable members of Congress propose that undocumented immigrants can become citizens by joining the military. These respected leaders realize that immigrants without proper papers could be arrested and deported. Instead of imposing this sanction, the legislation would remove the penalty and instead entail that the immigrants join the military and serve four years. Successfully completing this requirement could result in their becoming citizens. This would be a momentous opportunity for immigrants and critical to their gaining citizenship.

WORD	SYNONYM	WORD MEANING
reputable	respected	considered good or reliable
sanction	penalty	punishment
entail	result in	require
momentous	critical	significant

CCSS Vocabulary: 4.a.; Reading (Informational Text): 4. (See pp. T16–17.)

Practice for Tests

For a quiz and additional practice for this lesson, go to vocabularyforsuccess.com.

Fill in the bubble next to the answer that best completes the sentence or answers the question.

1. The weather event that is most likely to be *concurrent* with lightning is:

   ○ **A** wind
   ○ **B** meteors
   ○ **C** snow
   ● **D** thunder

2. When you want to *append* an idea to a letter you have already written, you can:

   ● **A** add a note at the bottom
   ○ **B** use a stamp
   ○ **C** take it to the post office
   ○ **D** deliver it in person

3. Read this sentence.

   By the time she was five, it was *self-evident* to Karina that the Tooth Fairy did not exist.

   Self-evident means:

   ○ **A** unfair
   ○ **B** depressing
   ○ **C** humorous
   ● **D** obvious

4. You would speak in a *vehement* manner if you:

   ○ **A** wanted people to like you
   ○ **B** didn't want to be too loud
   ● **C** felt very strongly about something
   ○ **D** didn't want to offend anyone

5. Police officers use a dog to patrol the *perimeter* of a crime scene. That means they:

   ○ **A** cover the entire area
   ○ **B** guard the interior
   ● **C** check the border
   ○ **D** witness the crime

6. Read this sentence.

   One of the goals of the civil rights movement was to completely *enfranchise* African Americans so they could have a voice in elections.

   Enfranchise means to:

   ○ **A** deny work to
   ● **B** give the right to vote
   ○ **C** lend money to
   ○ **D** recognize

7. Bryce has great *acumen* for numbers, so his parents have him:

   ○ **A** get tutoring in math
   ● **B** balance their checkbooks
   ○ **C** memorize their grocery list
   ○ **D** decide what allowance he deserves

8. To *motivate* yourself to do chores:

   ● **A** promise yourself a reward afterward
   ○ **B** ignore the chores completely
   ○ **C** put off the chores until later
   ○ **D** think about how you hate chores

9. If someone were *subordinate* to you at your job, that person would

   ● **A** do as you tell him or her
   ○ **B** work overtime
   ○ **C** make more money than you
   ○ **D** evaluate your performance

10. When you want to *acknowledge* a friend's success, you should NOT:

    ○ **A** praise him or her
    ○ **B** wish him or her well
    ○ **C** offer congratulations
    ● **D** ignore him or her

If students choose D for Item 6, explain that to recognize the concern occurs first; the goal is to enfranchise, "to give the right to vote."

Synonyms and Antonyms

In the following Word Bank, you will find synonyms and antonyms for some of the words in Lessons 10–12. (Remember: Some words have both synonyms and antonyms.) Study these words; then complete the exercises below.

excited	celebrate	enslave	various	release	luxurious
trivial	discourage	dilemma	error	subtlety	neutral

A. For each sentence, fill in the blank with a SYNONYM for the word in boldface.

1. Every year, our extended family tries to **commemorate** all the spring birthdays on one Saturday in May to make it easier for everyone to _____celebrate_____ together.

2. Joanie and her brother always **liberate** the wasps they find in the house, though their mother is not sure it's a good idea to _____release_____ stinging insects.

3. The food was delicious, with a delicate **nuance** in each dish that gave it a delightful _____subtlety_____ of flavors.

4. Trish was in a **quandary** over which colleges to apply to, and this _____dilemma_____ only added to her stress over the project.

5. Ricky's _____error_____ in adding up the budget numbers was a costly **inaccuracy**.

B. For each sentence, fill in the blank with an ANTONYM for the word in boldface.

6. Visitors to the national park spend a **significant** amount of money on supplies and food; in comparison, their souvenir spending is _____trivial_____.

7. I find that optimism and goal setting do more to **motivate** me to try harder, whereas fear of failure and pressure from my parents just _____discourage_____ me.

8. The _____neutral_____ response from supporters of the new dam stood in distinct contrast to the **vehement** protests of those against it.

9. Many people think that all ants are **homogeneous**, but a closer look reveals that within one ant colony you will see ants with _____various_____ body types and jobs.

10. The aid workers stayed in a modest house in the village, which seemed _____luxurious_____ compared to the **wretched** conditions of the people in the neighborhood.

CCSS Vocabulary: 4.a., 5, 6. (See pp. T16–17.)

Word Study: Denotation and Connotation

You know that words that are synonyms have the same literal meaning, or **denotation**, but that they may have different **connotations**, or emotional associations. Words can have neutral, positive, or negative connotations.

POSITIVE	NEGATIVE	NEUTRAL
masterful	bossy	dominating
haven	lair	hideout

Look at some of the synonyms for the word *vehement*, from Lesson 12.

| spirited | forceful | passionate |
| fierce | violent | earnest |

Most of these words are either positive or negative. They suggest either a powerful expression of belief or an extreme feeling. The words *spirited*, *passionate*, and *earnest* are all positive. The words *fierce* and *violent* are negative. The word *forceful*, however, is neutral. It has neither a positive nor a negative connotation.

Practice

A. Circle the word in parentheses that has the connotation (positive, negative, or neutral) given at the beginning of the sentence.

positive **1.** Mr. Thompson promised to (**clear,** (**forgive**)) his daughter's debt if she got straight A's.

negative **2.** The company president's (**subordinate,** (**inferior**)) drove him to the airport.

negative **3.** The investor showed (**acumen,** (**cunning**)) in choosing companies to buy out.

neutral **4.** I stayed home from school because I was feeling (**wretched,** (**unwell**)).

negative **5.** Being stuck in the car for four hours could account for the (**situation,** (**bickering**)) between my sister and me.

positive **6.** A tall glass of ice water at the end of the hike was a (**benefit,** (**blessing**)).

positive **7.** I will (**win,** (**triumph**)) at the track meet because I have trained more than my rivals.

B. Work with a partner. Write a plus sign (+) if the word has a positive connotation. Write a minus sign (–) if the word has a negative connotation. Or write a zero (0) if the word is neutral.

1. malicious `–`   **3.** disagree `0`   **5.** pale `–`   **7.** honest `+`

2. spiteful `–`   **4.** abundance `+`   **6.** cradle `+`   **8.** foresee `0`

Vocabulary for Comprehension

Read the following passage, in which some of the words you have studied in Lessons 10–12 appear in boldface type. Then, answer questions 1–6.

Building an Entrance

Cousins Javier and Katrina looked down as the airplane banked for the landing. The vivid green colors in the landscape contrasted with the **homogeneous** red-tiled roofs of the houses
5 outside Lima, Peru. Javier and Katrina were on an international volunteering adventure to help at a school serving students with special needs. The volunteers and the students would all get a **psychological** boost from the interaction.

10 When Katrina rolled her wheelchair into the classroom, the students were intrigued. She had them **acknowledge** that they had never seen a volunteer in a wheelchair. Katrina took the opportunity to **exhibit** how she used it. Sharing
15 how she dealt with the wheelchair was a great way to **assimilate** with the class. One student asked Katrina how she felt about needing the

wheelchair. "I accept it. And I can still do so many things." Another student asked if all Americans
20 were as optimistic as Katrina. She answered, "That's an **overgeneralization**, and maybe even an **inaccuracy**! I have my bad days." Then, she said, "Javier and his team are building a ramp for students who use wheelchairs. You can help!"

25 Next, Katrina had the students begin painting ceramic tiles and was pleased to see the students' **acumen** for art. When students asked what the tiles were to be used for, Katrina said, "You'll see!"

Finally Javier's team unveiled the new ramp.
30 The cement at the new **threshold** was still wet. Katrina's students placed their tiles there. It was a **significant** moment, and one to celebrate.

---

1. In sentence 2, **homogeneous** means
   - ● **A** uniform
   - ○ **B** spacious
   - ○ **C** attractive
   - ○ **D** smooth

2. The word **psychological** (line 9) refers to something that is
   - ○ **A** up in the air
   - ○ **B** encouraging
   - ○ **C** hard to understand
   - ● **D** in the mind

3. To **acknowledge** (line 12) something is to
   - ○ **A** deny it
   - ○ **B** talk about it
   - ● **C** admit it
   - ○ **D** correct it

4. To **exhibit** (line 14) something is to
   - ○ **A** build it
   - ● **B** show it
   - ○ **C** mean it
   - ○ **D** find it

5. Someone who does NOT **assimilate** (line 16) will
   - ○ **A** get along
   - ○ **B** blend in
   - ● **C** stand out
   - ○ **D** join up

6. A **threshold** (line 30) is located
   - ○ **A** on a roof
   - ○ **B** on a street
   - ○ **C** on a sidewalk
   - ● **D** in a doorway

If students choose an answer other than C for Item 5, review the meaning of *assimilate*. Point out that all the answer choices except C are synonyms for the word.

Using Context

Circle the word that best completes each sentence. Note that the choices are related forms of the vocabulary words in the box.

accommodate	deconstruct	overgeneralization
anonymous	ethical	practitioner
articulation	ethnicity	regenerative
buoyancy	illustrative	restoration
catalyst	implementation	specialization
commemorate	motivate	usurp

1. If you become famous, you will lose your (**anonymity**/articulateness).

2. Yuen Lee was a (regenerating/**buoyant**) person, always lifting other people's spirits with his cheerfulness.

3. It is not (ethnically/**ethically**) appropriate to give your friends the best jobs.

4. The entire village celebrates the event with an elaborate (**commemoration**/usurpation) every year.

5. In order to play the role convincingly, the actor tried to find the (**motivation**/illustration) for his character's behavior.

6. Diego's friendly criticism had a (deconstructive/**catalytic**) effect on Frida, inspiring her with the will to paint.

7. After three years of discussion, the two countries were finally able to agree on a mutual (**accommodation**/regeneration).

8. The dentist successfully (practiced/**restored**) the tooth by putting a crown on it.

9. Professor Daniels (**specializes**/overgeneralizes) in the study of one particular species of tropical plant.

10. We are going to (illustrate/**implement**) a new procedure by limiting game-playing time to one hour.

MID-YEAR REVIEW

Analogies

Read each sentence stem carefully. Then complete the sentence so that it makes sense. Use the relationship between the words in italics to help you.

1. When *copyright* laws are enforced, artists make money from their work, but when their music is sold by an *illicit* dealer, <u>they do not earn their rightful share.</u>

2. When you are honest with your client, you uphold your *fiduciary* relationship, but when you commit *fraud*, <u>you betray the relationship.</u>

3. In *tempestuous* times, rulers may be violently overthrown, while during a stable *regime*, <u>the rulers continue to hold power.</u>

4. It takes *hubris* to steal from the poor, while it takes a *humanitarian* outlook <u>to give</u> <u>to the poor.</u>

5. To *avert* disaster, be flexible in your responses; if you show *rigidity*, <u>you may not be</u> <u>able to respond effectively.</u>

6. When people are *vehement* in their opinions, they might displease listeners, although when they *vacillate*, <u>they may also be criticized.</u>

7. The best way to deal with a problem is to *acknowledge* it, because there could be *deleterious* results if <u>you make no attempt to address it.</u>

8. A human being's *persona* is visible on the surface, but the *psyche* <u>is not physically visible.</u>

C CCSS Vocabulary: 4.a., 5, 6. (See pp. T16–17.)

Word Relationships

You may wish to have students work in pairs or small groups to complete these exercises.

Read each question carefully. Think about the relationship between the two vocabulary words in italics. Then write an explanation that answers each question.

1. Why might a *depressed* person be *discreet*?

A depressed person might be shy, or might not want others to know that he or she

is depressed.

2. What *demographic* fact or situation do you think is *incontrovertible* today?

It is incontrovertible that the world's population is growing.

3. If you could undergo a *metamorphosis,* what kind of *entity* would emerge?

If I could undergo a metamorphosis, I would become a beautiful, free entity such as a butterfly.

4. In what way is a *tsunami traumatic*?

A tsunami is traumatic in that it causes sudden, massive death and destruction.

5. Why might there be an *exodus* of people from a country's *capitol*?

Everyone working in the capitol might leave because when the legislature is on a break, they

leave the city and return to their home states or take a vacation.

6. In your view, what *paradigm* is *integral* to the American way of life?

The paradigm of individual freedom and opportunity is integral to the American way of life.

MID-YEAR REVIEW

Generating Sentences

Follow the directions to write sentences with the vocabulary words in italics. Be sure your sentences make sense both grammatically and in meaning.

1. Use the word *hence* in a sentence.

Gabe loves animals; hence he volunteers in a vet's clinic.

2. Use the word *cower* in a sentence.

You weaklings will cower before the mighty Thor!

3. Use the word *eminent* in a sentence about a scientist.

She is eminent in her field because she knows everything there is to know about volcanoes.

4. Use the word *unlicensed* in a sentence of at least 8 words.

It is better not to use an unlicensed professional.

5. Use the word *chemical* in a sentence about health or disease that is at least 10 words long.

Many doctors think that mental illness has a chemical cause.

Extend Your Sentence

Choose one of your sentences and turn it into a paragraph. Use at least four other words from Units 1–4 in your paragraph.

CCSS Vocabulary: 6; Writing: 2.d. (See pp. T16–17.)

Where Will We Go Next?

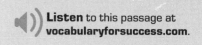

Watch a video introduction to this passage at **vocabularyforsuccess.com**.

Listen to this passage at **vocabularyforsuccess.com**.

C CCSS Vocabulary: 4; Reading (Informational Text): 4, 6. (See pp. T16–17.)

The World's Strangest Place

<expository essay> An expository essay is a nonfiction text that tells about a topic in content areas such as science, history, music, or political events.

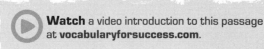

In 2012, a film director piloted a 24-foot-long submersible capsule to the deepest part of the ocean bed, in the Mariana Trench in the Pacific Ocean, 6.83 miles below the surface. Humans had twice previously reached that depth, but only for brief periods. He remained there for hours, taking samples of aquatic life and shooting 3-D film. Those findings could greatly expand human knowledge of Earth's strangest habitat: the deep sea.

Oceans cover almost three-quarters of the world's surface. However, humans have explored only five percent of that vast realm. The ocean floor contains wonders that can be found solely at those depths. For example, the mid-ocean ridge, an underwater mountain range, spreads for 50,000 miles. It contains valleys deeper than the Grand Canyon. Scientists estimate that eighty percent of the world's volcanoes are at the sea bottom beneath this ridge. Their activity creates areas of sea floor made of liquid rock.

Most impressive is the eclectic array of life at the sea bottom. There we find more diversity of life than in the Amazon rain forest. Creatures at sea bottom display adaptations whereby they can survive without sunlight, in extreme cold, under water pressure that could crush an ordinary steel ship. On the sea floor are volcanic hot-water vents. These vents are the portal through which heat energy enters the water. Specialized bacteria live at the rims of the vents and make food energy from chemicals such as hydrogen sulfide (H_2S). Larger creatures eat the bacteria. Even larger creatures feed on *them*.

Deep-sea species range from one-celled creatures to fish several feet long. There is an immense protozoan called the Xenophyophore, which can grow to eight inches long and contains four nuclei inside one huge cell. About ninety percent of deep sea species are bioluminescent. That is, they glow in the dark. Bioluminescent species include octopods with bright yellow rings around their mouths, vampire squid with glowing tentacles and black capes that they draw over themselves to hide from predators, and see-through sea cucumbers that vacuum the ocean floor in search of food protein. Some deep-sea creatures are migratory. Tube worms, which live at the hot-water vents, travel ocean currents for 190 miles in search of vents at which to feed.

Conditions in the deep sea are so strange that life forms there may offer us insights into possible life on other planets. The ocean floor is a prototype of an environment that seems hostile to life. If life can emerge at the sea bottom, it is reasonable to postulate that life can appear on cold, dark worlds such as the moons of Saturn.

As scientists analyze data from submersibles many new discoveries will be forthcoming. In any story about deep-sea life, perhaps the deep sea itself is the most mysterious protagonist of all.

Left: A squid

Above: Giant tube worms

VOCABULARY

aquatic	portal	prototype
solely	protozoan	postulate
eclectic	protein	forthcoming
whereby	migratory	protagonist

TALK ABOUT IT

With a partner, answer the questions below. Use as many of the highlighted words in the selection as you can.

1. **What other types of explorations or discoveries do you think will be *forthcoming* in the next decade or two?**

2. **Think about the world of living things on land. How do they, like life forms in the deep sea, show an *eclectic* array of adaptations?**

Deep-sea diving submersible in the Pacific Ocean

Word Meanings

For each highlighted word on pages 142–143, the meaning or meanings are given below.

For practice with synonyms, see page 172.

1. **aquatic** (uh-KWAT-ik) **adj.** having to do with, or living mainly in, the water. *Aquatic* life includes all the plants and animals of the oceans, lakes, and rivers. **SYNONYMS:** water-dwelling, watery

2. **eclectic** (i-KLEK-tik) **adj.** widely varied. An *eclectic* collection is one that contains items from many different sources. **SYNONYMS:** diverse, mixed

3. **forthcoming** (FORTH-kum-ing) **adj.** about to appear or to occur. *Forthcoming* refers to something in the near future. **SYNONYMS:** imminent, emerging

4. **migratory** (MYE-gruh-tor-ee) **adj.** moving from one region or area to another. Canadian geese are *migratory* because they travel south to the lower United States and Mexico for the winter and then travel north to Canada for the spring and summer. **SYNONYMS:** roving, wandering

5. **portal** (POR-tuhl) **n.** a doorway or entryway. A person passes through a *portal* whenever he or she enters a room. **SYNONYMS:** entrance, passage

6. **postulate** (POSS-chuh-late) **v.** to assume or claim to be true. Scientists *postulate* that there might have been a lot of water on Mars in the past. **SYNONYMS:** propose, theorize, guess, suppose; (POSS-chuh-luht) **n.** a statement that is assumed or claimed to be true. A *postulate* is considered true without proof, but it is based on reasoning. **SYNONYMS:** premise, given

7. **protagonist** (proh-TA-guh-nist) **n.** the main character in a story or real event. The *protagonist* is the most important person in a competition, conflict, or cause. **SYNONYMS:** hero, heroine, lead

8. **protein** (PROH-teen) **n.** any of a group of complex molecules consisting of carbon, hydrogen, oxygen, nitrogen, sulfur, and sometimes other elements, that are necessary to life. Animals are a source of *protein* for the living organisms that eat them.

9. **prototype** (PROH-tuh-tipe) **n.** the first model of something. Before building a complex, expensive machine, designers often use a *prototype* to test what they plan to make. **SYNONYMS:** pattern, original, standard

Watch a video introduction for each word at **vocabularyforsuccess.com**.

Listen to iWords at **vocabularyforsuccess.com**.

Refer to the online dictionary at **vocabularyforsuccess.com**.

10. **protozoan** (proh-tuh-ZOH-uhn) **n.** an organism that has only one cell. A *protozoan* contains a nucleus, a cell body, and a cell membrane or cell wall.

11. **solely** (SOHL-lee) **adv.** only. If something occurs *solely* in one place, it does not occur anywhere else. **SYNONYMS:** entirely, completely

12. **whereby** (WAIR-bye) **adv.** by which, according to, or as a result of which. The school created a program *whereby* students can attend dance, music, art, and gymnastics classes after school.

More on Meanings: Multiple-Meaning Words

As you know, there are many words in the English language that have more than one meaning. To understand the meaning of these words, see how they are used in context in a sentence. Also consider the words' part of speech.

Compare these sentences:

Just for the sake of argument, let's **postulate** that J. Q. Woodstone IV wins the senatorial election in November.

Our **postulate** is that a successful election requires wide voter support.

The word *postulate* is used in two different senses in the sentences above. In the first sentence, *postulate* is a verb meaning "to assume or claim to be true." In the second sentence, *postulate* is a noun meaning "a statement that is assumed or claimed to be true." Those two meanings are related but different, and the word's part of speech changes.

Many other words can be two different parts of speech as well. Consider the following:

We burned **incense** to make the room seem more exotic.

Having to wait in a long line always seemed to **incense** him.

I caught a **flounder** on my very first fishing trip!

The big waves and deep mud made me **flounder** about in the water.

In each of the cases above, the first usage is the noun form of the word, and the second usage is the verb form. It's possible to use these words in the same sentence, as subject and verb.

Does burning **incense incense** you?

Can a **flounder** ever **flounder**?

Challenge

1. Choose two of the multiple-meaning words below. For each word, write two sentences, each for a different meaning of the word.

   key   *quake*   *degree*   *point*

2. Now try to use both meanings of the words in the same sentence.

If students have difficulty using both meanings of a multiple-meaning word in the same sentence, suggest that they find other pairs whose meanings relate to the same content area.

C CCSS Vocabulary: 4.a., 5. (See pp. T16–17.)

vocabularyforsuccess.com   **145**

Word Talk

Each lesson word has been placed in a category. With a partner, discuss and list items that belong in each category. Compare your results with those of another pair of students.

C CCSS Vocabulary: 6. (See pp. T16–17.)

Things That Exist *Solely* in the Imagination

unicorns, giants, demons

Parts of a *Protozoan*

nucleus, cell body, cell wall

Objects for Which a *Prototype* Might Be Built

skyscraper, spacecraft, new model car

Reasons *Whereby* People Are Happy

good health, love, rewarding career

Characteristics of an *Eclectic* Collection

many different types, sizes, shapes, sources; not all the same

---

Aquatic Creatures

fish, whales, otters, squid, octopi

Where You Would Find a *Protagonist*

movies, novels, news stories

Events That Are *Forthcoming* in Your Life

birthday, spring break, English test

Migratory Creatures

robins, geese, whales

Places Where *Protein* Is Found

in the human body, in meat, in living things

Ideas That People May *Postulate* about Life

Exercise is important; jobs are necessary, love is the key to happiness.

Examples of a *Portal*

the doorway to my room, the entrance to the school building, a tunnel opening

Check for Understanding

Choose the lesson word that completes each sentence. Write the word on the line provided. Some words will be used twice.

aquatic	migratory	protagonist	protozoan
eclectic	portal	protein	solely
forthcoming	postulate	prototype	whereby

1. The _____protagonist_____ of this novel is too selfish for readers to care about her.

2. Every October, V-shaped flocks of _____migratory_____ geese cross the northern skies.

3. I came to this concert _____solely_____ to hear the world's greatest trombone player.

4. Through the microscope, the students were able to observe a/an _____protozoan_____ dividing into twin one-celled creatures.

5. This neighborhood meeting is the only means _____whereby_____ the traffic problem can be discussed in a reasonable way.

6. The new school is a/an _____prototype_____ of an environmentally green building.

7. _____Aquatic_____ mammals have lungs, not gills, and breathe air just as human beings do.

8. Our earth science study group will _____postulate_____ that if a planet has water, it can sustain life.

9. Lao was greatly excited to be able to ride in the _____prototype_____ of a new glider.

10. A bonus for every employee is _____forthcoming_____ at the end of the month.

11. To begin the discussion, let us _____postulate_____ that both sides consist of people of good will.

12. In the movie, the travelers crossed a/an _____portal_____ into another universe.

13. Joni's house was decorated in a/an _____eclectic_____ way, containing everything from Southwestern clay pots to a seventeenth-century chair.

14. "Eat enough _____protein_____, so you can stay healthy and grow," said Fritz's father.

If students have difficulty answering Item 12, have them review the meaning of *portal*. Then have partners brainstorm places, including unusual ones, that could have a portal.

Word Associations

Use what you know about the lesson word in italics to answer each question. Circle the letter next to the phrase that best answers the question. Be prepared to explain your answers.

1. Which of these contains *protein*?

   a. animals
   b. vegetables
   c. both

2. If an event is *forthcoming*, when does it take place?

   a. in the past
   b. in the present
   c. in the future

3. In which element does an *aquatic* plant grow?

   a. wood
   b. water
   c. air

4. How do we decide that a *postulate* is true?

   a. by assuming it
   b. by rejecting it
   c. by proving it

5. In which of the following would you expect to find a *protagonist*?

   a. a scientific report
   b. a short story
   c. the pledge of allegiance

6. Which situation demonstrates *migratory* behavior?

   a. A family moves from its old house after ten years.
   b. A tribe follows the herds of buffalo from season to season.
   c. A nation sends explorers on a mission into outer space.

7. In the sentence, "Carolina took a nap, *whereby* she felt much better," what relationship is expressed by *whereby*?

   a. She felt better despite taking a nap.
   b. She felt better while she took the nap.
   c. She felt better because of the nap.

8. If you create a *prototype*, what do you make?

   a. an exact copy of something old
   b. an example of something new
   c. a dozen of something

9. Which of the following is a *portal*?

   a. the gate of an ancient city
   b. the tower of a castle
   c. the path to a garden

10. If a disease is due *solely* to poor sanitation, how many causes does the disease have?

    a. one
    b. two
    c. three

11. Which person shows *eclectic* interests?

    a. someone who builds solar panels
    b. someone who eats the same foods every day
    c. someone who paints, plays music, and practices medicine

12. Where are you most likely to find a *protozoan*?

    a. in a layer of rock
    b. in fresh air
    c. in pond water

CCSS Vocabulary: 4.a. (See pp. T16–17.)

Check Again

Use what you know about the lesson words in italics to complete each sentence. Be sure your sentences make sense.

1. You might encounter a *portal* if you were _____ visiting a museum.

2. Scientists sometimes state a *postulate* when they _____ are explaining something they are working on. _____

3. The life of a *protozoan* includes _____ eating, growing, and dividing.

4. A *prototype* serves the purpose of _____ testing a new design or invention.

5. If you were a *migratory* creature, you would _____ travel with your group from place to place. _____

6. One drawback of being too *eclectic* might be _____ that you don't have a unified style. _____

7. If you are *solely* interested in indoor sports, you _____ don't participate in outdoor activities. _____

8. A situation *whereby* you might win an award is _____ being ranked first in your class.

9. A story can have only one *protagonist* because _____ it can have only one central character. _____

10. Some people wish they were *aquatic,* because _____ they feel they would be freer in the water. _____

11. *Protein* is necessary for _____ maintaining life.

12. A *forthcoming* television program is one that _____ will be on during the next season.

Write Your Own

Reread the passage on pages 142–143. Then, on a separate sheet of paper, write a one-paragraph response to the question, "How is the deep sea an example of the diversity of life on Earth?" Use at least two words from the lesson word list and support your answer by referring to the text of the passage.

Word-Solving Strategies: Latin and Greek Roots

Greek Root prot, proto: "first, primary"

Many English words have roots that originally came from ancient Greek, Latin, Old English, or other languages. For example, the root *proto* comes from the ancient Greek word *protos*, meaning "first, primary." *Prot* is used before a vowel; *proto* is used with consonants; otherwise, they are the same root.

The reading passage on pages 142–143 uses four *prot* or *proto* words: *protagonist*, *protein*, *prototype*, and *protozoan*. By combining the meaning of the root with the meaning of other word parts, you can guess the meaning of the English word. For example, let's look at the word *protagonist*. You know that the Greek root *prot* means "first, primary." The root *agon* also comes from the Greek and means "conflict" or "contest." The suffix *-ist* means "someone who does something." When you put all of these meanings together, you find that *protagonist* means "the primary character or participant in the action of a story or event."

More Examples

Look at the word *protozoan*. We can combine *proto* with the Greek root for animal, *zoion*, to discover its meaning, "first animal," or "early life form." Here's another example: the word *prototypical*.

proto → first, earliest

prototype → an early model

-ic, -al → having to do with, characteristic of

prototypical → characteristic of a prototype, or early model

> **BE CAREFUL!**
> The root *proto* may be confused with the prefix *pro-*, meaning "for." An example is the word *proceed*, which means "to move forward." *Proceed* does not have to do with being first.

Practice

Write a sentence using each of these words with the root *proto*. Use a dictionary if you're not sure about the meaning of a word.

1. protostar

A protostar is the beginning of a star.

2. proton

The proton is one of the elementary

particles that make up an atom.

3. Protozoic

Professor Smith is an expert on the Protozoic

era, the era of earliest life.

4. protogalaxy

A protogalaxy is the

beginning of a galaxy.

5. protoplasm

Protoplasm is the basic

form of living tissue.

6. protozoology

Fascinated by how a protozoan behaves,

my science teacher studied protozoology.

Point out to students that all of the Practice words have the root *proto* because in each instance the root comes before a consonant.

C CCSS Vocabulary: 4.c. (See pp. T16–17.)

Practice for Tests

For a quiz and additional practice for this lesson, go to vocabularyforsuccess.com.

Fill in the bubble next to the answer that best completes the sentence or answers the question.

1. A *prototype* is built:
   - ○ **A** to sell to the public
   - ○ **B** to correct a flaw
   - ○ **C** to reach a market
   - ● **D** to test a design

2. In a narrative, a *protagonist* is NOT:
   - ● **A** a minor character
   - ○ **B** a sympathetic figure
   - ○ **C** the hero of the plot
   - ○ **D** introduced early

3. An *eclectic* style:
   - ○ **A** changes often
   - ● **B** selects from many styles
   - ○ **C** comes from another culture
   - ○ **D** focuses on one thing

4. Read this sentence.
   Luck is part of the reason *whereby* James won.

   Whereby means:
   - ○ **A** before which
   - ○ **B** after which
   - ● **C** because of which
   - ○ **D** in spite of which

5. To work *solely* at one job is to work:
   - ● **A** only at that job
   - ○ **B** happily at that job
   - ○ **C** hard at that job
   - ○ **D** at a variety of jobs

6. To *postulate* is to state:
   - ○ **A** that something is unusual
   - ○ **B** a belief in something
   - ● **C** that something is true
   - ○ **D** what everyone believes

7. You might call someone *aquatic* if he or she:
   - ○ **A** lives near the water
   - ○ **B** studies water life
   - ○ **C** drinks a lot of water
   - ● **D** loves to swim

8. A *migratory* creature:
   - ○ **A** remains at home
   - ● **B** moves at regular times
   - ○ **C** wanders without a goal
   - ○ **D** damages the environment

9. Read this sentence.
   The *forthcoming* announcement is paid for by Citizens for Goodness.

   Forthcoming means:
   - ○ **A** having to do with goodness
   - ● **B** about to be delivered
   - ○ **C** especially important
   - ○ **D** taking a position

10. A *portal* is a kind of:
    - ● **A** entrance
    - ○ **B** barrier
    - ○ **C** picture
    - ○ **D** offering

If students answer Item 7 incorrectly, remind them that an aquatic creature lives in water. Tell them to choose the answer that comes closest to that meaning or expresses the meaning figuratively.

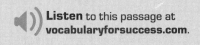

▶ **Watch** a video introduction to this passage at **vocabularyforsuccess.com**.

◀) **Listen** to this passage at **vocabularyforsuccess.com**.

CCSS Vocabulary: 4; Reading (Informational Text): 4, 6. (See pp. T16–17.)

Countdown to Curiosity

\<scientist's log\>

This is a fictional account of a real event.

August 3, 2012: The Mars rover *Curiosity* is only two days away from landing! Its trip so far has been a walk in the park—smooth and easy. In fact, it's been an exquisite journey, a thing of beauty. That's a tribute to NASA's pre-flight testing of all the rover's mechanics and software. Through computer visualization, every step of the journey has been examined in advance. The rover's mobility was tested on the sands of the California desert. Its robot arm was checked out in a lab. It's thrilling to watch videos of the pantomime of the 73-pound robot arm picking up an object the size of an aspirin and placing it into a container the size of a thimble.

NASA's decision to fully automate its early Mars missions, rather than to send astronauts, was a wise one. In this way, the rover can be a "stunt double" that tests how a spacecraft would respond to radiation from solar storms. That kind of knowledge is a prerequisite to safeguarding astronauts' health.

Despite earlier doubts, NASA's program of unmanned missions, followed by possible manned ones, now seems like a coherent plan that builds from early success to later triumph. The most recent rovers, *Spirit* and *Opportunity*, have explored Mars for several years—far longer than their primary missions stated. They've sent us masses of data about regions of Mars that were wet in the past. Water, of course, is one of the necessary factors to support life as we know it. *Curiosity* will take the next step.

August 4, 2012: Only one day away! With each moment, I appreciate more and more the unparalleled opportunity *Curiosity* will give us to pinpoint ancient Martian environments that may have hosted life. For the first time, a rover will be able to land on the narrow strip of flat surface at the foot of Mount Sharp, inside Gale Crater. The

A scientist's log is a day-by-day record of events written by a scientist during a scientific process or experiment that he or she considers significant.

VOCABULARY

exquisite	prerequisite	inquisitive
visualization	coherent	acquisitive
pantomime	unparalleled	vast
automate	optical	requisition

three-mile-high peak may hold geological clues as to where life could have existed. Taking geological samples with sophisticated optical instruments using X-ray beams, *Curiosity* will enable us to analyze chemical elements in layers of mountain rock. The data should allow us to understand how the Martian climate went from wet to dry and how wind and water eroded the mountain. *Spirit* and *Opportunity* found trace evidence of water on the red planet. That supports the theory that life once existed on Mars. Now *Curiosity* is expected to show us where such life could have been found.

Curiosity will live up to its name because it is both inquisitive and acquisitive. It's inquisitive in traveling adventurously over the rocky, sandy landscape of Mars. It's acquisitive in picking up samples as it goes. Meanwhile, down here on Earth, we human beings will look on in wonder.

I, for one, will be grateful for the vast amount of information *Curiosity* sends back. If the experiences of *Spirit* and *Opportunity* are a guide, I might have to requisition more lab space to deal with the data from *Curiosity*!

Mars rover *Spirit*, its solar panels gleaming, and the Martian surface

TALK ABOUT IT

With a partner, answer the questions below. Use as many of the highlighted words in the selection as you can.

1. Do you think it's better to *automate* missions to Mars or to send astronauts? Give reasons to support your opinion.

2. The discoveries made by Mars rovers show the importance of being *inquisitive*. What aspects of Mars are you most inquisitive about?

Opposite: Mars rover *Curiosity*, right side view

Bottom: Panoramic view of the "Santa Maria" crater on Mars

Word Meanings

For each highlighted word on pages 152–153, the meaning or meanings are given below.

For practice with synonyms, see page 172.

1. **acquisitive** (uh-KWIZ-uh-tiv) **adj.** eager to gain possessions. *Acquisitive* implies an especially strong desire to possess things. **SYNONYMS:** grasping, greedy, desirous

2. **automate** (AW-tuh-mate) **v.** to create a system operated by devices that take the place of human labor. To *automate* a factory is to have machines manufacture the factory's product. **SYNONYM:** mechanize

3. **coherent** (koh-HIHR-uhnt) **adj.** clear and logical. A well-organized speech that builds its main points step by step is *coherent*. **SYNONYMS:** unified, connected, consistent, understandable

4. **exquisite** (ek-SKWIZ-it) **adj.** finely or beautifully crafted. *Exquisite* implies something that has tremendous appeal to a viewer because of its delicate beauty. **SYNONYMS:** delightful, beautiful, delicate

5. **inquisitive** (in-KWIZ-uh-tiv) **adj.** given to asking questions. An *inquisitive* person wants to know more about everything he or she encounters. **SYNONYMS:** curious, questioning, inquiring

6. **optical** (OP-tuh-kuhl) **adj.** having to do with vision. *Optical* devices such as eyeglasses and *optical* instruments such as microscopes assist sight. **SYNONYM:** visual

7. **pantomime** (PAN-tuh-mime) **n.** a performance that includes silent dramatic movement. A *pantomime* is often a skit or play that is acted without words. **SYNONYM:** mime; **v.** to act out by gestures without speaking. When people *pantomime,* they do not talk but instead use their hands and facial expressions to communicate. **SYNONYM:** mime

8. **prerequisite** (pree-RE-kwi-zit) **n.** something that is necessary before something else can be done or accomplished. A *prerequisite* for taking Spanish II is taking Spanish I. **SYNONYM:** requirement

9. **requisition** (re-kwuh-ZI-shuhn) **v.** to make a formal request for an item. In the military, for example, an officer may *requisition* more uniforms. **SYNONYMS:** demand, order, apply; **n.** a formal request for an item. A *requisition* is often an application for more supplies. **SYNONYMS:** demand, order, application

C CCSS Vocabulary: 4.c., 4.d. (See pp. T16–17.)

Watch a video introduction for each word at **vocabularyforsuccess.com**.

Listen to iWords at **vocabularyforsuccess.com**.

Refer to the online dictionary at **vocabularyforsuccess.com**.

10. **unparalleled** (uhn-PA-ruh-leld) **adj.** having no equal or match. If an athlete's performance is *unparalleled,* no other athlete has reached that level. **SYNONYMS:** unequaled, unmatched

11. **vast** (VAST) **adj.** extraordinarily large. *Vast* is usually applied to physical size, but it can also be used to describe abstract concepts, such as *vast* knowledge. **SYNONYMS:** huge, immense, gigantic, giant, enormous, colossal

12. **visualization** (vizh-oo-uh-luh-ZAY-shuhn) **n.** the act of forming an image. When we see a picture in our minds, it is a *visualization.* **SYNONYMS:** envisioning, conceiving, imagination; **n.** an example of a created image. Making a *visualization* is a way of showing others an idea. **SYNONYMS:** image, picture, model

More on Meanings: Denotation and Connotation

Reread this sentence from the passage on page 153:

I, for one, will be grateful for the **vast** amount of information *Curiosity* sends back.

The writer could have chosen many words other than *vast*. Possible choices include *large, great, immense, huge,* and *enormous.* The writer chose *vast* because its shade of meaning—its connotation—fits the writer's purpose. *Vast* usually connotes something exceptionally large rather than merely a bit large and has a positive connotation. When people look at something vast, they often feel a sense of wonder. The universe itself is often called *vast.*

In contrast, if the writer had used *large,* the connotation would have been neutral and bland. The writer wanted a more specific connotation.

On the other hand, the synonym *monstrous* usually has a negative connotation. If an amount of data is monstrous, the researcher probably doesn't want to deal with it very much!

Many words have special connotations that go beyond the word's denotation. When you write or speak, choose words whose connotations create the feelings that you intend. Use the dictionary, the thesaurus, and your prior knowledge of words to help you.

Here are more examples of words with similar denotations and different connotations:

POSITIVE	NEGATIVE	NEUTRAL
peace	surrender	accord
wish	crave	desire

Challenge Choose two of the words below. For each, suggest two synonyms, one with a positive connotation and one with a negative connotation. Then use each synonym in a sentence that demonstrates the feeling associated with it.

adventurous   unlucky   quick

simple   important

If students have difficulty finding connotative synonyms, have them think of situations where they have experienced what the words describe. For *adventurous,* suggest *daring* (positive) and *reckless* (negative). Invite students to suggest others.

C CCSS Vocabulary: 5.b. (See pp. T16–17.)

vocabularyforsuccess.com   155

Word Talk

Each lesson word has been placed in a category. With a partner, discuss and list items that belong in each category. Compare your results with those of another pair of students.

C CCSS Vocabulary: 6. (See pp. T16–17.)

Optical Phenomena in the Everyday World

sunlight, rainbows, digital cameras

Items That Are Exquisite

diamonds, art masterpieces, delicious pastries

Actions That Someone Could Perform as a Pantomime

climbing a rope, running, shooting a basketball

Things Someone Might Requisition

supplies for an expedition, bandages for a military hospital, movie props

---

Unparalleled Events

moon landing, Mars rover explorations, an athletic record

Things That Should Be Coherent

plans, arguments, directions, explanations, descriptions

Things Visualization Helps You Understand

directions to a place, what someone looks like

Things You Are Inquisitive About

the future, outer space, summer jobs

Activities That Have Been Automated

manufacturing, checking out at a store, getting money from a bank

---

Things Acquisitive People Want

money, jewelry, luxury cars

Activities with a Prerequisite

taking advanced courses, becoming a doctor, getting a driving license

---

Vast Things

the Milky Way, encyclopedia entries, a billionaire's wealth

Check for Understanding

Choose the lesson word that completes each sentence. Write the word on the line provided. Some words will be used twice.

acquisitive	exquisite	pantomime	unparalleled
automate	inquisitive	prerequisite	vast
coherent	optical	requisition	visualization

1. Zach presented a/an _____pantomime_____ of a camel, but we all thought he was acting out the movements of a horse.

2. Raimondo had to take a biology course as a/an _____prerequisite_____ for nursing school.

3. "If the colonel doesn't _____requisition_____ coats," said the private, "we'll freeze."

4. Seeing spots in front of your eyes can be a troubling _____optical_____ event.

5. Too many people in our society are _____acquisitive_____, buying things they don't need.

6. "What a/an _____exquisite_____ wedding dress!" one of the guests cried out upon seeing the beautiful bride.

7. Some people find _____pantomime_____ hard to understand because of the absence of words.

8. Although the topic was complicated, Chelsea prepared a/an _____coherent_____ presentation.

9. The speaker's vivid description gave us a/an _____visualization_____ of his mountain-climbing expedition.

10. My cat is so _____inquisitive_____, he looks inside every empty box or paper bag.

11. The factory will _____automate_____ its operations and human workers won't be needed.

12. Cody created his own _____visualization_____ of the characters and events as he read the story, seeing the things he imagined as if they were really in front of him.

13. Ms. Ramirez claimed such a/an _____vast_____ amount of work takes days to finish.

14. NASA hopes to achieve the _____unparalleled_____ feat of landing humans on Mars.

If students have difficulty answering Item 11, tell them to look at nearby words and phrases in the sentence for clues. The clue is that human workers will not be needed in the factory.

Word Associations

Use what you know about the lesson word in italics to answer each question. Circle the letter next to the phrase that best answers the question. Be prepared to explain your answers.

1. Which sense organ is associated with *optical* phenomena?

   a. eyes
   b. nose
   c. ears

2. Why might someone write a *requisition*?

   a. to file a complaint
   b. to ask for materials
   c. to deliver a report

3. Which of the following is a *prerequisite* for a high school diploma?

   a. having a life or career goal
   b. an average of B or higher
   c. a certain number of course credits

4. Which of the following represents something that is *coherent*?

   a. a factual newspaper article
   b. the moans and mumblings of someone with a high fever
   c. baby's cooing

5. What event is most likely to be called *exquisite*?

   a. a performance of a love song
   b. a trip to the grocery store
   c. a subway ride

6. Whose work most closely resembles *pantomime*?

   a. a writer's
   b. a dancer's
   c. a director's

7. Which of the following is most likely to be called *vast*?

   a. an ocean
   b. a lake
   c. a river

8. How could you *automate* housework?

   a. do it on a strict schedule
   b. pay someone to do it
   c. have robots do it

9. Which job requires being *inquisitive*?

   a. a crossing guard
   b. a ticket taker
   c. a news reporter

10. Which of the following is *unparalleled*?

    a. the height of the highest mountain on Earth
    b. the length of the average movie
    c. the distance from New York to Los Angeles

11. How is an *acquisitive* person most likely to spend leisure time?

    a. texting
    b. shopping
    c. sightseeing

12. Which of the following is an example of a *visualization*?

    a. a computer model of a DNA molecule
    b. a sound recording of whales' communication
    c. an astronaut's first glimpse of the moon

 CCSS Vocabulary: 4.a. (See pp. T16–17.)

Check Again

Use what you know about the lesson word in italics to complete each sentence. Be sure your sentences make sense.

1. You can tell I'm not *acquisitive* by the fact that _____ I don't own many possessions.

2. I need to take algebra this year as a *prerequisite* before _____ taking geometry.

3. Because of your *vast* camping experience, you _____ are the best person to set up the tent. _____

4. If we *automate* all the jobs in the world, _____ there will be no jobs for people to do. _____

5. One thing that's *unparalleled* in my own experience is _____ the amount I grew this year.

6. That painting is *exquisite* because of its _____ fine brushwork and exact details.

7. Gloria's graphic *visualization* of Mars _____ showed every detail of the landscape.

8. Before my wilderness trek, I'm going to *requisition* _____ dehydrated food and five liters of water. _____

9. That *inquisitive* child _____ never stops asking questions. _____

10. The *pantomime* artist surprised the audience by _____ saying "Thank you" at the end of the show. _____

11. *Optical* illusions show us _____ images that trick our eyes.

12. I was at my most *coherent* when _____ I participated in the debate.

Write Your Own

1. **Write a ten-word sentence about a place using the word *vast* in the second position.**

   The vast expanse of the desert spread out before us.

2. **Write an eleven-word sentence about someone you heard speak and use the word *coherent* in the fifth position.**

   The speaker was so coherent, we could follow all his ideas.

Word-Solving Strategies: Latin and Greek Roots

Latin Root *quis*: "to ask, seek, or obtain"

You've learned about the roots *vert* and *vers* (meaning "turn around") and *prot* and *proto* (meaning "first") in previous lessons, and you know that a root can help you figure out word meaning. You know that the root is the part of a word that contains the word's main content. Many English words have ancient Greek, Latin, or Old English roots. The Latin root *quis* comes from the Latin *quirere* and means "to ask, seek, or obtain." The reading passage on pages 152–153 uses four "quis" words: *acquisitive, inquisitive, prerequisite,* and *requisition.* In each word, the root combines with a prefix and suffix to create the word's meaning.

For example, let's look at the word *acquisitive.* You know that *quis* means "to ask, seek, or obtain." The prefix *ac-* or *ad-* means "to or toward." The suffix *-ive* means "having the trait of." When you put the meanings of root, prefix, and suffix together, you might be able to figure out that *acquisitive* means "inclined toward or eager to obtain or possess things."

Another Example

Here's a different kind of example: *quest.* This word contains no prefixes or suffixes. However, it comes directly from the root *quis* and *quirere. Quest* means a pursuit or search. For another example, you can figure out the meaning of the word *quester* by using the meaning of the root and the suffix *-er.*

quest → a pursuit or search

-er → a person connected with

quester → someone who conducts a quest

> **BE CAREFUL!**
>
> Words with the root *qui,* meaning "rest," are not closely related to words with the root *quis. Qui* is related to *quiet*; the Latin form is *quies,* "quiet, rest."

Practice

Read each sentence below. Then use what you know about the Latin root *quis* to write the meaning of the word in italics. Check your answers in a dictionary.

1. In order to learn anything, it is *requisite* to listen.

needed for a particular purpose

2. The king ordered an *inquisition* to root out his enemies.

an investigation seeking out answers

3. The police officer behaved like an *inquisitor* when she asked questions.

a person who asks questions in

a pointed way

4. "Come see my new *acquisition*, a sports car," boasted my wealthy neighbor.

something obtained or purchased

Encourage students to compare answers with a partner before they check their answers in a dictionary.

C CCSS Vocabulary: 4.c. (See pp. T16–17.)

Practice for Tests

For a quiz and additional practice for this lesson, go to **vocabularyforsuccess.com**.

Fill in the bubble next to the answer that best completes the sentence or answers the question.

1. A text that is *coherent* is:

   ○ **A** on an easy level
   ● **B** logically connected
   ○ **C** intended for experts
   ○ **D** formal in its tone

2. If a detail is *optical*, it can be:

   ○ **A** erased
   ○ **B** used
   ○ **C** analyzed
   ● **D** seen

3. In *pantomime*, the performer does NOT use his or her:

   ○ **A** body
   ○ **B** hands
   ● **C** voice
   ○ **D** face

4. To be *inquisitive* is to be:

   ● **A** curious
   ○ **B** suspicious
   ○ **C** guilty
   ○ **D** misunderstood

5. Read this sentence.

   Management's decision to *automate* its payroll was a good one.

   Automate means:

   ○ **A** to produce around the clock
   ● **B** to have done by machines
   ○ **C** to do as fairly as possible
   ○ **D** to do at maximum speed

6. Someone who is *acquisitive* wants to:

   ○ **A** know things
   ○ **B** destroy things
   ○ **C** make things
   ● **D** own things

7. A *requisition* is a kind of:

   ○ **A** friendly invitation
   ○ **B** stern warning
   ● **C** formal request
   ○ **D** casual agreement

8. *Vast* implies that something is:

   ○ **A** average
   ○ **B** somewhat large
   ● **C** extremely large
   ○ **D** too small to measure

9. If earth science is a *prerequisite* for environmental studies, then a student will need to:

   ○ **A** take environmental studies first
   ○ **B** take both classes at the same time
   ● **C** take earth science first
   ○ **D** miss out on environmental studies

10. Read this sentence.

    The students admired the car maker's *visualization* of the new convertible.

    Visualization means:

    ● **A** model
    ○ **B** discussion
    ○ **C** opinion
    ○ **D** analysis

If students choose A for Item 9, remind them that the prefix *pre-* means "before" or "prior to." Then ask them which course comes first.

 Watch a video introduction to this passage at **vocabularyforsuccess.com**.

Listen to this passage at **vocabularyforsuccess.com**.

C CCSS Vocabulary: 4; Reading (Informational Text): 4, 6. (See pp. T16–17.)

Let's Do Nanotechnology

<how-to>

A new word has been added to the scientific lexicon. The word is nanotechnology, and you'll probably be hearing more about it with every passing year. Nanotechnology is still at the early stages of development. If you have an affinity for science and want to get in on this ground-breaking field, here's what you need to know.

What Is Nanotechnology? Nanotechnology is the engineering or manipulation of extremely small-size materials, usually ranging from one nanometer to 100 nanometers in length. To imagine how small that is, consider that a nanometer is one billionth of a meter. That's less than one twenty-five-millionth of an inch. It's not quite as small as the smallest atoms: a hydrogen atom is one tenth of a nanometer. But nano-scale is still infinitesimal.

How to Get Started The first step in the birth of nanotechnology was to develop instruments that could sense objects on an extremely small scale. This advance took place during the 1980s with the invention of the scanning tunneling microscope (STM) and the atomic force microscope (AFM). These instruments do not "see" nanoparticles. Instead, the AFM uses a mechanical probe to "feel" their surfaces. You can think of these methods as a virtual form of seeing and feeling.

Manipulating Nanomaterials To work at that tiny scale, you might use an STM, a sensing device that is also a tool that can move nanoparticles. In 1989, a researcher manipulated atoms so that they spelled the name of his company. Since that auspicious beginning, scientists have been able to move even smaller particles. There are different kinds of nanomaterials, with shapes such as films, flakes, particles, shells, tubes, and wires. Each is a different permutation of the kinds of substances we will have to manipulate at the nano level, and each poses a different challenge.

Progress So Far So far, nanotechnology's main achievements have been in creating new materials out of old ones. Nanoscale materials have led to everything from stronger, wrinkle-free fabrics to more resistant electric wires to lighter, stronger baseball bats. The future, however, may

Artist's renderings of nanoparticles in the blood

162

A how-to is a text, such as an article or book, that informs readers about how a particular process is carried out.

bring even more of a revelation in how much the nano-size world can be altered. Medicine is already benefitting; for example, using nanocrystals known as "quantum dots," scientists have created improved dyes for the imaging of diseases in the body. And scientists are already using nanomaterials to help grow new nerve cells in damaged spines and brains.

Nanotechnology may someday help ensure a clean environment by cleaning up or filtering out pollutants and by converting waste heat into electrical energy. Instead of waste being lost, it could become part of a cyclical process to make more fuel. Thus, a finite amount of material may be able to produce more energy than in the past.

Potential Hazards In the future, it may be possible to build nanomachines that can repair themselves and nanomachines that can build other nanomachines. But there are hazards involved; for example, will such devices escape the control of their creators? Will it be possible to insure a nanomachine against a dangerous malfunction? Many questions about nanotechnology remain to be solved!

TALK ABOUT IT

With a partner, answer the questions below. Use as many of the highlighted words in the selection as you can.

1. Based on the reading passage and your own imagination, what exciting developments do you think will be possible in the future of *nanotechnology*?

2. *Nanotechnology* is one *auspicious* scientific development. What other great advances in science might occur?

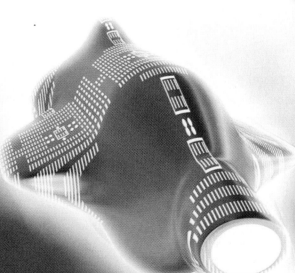

Above: Artist's rendering of a medical device for delivering therapeutic nanoparticles into a patient's bloodstream

Below: Artist's rendering of nanobot (left) and nanoparticle (right)

Word Meanings

For each highlighted word on pages 162–163, the meaning or meanings are given below.

For practice with synonyms, see page 172.

1. **affinity** (uh-FIN-i-tee) **n.** attraction to, liking for, sympathy with. People may have an *affinity* for other individuals or for activities or for subjects. **SYNONYMS:** connection, resemblance, kinship

2. **auspicious** (aw-SPISH-uhs) **adj.** indicating success in the future. An excellent grade on the first exam is an *auspicious* sign for the rest of the quarter. **SYNONYMS:** fortunate, promising

3. **cyclical** (SIK-luh-kuhl) **adj.** having to do with or occurring in fixed periods of time. *Cyclical* often refers to a time when a series of regular events, such as the change of seasons, is completed. **SYNONYMS:** cyclic, periodic, recurrent, continuous

4. **ensure** (en-SHUR) **v.** to make sure, to make certain. When you *ensure* that something will happen, you do everything you can in order for it to happen. **SYNONYMS:** assure, secure, guarantee

5. **finite** (FYE-nite) **adj.** having an end. Something that is *finite* has limits and cannot go on forever, such as a life span. **SYNONYMS:** limited, bounded

6. **infinitesimal** (in-fi-nuh-TE-suh-muhl) **adj.** extremely small; too small to be measured. Objects of molecular size or smaller—such as atomic or subatomic size—are *infinitesimal*. **SYNONYMS:** minute, tiny, microscopic

7. **insure** (in-SHUR) **v.** to take precautions to assure against loss; to provide a policy of coverage of loss. People *insure* items of importance, such as their house or car, so that they will be paid in case the items are damaged or destroyed. **SYNONYMS:** secure, protect

8. **lexicon** (LEK-suh-kon) **n.** the vocabulary of a language, a subject, or a people. The word "byte" is a computer term that has entered the *lexicon* of the general population. **n.** a book listing all the words of a language with their pronunciations and definitions. The dictionary is a *lexicon* of the English language. **SYNONYM:** dictionary

9. **nanotechnology** (na-noh-tek-NOL-uh-jee) **n.** the science of working with extremely small objects, usually between one billionth of a meter to 100 billionths of a meter in length. *Nanotechnology* refers both to manipulating extremely small objects and to building with them. **SYNONYM:** nanotech

Watch a video introduction for each word at **vocabularyforsuccess.com**.

Listen to iWords at **vocabularyforsuccess.com**.

Refer to the online dictionary at **vocabularyforsuccess.com**.

10. **permutation** (pur-myuh-TAY-shuhn) **n.** one of the many different ways that something can be arranged. A T-shirt is just one *permutation* of the many things that can be made of cotton cloth. **SYNONYMS:** combination, arrangement

11. **revelation** (rev-uh-LAY-shuhn) **n.** something that is made known. *Revelation* often implies a surprising and sudden awareness. **SYNONYMS:** disclosure, unveiling

12. **virtual** (VUR-choo-uhl) **adj.** being nearly the same as something without being that thing. Objects that can substitute effectively for each other, or be mistaken for each other, without being identical may be called *virtual* copies. **SYNONYMS:** essential, substantial; **adj.** existing in the world of computers rather than in the physical world. Many video games take the player into a *virtual* world of fictional settings and characters. **SYNONYM:** cyber

More on Meanings: Confusing Word Pairs

Some pairs of words in English do not have similar meanings but are often confused with each other because of similar sounds or spellings. Compare these sentences:

The hospital staff will **ensure** that the operating room is clean.

The insurance agency agreed to **insure** this property if the owner pays for a policy.

In the first sentence, *ensure* is a verb meaning "to make sure." In the second sentence, *insure* is also a verb but means "to provide insurance for."

Confusing word pairs can also be the same or different parts of speech. These two confusing words are nouns:

When we traveled across the country by train, we slept in a **berth**.

The siblings were thrilled at the **birth** of their newest brother.

In the first sentence, *berth* means "a place to sleep on a train, ship, or airplane." In the second sentence, *birth* means "the act of coming into life."

Confusing word pairs can occur regularly in daily language. Compare these two words:

Every morning Lilianna eats the same **cereal**.

Every week Troy looks for the next installment in his favorite **serial** novel.

Cereal is a noun that means "food made from grain." *Serial* is an adjective that means "happening in parts or installments."

Challenge Choose one word pair below. Then use the words correctly in the same sentence.

chord, cord   human, humane

loose, lose

If students have difficulty using both words in the same sentence, have them write two sentences. Then challenge students to combine them.

CCSS Vocabulary: 4.a., 5. (See pp. T16–17.)

vocabularyforsuccess.com   165

Word Talk

Each lesson word has been placed in a category. With a partner, discuss and list items that belong in each category. Compare your results with those of another pair of students.

C CCSS Vocabulary: 6. (See pp. T16–17.)

Things Valuable Enough to *Insure*

a boat, a house, a pianist's fingers

Activities, Places, and People for Which You Feel an *Affinity*

clowns, ice skating, mountains

Groups That Have a Specialized *Lexicon*

baseball players, musicians, scientists, knitters, painters, food critics

Things That Are a *Permutation* of Something

different kinds of vehicles, different kinds of clothing, different kinds of ball games

Things That Can Seem To Be *Virtual* Copies

different locations of the same fast-food restaurants, different locations of the same brand-name stores

Uses of *Nanotechnology*

medicine, consumer products, sports equipment

Auspicious Beginnings to a New Friendship

lots of interests in common, easy conversation, laugh at the same things

Infinitesimal Things

subatomic particles, numbers smaller than one billionth, molecules

Activities on Which You Spend a *Finite* Amount of Time

brushing teeth, taking a shower, mowing the lawn

Ideas or Feelings That May Come as a *Revelation*

understanding one's problems, discovery of a hidden skill

Cyclical Processes in Nature

day and night, life cycle, water cycle, oxygen cycle

Outcomes You Would Like to *Ensure*

a happy life, an A on a test, a large income

Check for Understanding

Choose the lesson word that completes each sentence. Write the word on the line provided. Some words will be used twice.

affinity	ensure	insure	permutation
auspicious	finite	lexicon	revelation
cyclical	infinitesimal	nanotechnology	virtual

1. An atom is not the most _____infinitesimal_____ object that exists, but it's extremely small.

2. The library has a thousand-page _____lexicon_____ of all the words in science.

3. If _____nanotechnology_____ becomes widely used, medicine may change drastically.

4. I prefer real people to _____virtual_____ ones.

5. No one is certain whether severe weather occurs in a/an _____cyclical_____ pattern or not.

6. "You must _____insure_____ this priceless diamond necklace before you wear it in public," the Count warned the Countess.

7. Ned and Nat look so much alike that they are _____virtual_____ twins, even though they are only brothers.

8. The _____auspicious_____ beginning to the new year was signaled by warm temperatures and clear skies.

9. My patience is not endless; it is _____finite_____.

10. I have been through every possible _____permutation_____ of ways to say, "Please," and you still don't answer politely.

11. It was not just a surprise, but an absolute _____revelation_____, when Gustavo announced that he was the heir to a fortune.

12. Nik's great _____affinity_____ for dogs led him to volunteer at the animal shelter.

13. It was the river guide's duty to _____ensure_____ that all the rafters wore life jackets.

14. "I watch very little television," Jo Ellen said. "The amount is _____infinitesimal_____."

If students have trouble answering Item 6, explain that to *ensure* against loss, someone would *insure* the necklace.

Word Associations

Use what you know about the lesson word in italics to answer each question. Circle the letter next to the phrase that best answers the question. Be prepared to explain your answers.

1. What is true of a *virtual* world?

   a. You cannot breathe in it.
   b. You can feel the objects in it.
   c. You can eat actual food in it.

2. If you have an *affinity* for poetry, which are you most likely to do?

   a. read it
   b. avoid it
   c. criticize it

3. Which of the following is NOT *cyclical*?

   a. Earth's orbit
   b. a road map
   c. the tides

4. By practicing a musical instrument, what can you *ensure*?

   a. that you will love practicing
   b. that you will become a professional
   c. that you will play your best

5. Which of the following numbers is *infinitesimal*?

   a. 1.000000000
   b. 0.000000001
   c. 1,000,000,000

6. What is it possible to *insure*?

   a. that your car will not crash
   b. that you will not be injured in a crash
   c. your car

7. Which of the following describes a *nanotechnology* project?

   a. sandbagging a rising river
   b. programming microscopic robots
   c. running computer analyses

8. Which has a *permutation* that is a code?

   a. a locker combination
   b. an anonymous letter
   c. a secret pal

9. Which of the following is an example of a *lexicon*?

   a. an atlas
   b. a dictionary
   c. an encyclopedia

10. Which of the following would be a *revelation*?

    a. suddenly realizing that you can dance
    b. attending a play and liking it a bit
    c. putting on a stage production

11. If someone experienced an *auspicious* event, what would it be?

    a. acceptance on the school swim team
    b. failure to attend the tryouts
    c. rejection from the swim team

12. Which of the following is NOT *finite*?

    a. the number of days in a year
    b. the number of numbers in mathematics
    c. the number of bones in a human body

CCSS Vocabulary: 4.a. (See pp. T16–17.)

Check Again

Use what you know about the lesson word in italics to complete each sentence. Be sure your sentences make sense.

1. I have only a *finite* _____ amount of patience for nasty gossip. _____

2. Playing the word game, Sherri Lynn considered every *permutation* of the letters she had been given. _____
_____

3. Mr. and Mrs. Powers decided they needed to *insure* _____ their belongings for a larger amount. _____

4. My personal *lexicon* doesn't include _____ the phrase "I can't." _____

5. It's amazing how *nanotechnology* might _____ change the way materials are manufactured. _____
_____

6. The dancer experienced a powerful *revelation* when _____ he realized he could perform a dance that he _____
never thought possible. _____

7. It is a *virtual* certainty _____ that our baseball team will do well this season. _____

8. If you have an *affinity* for writing, _____ you might want to try working on the school newspaper. _____
_____

9. Casey believed it was an *auspicious* sign when _____ the power was restored after the storm. _____
_____

10. To be able to see *infinitesimal* objects, _____ humans have to use powerful microscopes. _____
_____

11. A *cyclical* process is _____ one that repeats over and over. _____

12. I hope to *ensure* _____ that I will attend college after I graduate high school. _____

Write Your Own

Reread the passage on pages 162–163. Then, on a separate sheet of paper, write a one-paragraph response to the question, "Will nanotechnology turn out to be mainly a positive thing or mainly a negative thing?" Use details from the passage to support your answer.

Word-Solving Strategies:
Latin and Greek Roots

Latin Root fin: "limit, end"

Thousands of English words contain roots that derive from ancient Greek, Latin, or Old English, three languages that are no longer spoken but that contributed to the development of modern languages. The Latin root *fin* is found in many common English words. It comes from the Latin word *finitus*, meaning "limit, end."

The reading passage on pages 162–163 includes three words that contain the root *fin*: *affinity*, *finite*, and *infinitesimal*. By combining the meaning of the root with the meaning of other word parts, you can guess the approximate meaning of the English word. Let's look at the word *infinitesimal*. You know that the root comes from the Latin word *fin*. The prefix *in-* means "not, without." The suffix *-al* means "having to do with." And

the suffix *-esimus* means "order or rank." When you put the meaning of the word parts together, you can see how *infinitesimal* means "having to do with something small that has no limit."

Another Example

Now let's look at the word *affinity*:

a- → to, toward

fin → limit, end

-ity → state of being

When two things have an affinity, you might think of them as sharing a space that is the limit of each, that is, where they overlap. The origin of *affinity* is a good example of how language develops.

BE CAREFUL!

Fin as it relates to the fin of a fish comes from another Latin root, *spinus*, meaning "spine." Meanwhile, *finger* comes from an Old English root, *fif*, meaning "five."

Practice

Write a sentence using each of these words with the root *fin*.

1. final

This discussion is over, and that's final.

2. infinite

There are infinite ways to find happiness if you really want to.

3. infinity

Looking up at the stars, Deb thought about the vastness of infinity.

4. finish

When you finish a task, you bring it to an end.

5. fine (penalty)

Instead of arguing with the librarian, just pay the fine and end the matter.

6. finale

The finale of the concert was the most impressive part.

Encourage students to look up words they don't know in a dictionary.

CCSS Vocabulary: 4.c. (See pp. T16–17.)

Practice for Tests

For a quiz and additional practice for this lesson, go to **vocabularyforsuccess.com**.

Fill in the bubble next to the answer that best completes the sentence or answers the question.

1. The number of grains of sand on all the world's beaches is *finite*, because:
   - ○ **A** the number is too large for anyone to count
   - ● **B** though the number is huge, it does not go on forever
   - ○ **C** sand is found other places besides beaches
   - ○ **D** it is always changing

2. A *lexicon* consists of:
   - ● **A** words
   - ○ **B** numbers
   - ○ **C** synonyms
   - ○ **D** articles

3. Read this sentence.

   "We want to *ensure* that nothing goes wrong on this expedition," said the group leader.

   Ensure means:
   - ○ **A** stop worrying
   - ○ **B** buy insurance
   - ● **C** make certain
   - ○ **D** pay to guarantee

4. A phenomenon is NOT *cyclical* if:
   - ○ **A** it repeats
   - ○ **B** it happens often
   - ● **C** it occurs only once
   - ○ **D** it can be predicted

5. A *permutation* of something is:
   - ○ **A** not related to it
   - ○ **B** in a separate category entirely
   - ○ **C** its opposite
   - ● **D** one aspect of it

If students choose A for Item 1, remind them that *finite* means "having an end." Something may be too large for human beings to count and still have an end at some distant point.

6. Read this sentence.

   Jen and Isabelle go everywhere together and show a strong *affinity*.

   Affinity means:
   - ● **A** a liking for each other
   - ○ **B** an inability to get along
   - ○ **C** a pattern of late arrival
   - ○ **D** a tendency to laugh at everything

7. An example of something *infinitesimal* is:
   - ● **A** a molecule of salt
   - ○ **B** a pinch of salt
   - ○ **C** a teaspoon of salt
   - ○ **D** a shaker of salt

8. A professor in the field of *nanotechnology* would be most likely to invent:
   - ○ **A** new diseases
   - ○ **B** new computer applications
   - ○ **C** new sports
   - ● **D** new materials

9. An example of a *revelation* is:
   - ○ **A** forgetting where you left your keys
   - ● **B** seeing, in a flash, that you must be kinder to others
   - ○ **C** struggling to solve a problem
   - ○ **D** worrying that you said the wrong thing to a friend

10. If two brands of telephone are *virtual* copies of each other:
    - ○ **A** they are different from each other
    - ○ **B** they are alike in most ways
    - ● **C** they are almost exactly alike
    - ○ **D** they are exactly alike

Synonyms and Antonyms

In the following Word Bank, you will find synonyms and antonyms for some of the words in Lessons 13–15. (Remember: Some words have both synonyms and antonyms.) Study these words; then complete the exercises below.

backup	boundless	broad	crude	disconnected	discovery
exit	gateway	matchless	nomadic	statement	troubled

A. For each sentence, fill in the blank with a SYNONYM for the word in boldface.

1. Crossing the **portal** to the auditorium for the graduation ceremony, I felt I was also at the ___gateway___ to my future life.

2. The sudden, surprising ___discovery___ that Delores had moved out of town came as a complete **revelation** to us.

3. The open country, with its night sky of **unparalleled** clarity, gave us a/an ___matchless___ opportunity to view the meteor shower.

4. Ezekiel sometimes felt like a **migratory** animal since his parents did not like to settle in one place for too long and preferred a/an ___nomadic___ lifestyle.

5. Darcy's reading interests are ___broad___, and her musical taste is **eclectic** too.

B. For each sentence, fill in the blank with an ANTONYM for the word in boldface.

6. We had hoped for an **auspicious** beginning for our project, but the delayed start indicated its true ___troubled___ nature.

7. My interest in playing soccer is ___boundless___, but my interest in watching it on television is **finite**.

8. Christopher said, "I want to be the **protagonist** of my own life, not the ___backup___ of someone else's."

9. Considering how **exquisite** the museum building was, it was shocking how ___crude___ the paintings inside were.

10. The candidate's speech, far from being **coherent**, was ___disconnected___ and lacked sense.

CCSS Vocabulary: 4.a., 5, 6. (See pp. T16–17.)

Word Study: Idioms

In the reading passage "Countdown to *Curiosity*" on page 152, the author writes, "Its trip so far has been a walk in the park—smooth and easy." That doesn't mean that the Mars rover *Curiosity* has been walking in a park. It means that the trip has been easy, just as a walk in a park is usually easy. "A walk in the park" is an idiom—an expression whose meaning goes beyond the literal meaning of its words.

The selections in this unit often use words that could be expressed by idioms. For example, a coherent plan could be a plan that "sticks together" or "holds together." Or, if the Mars exploration is unparalleled, you could say that it's "over the top."

Practice

Read each sentence. Use the context clues to figure out the meaning of each idiom in bold print. Then write the letter of the definition for the idiom in the sentence.

___d___ **1.** Jed thinks he can skip practice and still be a star, but he'll learn that he can't **have his cake and eat it, too**.

___g___ **2.** Perhaps you should have bought the sports car rather than the SUV, but it's too late to **cry over spilled milk**.

___e___ **3.** Seeing that the new art student was talented, Professor Schwartz did all she could to t**ake him under her wing**.

___c___ **4.** Senator Griffith gets in trouble when she speaks **off the cuff** rather than from her notes.

___b___ **5.** Don't worry about whether you'll be accepted into the drama camp; it's **in the cards**.

___f___ **6.** Mom is right that I should practice driving more, but I wish she would **get off my back** about it.

a. learn from your mistakes

b. almost certain to happen

c. without thinking much beforehand

d. benefit from two opposite possibilities

e. give help to someone younger or less experienced

f. stop criticizing or bothering someone

g. be upset about something that has already happened

Apply

Work with a partner to find out the meaning of each idiom. (Use an online or print dictionary.) Then work together to write a sentence for each idiom.

1. in a pickle

2. pot luck

3. other side of the coin

4. have an axe to grind

5. out of the blue

6. take a back seat

7. let bygones be bygones

8. dyed in the wool

Vocabulary for Comprehension

Read the following passage, in which some of the words you have studied in Lessons 13–15 appear in boldface type. Then answer questions 1–6.

What Is a Futurologist?

The future comes upon us with **unparalleled** swiftness, with new technologies arriving every year. What kinds of computers will we use as our need to process information keeps
5　expanding? How will our knowledge of the genetic code affect life on Earth? What new types of work will we **automate**? There is such great demand for predicting forthcoming breakthroughs that some people have added
10　a new word to the **lexicon** and begun to call themselves futurologists: scientists and writers who specialize in imagining where science will take us next. What's necessary for becoming a futurologist? The first **prerequisite** is to
15　be **inquisitive**. Be curious about all fields

of knowledge, for new advances may come from any of them. Be confident that each **permutation** may turn out to be the **portal** to a scientific revolution. Major change may
20　arrive on the scale of the **infinitesimal**, such as discovering minute new forms of **protein**, engineering DNA, or even creating entirely new living species. Or, new knowledge may come from the study of **vast** events such as the Big
25　Bang that began the universe some 15 billion years ago. Above all, be guided by the **postulate** that change is always happening. The only thing that never happens is that things always remain the same.

If students have difficulty answering some of the questions, encourage them to use nearby context clues, such as curious following inquisitive, to figure out word meanings.

1. In sentence 1, **unparalleled** means

　● **A** without equal
　○ **B** without warning
　○ **C** without results
　○ **D** without cause

2. If you **automate** (line 7) a job, you

　○ **A** perform it quickly
　● **B** use machines to do it
　○ **C** impress others with it
　○ **D** modernize the product

3. In line 14, a **prerequisite** is something that you need

　● **A** before you begin
　○ **B** in order to do your best
　○ **C** as an emergency backup
　○ **D** in order to finish properly

4. An action associated with a **portal** (line 18) is

　○ **A** asking and answering
　○ **B** searching and finding
　● **C** approaching and entering
　○ **D** accepting and rejecting

5. Things that are **infinitesimal** (line 20) are NOT

　○ **A** small and unable to be seen
　○ **B** being studied by scientists
　○ **C** the size of atoms
　● **D** visible to the naked eye

6. A **postulate** (line 26) is a statement that

　○ **A** is false and doesn't have to be proven
　○ **B** is false and has to be proven
　● **C** is true and doesn't have to be proven
　○ **D** is true and has to be proven

Politics and Revolution in the 21st Century

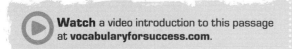
Watch a video introduction to this passage at **vocabularyforsuccess.com**.

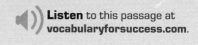
Listen to this passage at **vocabularyforsuccess.com**.

C CCSS Vocabulary: 4; Reading (Informational Text): 4, 6. (See pp. T16–17.)

Divided by a Wall

\<e-mail exchange\>

Dear Franz,

Thank you for hosting us on our recent trip to Berlin. It was amazing to see you again and to walk along the remains of the Berlin Wall. I will never forget how we disagreed over the meaning of the wall when it was built. I saw it as a Wall of Shame built to protect a dictatorial system, an unjust state. You saw it as an "anti-fascist protection wall" built to save East Germany from losing its citizens to the West. I am glad that now that the wall is gone, we can put our differences aside and forget our disagreement. But the wall will never be forgotten. I have never seen so many people weep as when we saw the statue "Wall Memorial 1000." It is an incredible image of the cruelty brought on by the wall. When we boarded the plane back to the United States, I felt as though I was fleeing my homeland all over again. I occasionally make an **allusion** to my escape from East Berlin in the 1960s, but I have never told anyone the full story. It is still too painful to relive—having to leave everything behind and knowing that others, including my cousin, died on the way. Our recent trip has led to some **introspection** on my part. I have been thinking a lot about the past and what I will do in the future. Knowing how my countrymen were able to **revolutionize** our country so that others could enjoy freedom is a great inspiration. —Peter

Dear Peter,

It was pure pleasure having you here. It has been more than twenty years since the Berlin Wall fell in 1989, but I am still getting used to a **geopolitical** reality in which friends and family can easily come into—and get out of— Germany and Berlin. At the time that you fled East Berlin during the Cold War, this was not so. It is fitting that you made it to America. Many others were brave, too, but as you related to me and I now realize, your cousin was considered a real **vigilante** by the Communist government because he could not tolerate the injustices of the regime that lashed out **arbitrarily** at its citizens. He spoke out against the oppressive **status quo** of the Communists. His **rhetoric** was so inspiring that he could move people to action with a single speech. Soon he had a whole **subculture** of rebels secretly plotting to undermine the regime from within. He **wrought** an elaborate system of escape. He forged papers, arranged safe houses on the other side, and found ways to get people out. He helped hundreds escape. But in the end, he paid a price for his lawlessness. As you know, I was far too **diffident** to join the rebels. I could not find the courage to voice any opinions other than those of the Communists in power.

It is **ironic** that today you and I, who were once on different sides of the wall, can now be friends. —Franz

176

An e-mail exchange is a series of electronic letters between two people.

Opposite: The Wall Memorial 1000, a statue commemorating the first East German killed at the Berlin Wall

Above: The fall of the Berlin Wall in November 1989

Below: East and West Germans mingle freely at the Brandenburg Gate after the fall of the Berlin Wall.

VOCABULARY

allusion	vigilante	subculture
introspection	arbitrarily	wrought
revolutionize	status quo	diffident
geopolitical	rhetoric	ironic

TALK ABOUT IT

With a partner, answer the questions below. Use as many of the highlighted words in the selection as you can.

1. What is the *geopolitical* reality in which you live? How is it different from that of a divided Germany, as described in the passage?

2. Why do you think Franz considers it *ironic* that he and Peter are now friends?

Word Meanings

For each highlighted word on pages 176–177, the meaning or meanings are given below.

For practice with synonyms, see page 206.

1. **allusion** (uh-LOO-zhuhn) **n.** an indirect reference to something, often to literature. When my teacher made an *allusion* to *Hamlet*, I was the only one who caught it.

2. **arbitrarily** (ar-buh-TRER-uh-lee) **adv.** not fixed by law; unrestrained in the use of power. A government that acts *arbitrarily* might overlook crimes committed by its allies and arrest its enemies for crimes they did not commit. **SYNONYM:** dictatorial; **adv.** in a random way. When someone makes a decision *arbitrarily*, he or she decides by chance, without basing the decision on rules, data, or logic. **SYNONYM:** haphazardly

3. **diffident** (DI-fuh-duhnt) **adj.** afraid to take action or speak out. A *diffident* person might give in to peer pressure for fear of standing out from others. **SYNONYMS:** shy, bashful, withdrawn

4. **geopolitical** (jee-oh-puh-LIT-uh-cuhl) **adj.** related to international policies or politics. The term *geopolitical* is often used to refer to international politics because the policies of one country usually have an impact on people in other countries.

5. **introspection** (in-truh-SPEK-shuhn) **n.** an examination of one's own thoughts and feelings; self-reflection. Those who engage in *introspection* before making major decisions are often happier because they understand the reasons for their choices. **SYNONYMS:** self-observation; soul-searching

6. **ironic** (eye-RON-ik) **adj.** marked by a contradiction between what is said and what is meant, or between what is expected and what actually happens. It would be *ironic* if, to save time, you decided to drive to the store instead of taking the bus, but then you had a flat tire that took hours to fix.

7. **revolutionize** (rev-uh-LOO-shuhn-ize) **v.** to completely change the way something is done, thought about, or made. The invention of the automobile would *revolutionize* the way people lived in the United States. **SYNONYMS:** innovate, change

8. **rhetoric** (RE-tuh-rik) **n.** a way of speaking or writing effectively. *Rhetoric* is the careful use of language to communicate with others clearly and persuasively. **SYNONYMS:** discourse, oratory, verbiage

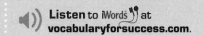

Watch a video introduction for each word at **vocabularyforsuccess.com**.

Listen to iWords at **vocabularyforsuccess.com**.

Refer to the online dictionary at **vocabularyforsuccess.com**.

9. **status quo** (STAT-uhss KWOH) **n.** the existing state of affairs. Those who are well off usually want to maintain the *status quo*, so they resist change. **SYNONYM:** normalcy

10. **subculture** (SUHB-cuhl-chur) **n.** a small group whose behavior goes against that of the larger culture or society. Young people often create a unique *subculture*, defined by music and fashion, to distinguish themselves from their parents.

11. **vigilante** (vij-uh-LAN-tee) **n.** someone who acts alone or as a member of a group to seek justice outside the legal system. A *vigilante* thinks the laws are not fair and therefore takes justice into his or her own hands. **SYNONYM:** avenger

12. **wrought** (RAWT) **v.** to have worked into shape by skill or effort. Things that artists have *wrought* include poems, paintings, and sculptures. **SYNONYMS:** crafted, worked, formed; **adj.** feeling very moved or excited. Usually used with *up* and *over*. A person might become *wrought* while listening to sad music or an inspiring speech. **SYNONYM:** emotional

More on Meanings: Denotation and Connotation

Words may have a positive or negative connotation. Compare these sentences:

This new computer program will **revolutionize** the business world.

This new computer program will **ruin** the business world.

Revolutionize and *ruin* are words that describe great change. But *revolutionize* suggests that the change will be a good one, so it has a positive connotation. *Ruin*, however, suggests that the change will be destructive. It has a negative connotation.

Now consider this pair of sentences:

Nina is **diffident** when sharing her opinions with the group.

Nina is **modest** when sharing her opinions with the group.

Diffident has a negative connotation. It suggests that Nina is hesitant and uncertain. But *modest* has a neutral or even positive connotation—that Nina does not want to draw unwanted attention to herself.

Challenge Choose two of the words below. For each, suggest two synonyms, one with a positive connotation and one with a negative connotation. Then, use each synonym in a sentence that demonstrates the feeling associated with it.

intelligent	*irregular*	*assertive*
reserved	*powerful*	*unyielding*

Students may differ about the connotation of a word. Some might consider *assertive* to be positive, conveying confidence. Others might consider *assertive* to be negative, suggesting aggression.

Word Talk

Each lesson word has been placed in a category. With a partner, discuss and list items that belong in each category. Compare your results with those of another pair of students.

C CCSS Vocabulary: 6. (See pp. T16–17.)

Geopolitical Issues in the News	Examples of a *Subculture* at Your School	Inventions That Would *Revolutionize* the World	People Who Use *Rhetoric*
war, unrest in the Middle East, issues regarding pollution and climate change	jocks, skateboarders, geeks, goths, punks, hippies	the wheel, the telephone, the smart phone, the computer, television, the printing press, the gun	politicians, professors, speakers at a convention

Words to Describe a *Vigilante*	People Who Like the *Status Quo*	*Ironic* Situations	Questions That Call for *Introspection*
tough, self-righteous, vengeful, justice-seeking	a king or queen, a wealthy person, a frontrunner, a record-breaking athlete	a clown making children cry instead of laugh, a race-car driver getting pulled over for going too slowly	How can I be a better person? What is the right thing to do?

Things That Are *Wrought* by Artisans	Situations in Which You Might Feel *Diffident*	Ways Tyrants Act *Arbitrarily*	Examples of an *Allusion*
jewelry, a chair, a lamp, a statue	meeting your girlfriend's or boyfriend's parents for the first time, going to the principal's or coach's office, starting at a new school	throwing enemies in jail, taking away citizens' rights, changing laws without considering the people	referring to school as "Hogwarts," referring to "Spidey senses"

Check for Understanding

Choose the lesson word that completes each sentence. Write the word on the line provided. Some words will be used twice.

allusion	geopolitical	revolutionize	subculture
arbitrarily	introspection	rhetoric	vigilante
diffident	ironic	status quo	wrought

1. The ___vigilante___ was not satisfied to let the authorities handle the situation, so he went after the criminal himself.

2. The speaker's ___rhetoric___ was uplifting, filling the audience with hope.

3. The silversmith had ___wrought___ a bracelet from metal and precious stones.

4. Lourdes was too ___diffident___ to admit that she did not like the movie her friends were raving about.

5. After much arguing, the political leaders

   ___arbitrarily___ withdrew their support from the candidate's campaign.

6. Before making a/an ___geopolitical___ decision, the leaders of the countries consulted many experts to assess possible benefits and consequences.

7. After much ___introspection___, I have realized that I do not really want to be a doctor.

8. The speaker used a/an ___allusion___ to Aesop's fable about the grasshopper and the ant to inspire us to take action now.

9. Tablets and e-readers are starting to ___revolutionize___ the way we read books.

10. Hippies were a major ___subculture___ of the 1960s.

11. It is ___ironic___ that aggressive salespeople make me not want to buy anything.

12. If you don't like the ___status quo___, do something to bring about change.

13. The poet had ___wrought___ such a lovely poem that I cried as she read it aloud.

14. When my grandmother made a/an ___allusion___ to her "closet of secrets," I realized there must be a lot about her that I didn't know.

If students answer *allusion* for Item 2, point out that a speech is a form of *rhetoric*, or persuasive speaking. If it were clear that the speech made a reference to literature or culture, then *allusion* might be a reasonable answer.

Word Associations

Use what you know about the lesson words in italics to answer each question. Circle the letter next to the phrase that best answers the question. Be prepared to explain your answers.

1. Which is a *geopolitical* action?

   a. lowering the driving age
   b. declaring war on a country
   c. announcing a new holiday

2. When would you be most likely to engage in *introspection*?

   a. on a long walk
   b. at a party
   c. during gym class

3. Which of the following is *ironic*?

   a. a popular movie star
   b. a talented singer
   c. a sad comic

4. Who would most likely want to change the *status quo*?

   a. a king
   b. a starving artist
   c. a wealthy businessperson

5. Which of the following is something a *diffident* person would do?

   a. listen quietly to others
   b. argue for a major change
   c. write a letter to the editor

6. If you make a decision *arbitrarily,* what have you done?

   a. not thought very much about it
   b. given it extensive consideration
   c. researched it thoroughly

7. Which of the following most helped *revolutionize* modern communication systems?

   a. the invention of the fountain pen
   b. the invention of the telephone
   c. the invention of the hair dryer

8. Why would a sad movie make people feel emotionally *wrought*?

   a. It moved them greatly.
   b. It won many awards.
   c. It was supposed to be funny.

9. In which situation would you most likely use *rhetoric*?

   a. when talking with a friend
   b. when discussing a book in class
   c. when running for student council

10. Which of the following is most likely true of the members of a *subculture?*

    a. They have similar interests.
    b. They go to the theater often.
    c. They have different interests.

11. What would a *vigilante* most likely do?

    a. break the law in the name of justice
    b. call the police for assistance
    c. read someone his or her rights

12. Which of the following is an *allusion*?

    a. a magic trick
    b. a reference to *Romeo and Juliet*
    c. a website about mythology

CCSS Vocabulary: 4.a. (See pp. T16–17.)

Check Again

Use what you know about the lesson word in italics to complete each sentence. Be sure your sentences make sense.

1. A presidential candidate would use *rhetoric* when ___trying to persuade people to vote for him or her.___

2. If you do not like the *status quo*, you should ___work to change the current conditions.___

3. A *diffident* person may feel nervous when ___asked to express his or her opinion.___

4. Something that has helped *revolutionize* the way people live today is ___the invention of the___ automobile or the Internet.

5. After several of his neighbors' houses were robbed, the *vigilante* ___set a trap and waited to catch___ the robber when he returned.

6. A good place for *introspection* would be ___a hot bath.___

7. A *geopolitical* event is one that ___affects countries around the globe.___

8. A mystery novel would have an *ironic* ending if ___the detective had committed the crime.___

9. Members of a *subculture* show that they are outsiders by ___acting out against the larger culture or___ society.

10. You can tell when someone is feeling *wrought* because ___he or she might be crying.___

11. When laws are passed *arbitrarily*, citizens are likely to ___band together and strongly object.___

12. I could tell by my friend's *allusion* to the popular TV show that ___he was about to act like one of the___ characters on the show.

Write Your Own

Reread the passage on pages 176–177. Then, on a separate sheet of paper, write a one-paragraph response to the question, "Based on what you have learned about East Berlin during the Cold War, why might people have wanted to tear down the Berlin Wall?" Use at least two words from the lesson word list and support your answer by referring to the text of the passage.

Word-Solving Strategies:
Context Clues

Inference

The meaning of an unfamiliar word is not always made clear by context clues in the sentence. Sometimes readers must look for clues and use their own prior knowledge to make inferences, or educated guesses, about the unfamiliar word. Read these sentences from "Divided by a Wall":

> As you know, I was far too diffident to join the rebels. I could not find the courage to voice any opinions other than those of the Communists in power.

The writer does not give any clues about the meaning of *diffident* in the sentence in which it appears. However, the writer does provide details in the next sentence—"courage," "voice any opinions." From these clues, readers can infer that *diffident* means "afraid to speak out or voice one's opinions."

Sometimes you must read deeply to understand how an author uses a word.

> . . . *your cousin was considered a real vigilante by the Communist government because he could not tolerate the injustices of the regime . . .*

The Communists considered the cousin to be a vigilante, or outlaw, because he defied their laws. But their laws were unjust. The writer is suggesting the cousin was in fact a hero who resisted a cruel regime.

BE CAREFUL!

Practice

Write six sentences using the highlighted words from the paragraph below. Provide clues that signal the meaning of the word.

It was difficult for Elizabeth to acclimate to Russian culture. In America, she could procure groceries easily. But in Russia, customers had to wait to give their lists to the clerk, who retrieved their items for them. The process was painstakingly slow. "Why do they keep everything behind the counter?" she asked. "Because Russians faced so many impediments during the Soviet days, we are not used to getting things easily," her friend replied. "The stores are afraid that people will simply take what they want."

1. In a foreign place, you must acclimate to a different and unfamiliar way of doing things.

2. To procure a passport, go to a government office and fill out the form for getting it.

3. The seamstress took weeks to painstakingly sew each tiny sequin onto the costume.

4. Impediments to enjoyable travel include high fares and crowded planes and highways.

5. The difficulties of learning a language should not be impediments to exploring a foreign place.

6. You will acclimate to life at college, but it will take time for you to get used to a new environment.

C CCSS Vocabulary: 4.a.; Reading (Informational Text): 4. (See pp. T16–T17.)

Practice for Tests

For a quiz and additional practice for this lesson, go to **vocabularyforsuccess.com**.

Fill in the bubble next to the answer that best completes the sentence or answers the question.

1. Read this sentence.

   The Internet has helped *revolutionize* the way people access information.

   Revolutionize means:

   ○ **A** speed up
   ○ **B** increase demand for
   ○ **C** attack violently
   ● **D** change dramatically

2. When you speak in an *ironic* way, you:

   ○ **A** say something that is mean
   ● **B** say the opposite of what you really think
   ○ **C** tell a long story
   ○ **D** say something angrily

3. The most likely reason to use *rhetoric* is:

   ● **A** to influence people
   ○ **B** to get things for free
   ○ **C** to show how hungry you are
   ○ **D** to earn a lot of money

4. If you belong to a *subculture*, you:

   ● **A** are different from most other people
   ○ **B** believe it is important to follow rules
   ○ **C** lack self-confidence
   ○ **D** think carefully before you act

5. Which of the following is NOT a *geopolitical* issue?

   ● **A** establishing guidelines for the height of new buildings in a city
   ○ **B** creating new rules for arresting international criminals
   ○ **C** writing new laws for protecting coral reefs around the world
   ○ **D** setting new regulations for shipping aid materials abroad

If students choose answer A for Item 1, point out that "speed up" might accurately describe an effect of the Internet, but it does not describe the correct meaning of the word *revolutionize*.

6. Which of the following is a way to maintain the *status quo*?

   ○ **A** starting a new company
   ○ **B** moving to a different town
   ○ **C** refusing to pay your taxes
   ● **D** preventing change

7. Read this sentence.

   The article's *allusion* to the Greek myth of Daedalus helped readers understand that being too ambitious is not always a good thing.

   Allusion means:

   ● **A** specific reference
   ○ **B** loaded language
   ○ **C** rhyming word
   ○ **D** vivid image

8. A dictator who governs *arbitrarily* is one who:

   ○ **A** establishes clear laws and enforces them consistently
   ○ **B** does away with all but the most necessary laws
   ● **C** acts on his or her own whims and without clear laws
   ○ **D** appoints others to govern in his or her absence

9. A *vigilante* is most likely to act when:

   ● **A** the authorities are viewed as ineffective
   ○ **B** the crime is petty
   ○ **C** the victim is a child
   ○ **D** the economy is bad

10. Some *introspection* is advisable before you:

    ○ **A** plan a party
    ○ **B** make your bed
    ○ **C** take a vacation
    ● **D** decide to get married

CCSS Vocabulary: 4.a., 6. (See pp. T16–17.)

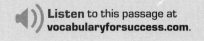
Social Media Spark Revolutions

<blog>

Posted by: iamblogger June 22, 2012 at 6:00 p.m.

Egyptians protesting in Cairo in December 2011

You have probably heard the expression, "A picture is worth a thousand words." When it comes to political revolution, this may be an understatement; a photo or video is worth far more. No journalist's observation can spark people's anger or match the power of the anecdotal evidence in an eyewitness's photograph. And today there is no more powerful vehicle for distributing influential images than social media.

The role of television in world affairs in the 1960s is analogous to social media's place in the world today. In the 1960s, television viewers saw images of the Vietnam War in their homes on a daily basis. Underestimating the power of these images, the military did little at first to confine photographers' movements. As a result, journalists and photographers were able to witness and record scenes that shocked Americans and helped erode their support for the war.

Public outrage led to massive protests against the war and divisions within American society. Many older Americans felt that young people were being impertinent by questioning the government's actions and writing satire that mocked officials and soldiers. Conversely, young people felt frustrated by their elders, who seemed to accept blindly what the government said without any effort to verify the facts. This division led to what is commonly referred to as the "generation gap," which incidentally brought about a cultural revolution of sorts in the United States.

College students in Boston, Massachusetts, protesting the war in Vietnam in 1965

Today images still have power. They can be spread quickly on the Internet and without any editorial review by newspapers and publishers. Uncensored images of conflicts around the world show up almost immediately on people's computers and smart phones. This ability to post news online is creating problems for

VOCABULARY

anecdotal	impertinent	incidentally
analogous	satire	so-called
confine	conversely	metaphor
erode	verify	albeit

oppressive world governments. In such places, the so-called state news organizations are essentially propaganda machines. But social media give citizens ways to voice their opinions and post photos and videos of what they see in the streets. The Internet allows them to organize quickly and inspire others to mobilize.

This was the case recently in Egypt. A young businessman, Khaled Said, posted a video exposing corruption in the police force. The police beat him to death in retaliation. When Said's friends posted a photo of his battered face on social media, his death became a metaphor for an oppressed population. For Egypt's youth, Said's death was the last straw. Using social media and texting, they quickly posted information about where and when to gather. Within days, thousands of people took to the streets to demand change. Just a few weeks later, Hosni Mubarak, who had ruled Egypt for three decades, resigned. Unrest in Egypt had been growing for many years, albeit without great interest from the outside world. But the introduction of social media—and its use to spread the disturbing image of Said—was a catalyst for the success of the people's revolution.

Events in Egypt are not the only instance of rebellion in the Middle East. An entire wave of revolutionary demonstrations and protests has swept across more than seventeen countries since December 2010. These protests have become known as the Arab Spring.

All of these movements have used similar tools, including social media, to organize, communicate, and create awareness.

The demonstrations have met with varying degrees of success, but the positive results can be attributed, at least in part, to the power and worldwide reach of social media.

TALK ABOUT IT

With a partner, answer the questions below. Use as many of the highlighted words in the selection as you can.

1. In what ways are television in the 1960s and social media today *analogous*?

2. What types of *anecdotal* evidence have you seen distributed to large numbers of people through social media?

Egyptians demonstrating in the streets in July 2011

Word Meanings

For each highlighted word on pages 186–187, the meaning or meanings are given below.

For practice with synonyms, see page 206.

1. **albeit** (awl-BEE-it) **conj.** even though; although. Use *albeit* when you want to acknowledge a contrast to or downside of something you've just referred to; for example, "I'm going to make a salary at my new job, *albeit* a small one." **SYNONYMS:** notwithstanding, whereas

2. **analogous** (uh-NAL-uh-guhss) **adj.** having similar traits. When two things are *analogous*, they share enough similarities that they can be compared to one another. **SYNONYMS:** comparable, alike, parallel

3. **anecdotal** (an-ik-DOTE-uhl) **adj.** based on personal experiences. *Anecdotal* evidence is based on the casual observations of individuals, not the careful gathering of scientific data.

4. **confine** (kuhn-FINE) **v.** to keep someone or something enclosed in an area. If you *confine* skateboarders to a particular area of the park, you restrict them to the space they can use. **SYNONYMS:** restrict, imprison; **v.** to limit or restrict. To *confine* your remarks means you will discuss only the topic at hand. **SYNONYM:** cap; (KON-fine) **n.** (usually presented as *confines*) borders or boundaries. A large crowd would feel cramped in the *confines* of a small room. **SYNONYMS:** limits, walls, fences

5. **conversely** (kon-VURSS-lee) **adv.** in contrast. The Internet has led to an increase in worker productivity; *conversely*, the Web has also led to great time-wasting activities. **SYNONYMS:** on the other hand, to the contrary

6. **erode** (i-RODE) **v.** to slowly reduce the strength, value, or importance of. To *erode* something, like public support for a law, is to wear down and weaken it, perhaps by speaking persuasively against it. **SYNONYM:** weaken; **v.** to slowly wear away, often by the action of a natural force. Over time, wind and rain will *erode* rocks. **SYNONYM:** corrode

7. **impertinent** (im-PUR-tuh-nuhnt) **adj.** rude and disrespectful. His *impertinent* reply to her polite question made us all dislike him. **SYNONYMS:** brash, sassy, audacious

8. **incidentally** (in-suh-DENT-uh-lee) **adv.** by the way; as a minor or additional side note. To say something *incidentally* is to offer a tidbit of information. **SYNONYM:** furthermore

C CCSS Vocabulary: 4.c., 4.d. (See pp. T16–17.)

Watch a video introduction for each word at **vocabularyforsuccess.com**.

Listen to iWords at **vocabularyforsuccess.com**.

Refer to the online dictionary at **vocabularyforsuccess.com**.

9. **metaphor** (MET-uh-for) **n.** a figure of speech in which one thing is described as another. A *metaphor* makes a direct comparison between two essentially unlike things without using the words *like* or *as,* as in "Life is a journey." **SYNONYM:** indirect comparison

10. **satire** (SAT-ire) **n.** the use of humor to make someone or something seem ridiculous. A fake news program that makes fun of real news by having seemingly clueless reporters cover absurd stories is a *satire.* **SYNONYMS:** caricature, lampoon

11. **so-called** (SOH-kawld) **adj.** improperly or falsely labeled. The *so-called* help function on most computer programs is often not helpful at all. **SYNONYMS:** supposed, doubtful

12. **verify** (VER-uh-fye) **v.** to check that something is true or accurate. You can *verify* that a fact is true by checking the encyclopedia or asking an expert. **SYNONYMS:** confirm, authenticate

More on Meanings: Denotation and Connotation

A word's *denotation*, or its dictionary definition, only gives the word's actual meaning. Many words also have a *connotation*, or an emotional association, that can be either positive or negative.

Consider these sentences:

The doctor says we must **confine** Leticia to her room.

The doctor says we must **imprison** Leticia in her room.

Both words mean "to limit to a particular location," but *confine* has a neutral connotation, whereas *imprison* has a more negative one. It suggests that Leticia will be locked up like a criminal while she recovers. Now read this pair of sentences:

The appearance of clouds began to **erode** our desire for a picnic.

The appearance of clouds began to **destroy** our desire for a picnic.

Both words mean "to break down," but *erode* has a more positive connotation than *destroy,* which suggests that any desire for a picnic is totally gone.

Challenge Choose two of the words below. For each, suggest two synonyms, one with a positive connotation and one with a negative connotation. Then, use both synonyms in a sentence that demonstrates the feeling associated with each word.

heavy	*colorful*	*surprise*
load	*cry*	*stout*

Remind students that assigning connotations can be a subjective process. Some might consider *stout* to have a positive connotation, while others may consider it to have a negative or neutral one.

Word Talk

Each lesson word has been placed in a category. With a partner, discuss and list items that belong in each category. Compare your results with those of another pair of students.

C CCSS Vocabulary: 6. (See pp. T16–17.)

Things That Are *Analogous*

a battle and a football game; bees and busy workers; a herd of sheep and people in a crowd

Examples of a *Metaphor*

The wind was a sharp whip against their faces. The snow was a blanket at our feet. The night was a cloak of darkness.

Ways to *Verify* Information

look in a dictionary or encyclopedia; check other sources; ask an expert

Ways to Be *Impertinent*

ask an older person his or her age; tell parents how to discipline their children; correct someone else's pronunciation

Places to *Confine* Someone

waiting room, the nurse's office, sickbed, prison

Information to Add *Incidentally* When Summarizing a Book

unimportant details, your thoughts about how good it was

Words to Describe a *Satire*

witty, sharp, funny, clever, bitter

Examples of the Correct Use of *Albeit*

My meal did come with a milkshake, *albeit* a very small one. The team has some great players, *albeit* mostly seniors.

Ways to *Erode* a Friend's Interest in Sports

telling him or her that the sport is silly; talking about the dangers of the sport; suggesting other, more interesting things to do

Examples of Things or People You Might Refer to as *So-called*

a tool that doesn't work properly; a doctor who is a "quack"; a lawyer who never graduated from law school

Examples of Ways to Use *Conversely* in a Sentence

She did not want to be his partner for the project; *conversely*, he desperately wanted to be her partner. The gym was freezing; *conversely*, the cafeteria was stifling hot.

Examples of *Anecdotal* Evidence

one person's version of an event; what someone told someone else happened; gossip

Check for Understanding

Choose the lesson word that completes each sentence. Write the word on the line provided. Some words will be used twice.

albeit	confine	impertinent	satire
analogous	conversely	incidentally	so-called
anecdotal	erode	metaphor	verify

1. That _____so-called_____ computer technician couldn't even hook up my keyboard.

2. Jessie is an amazing singer; _____conversely_____, her brother cannot carry a tune.

3. Hearing nothing but negative comments tends to _____erode_____ my good mood.

4. Her conclusion is interesting, but it is based entirely on _____anecdotal_____ evidence.

5. The book is a/an _____satire_____ that mocks politicians who contradict themselves.

6. The poem uses a/an _____metaphor_____ comparing youth to a flower.

7. A ferret is an amusing and loyal, _____albeit_____ unusual, choice for a pet.

8. We have to _____confine_____ our new puppy in its crate whenever we aren't home, or it will chew on our shoes and furniture.

9. We prepared a/an _____satire_____ to illustrate what we think about hypocrites.

10. The shoe store manager fired Monica for being _____impertinent_____ when she suggested the store should sell shoes that were actually fashionable.

11. Prime Minister Winston Churchill was one of the greatest leaders in European history; _____incidentally_____, he was a gifted amateur painter as well.

12. To enter the facility, you must _____verify_____ your identity by showing the guard a driver's license or other photo identification.

13. Running a marathon and working three jobs are _____analogous_____ in that both require extensive dedication and great endurance.

14. All the guests are suspects, so the police will _____confine_____ them to the lobby.

If students answer *albeit* for Item 2, point out that the sentence describes two people who are exact opposites in respect to singing. *Conversely* conveys a direct contrast more clearly than *albeit*.

Word Associations

Use what you know about the lesson word in italics to answer each question. Circle the letter next to the phrase that best answers the question. Be prepared to explain your answers.

1. Which is a synonym for *albeit*?

   a. often
   b. consequently
   c. although

2. What could *erode* rock over time?

   a. water
   b. disease
   c. sunlight

3. Which of the following might a train conductor mention *incidentally*?

   a. the name of the next stop
   b. the need for the train to make an emergency stop
   c. the fact that there is a newspaper stand at the next stop

4. What is something you might have to *verify* when logging on to a website?

   a. your favorite food
   b. your password
   c. your locker combination

5. If you are in the *confines* of a movie theater, where are you?

   a. in the parking lot
   b. inside the movie theater
   c. outside the movie theater

6. Which sentence uses *so-called* correctly?

   a. The *so-called* mechanic knew nothing about how to fix my car.
   b. The *so-called* professor was admired by her colleagues.
   c. The *so-called* doctor was able to diagnose my aunt's condition.

7. What is an example of *satire*?

   a. a comedian putting on a tutu and clumsily dancing around the stage
   b. a handsome actor playing the part of a hideous monster in a movie
   c. someone calling a stranger to tell him he's won a prize as a prank

8. Which of the following is a *metaphor*?

   a. The leaves twirled like dancers.
   b. The fighter's fist was a thunderbolt.
   c. The rain pelted his head like pebbles.

9. You like to stay up late and get up early; *conversely*, your best friend does what?

   a. goes to bed late and gets up early
   b. goes to bed early and gets up late
   c. goes to bed early and gets up early

10. Which is an *impertinent* question to ask your host?

    a. May I have a glass of water?
    b. Why does your house smell?
    c. How long have you lived here?

11. Where would you expect to encounter *anecdotal* evidence?

    a. in an infomercial
    b. in a scientific report
    c. in a courtroom

12. Which of the following would most likely be considered *analogous*?

    a. going to the prom and mowing a lawn
    b. riding a bus and driving a car
    c. persuading a parent and arguing a case in court

CCSS Vocabulary: 4.a. (See pp. T16–17.)

Check Again

Use what you know about the lesson word in italics to complete each sentence. Be sure your sentences make sense.

1. The support for her argument was largely *anecdotal* and based on _____ observations she gathered from a handful of people.

2. A good *metaphor* is one that _____ compares two unlike things in an interesting way.

3. Being a professional baseball player would be a great career, *albeit* _____ a short-lived one.

4. In order to *verify* the facts in your research report, you need to _____ provide a bibliography or footnotes.

5. We worried that not making the football team would *erode* his self-confidence, so we _____ tried to cheer him up and tell him he would do better next year.

6. I asked the *so-called* hairstylist to trim my hair just a bit, and now _____ my head is shaved.

7. The *impertinent* child asked the librarian _____ why all the books were so boring.

8. For the camping trip you will need a sleeping bag, a flashlight, bug spray, and *incidentally*, _____ any good campfire songs you know.

9. I really don't like cats; *conversely*, _____ they seem to love me.

10. If you want to *confine* your answer to a particular issue, then you must _____ be sure that everything you say addresses the issue and nothing else.

11. Driving a car is *analogous* to managing your life because _____ you should always know where you're going and keep your eyes on the road ahead.

12. The video was a *satire* of American consumer culture; it _____ made fun of Americans' love for buying in bulk.

Write Your Own

1. **Write an 8-word sentence about social media, using the word *confine* in the third position.**

   Texters must confine their texting to appropriate times.

2. **Write a 15-word sentence about a photo, using the word *incidentally* in the seventh position.**

   The photo is amazingly powerful, and, incidentally, I am on the edge of the crowd.

LESSON 17

Word-Solving Strategies:
Context Clues

Examples

Examples present one or more details to show a word's meaning. Reread this sentence from "Social Media Spark Revolutions":

> Many older Americans felt that young people were being impertinent by questioning the government's actions and writing satire that mocked officials and soldiers.

The writer provides "questioning the government's actions," and "writing satire that mocked officials and soldiers" as examples of impertinence. From these examples, a reader can determine that *impertinent* means "being rude or disrespectful toward authority figures."

You may have to read further to find examples in later sentences. Look at this sentence from "Social Media Spark Revolutions":

> *The role of television in world affairs in the 1960s is analogous to social media's place in the world today.*

Analogous is in the first sentence of the paragraph. Examples in the rest of the paragraph tell how TV in the 1960s is similar to social media in the 2010s.

BE CAREFUL!

Practice

Write a highlighted word from the passage below and the example or examples that help define it in the first two boxes. Then write the meaning of the word in the third box.

> Anouke watched the protest from her father's office window. She could sense how exasperated the crowd was—fed up with corruption, frustrated by the lack of jobs, impatient for change. Watching the exuberant protestors below waving signs, chanting slogans, and yelling for justice, she wanted to join them. Why would her father not let her? Was he too callous to care about justice or too hard-hearted to see her passion for the cause? It was futile to argue, however. Nothing would convince him to let her risk her safety.

WORD	EXAMPLES	WORD MEANING
exasperated	fed up with corruption, frustrated by the lack of jobs, impatient for change	frustrated and impatient
exuberant	waving signs, chanting slogans, and yelling for justice	full of energy and enthusiasm
callous	too hard-hearted	insensitive
futile	nothing would convince him	pointless

194   CCSS Vocabulary: 4.a.; Reading (Informational Text): 4. (See pp. T16–17.)

Practice for Tests

For a quiz and additional practice for this lesson, go to **vocabularyforsuccess.com**.

Fill in the bubble next to the answer that best completes the sentence or answers the question.

1. Read this sentence.

   My *so-called* friend told everyone that I cannot keep a secret.

   So-called means:

   ○ **A** best
   ○ **B** critical
   ○ **C** skeptical
   ● **D** alleged

2. When you *verify* a witness's story, you:

   ○ **A** decide that he or she is telling the truth
   ● **B** check that what he or she says is true
   ○ **C** fill in any details that were missing
   ○ **D** consider that what he or she says is worthless

3. The highway is the shortest way to get to school; *conversely*:

   ● **A** the traffic is usually so bad it takes the longest
   ○ **B** the highway is also the shortest way to get to the mall
   ○ **C** the city streets are often difficult for the bus to get through
   ○ **D** the highway is the best route to take

4. If someone is *impertinent,* then he or she is:

   ○ **A** outgoing and friendly
   ● **B** fresh and sassy
   ○ **C** selfish and vain
   ○ **D** popular with others

5. Something that a teacher mentions *incidentally* is:

   ○ **A** probably going to be on the test
   ● **B** not as important as other details
   ○ **C** the most interesting detail
   ○ **D** something you should write down

6. Read this sentence.

   The writer's latest story is a *satire* of modern technology.

   A *satire* is:

   ● **A** a mocking piece of humor
   ○ **B** a complete summary
   ○ **C** a broad overview
   ○ **D** a romantic tale

7. When two things are *analogous,* they are:

   ○ **A** joined together in some way
   ○ **B** complicated and hard to explain
   ● **C** similar in a number of ways
   ○ **D** totally different

8. An *anecdotal* story is:

   ○ **A** based on serious research
   ○ **B** intended to make people laugh
   ○ **C** meant to persuade others to change their ideas
   ● **D** about something that really happened to you

9. If the organizers of a concert want to *confine* the crowd to part of an arena, they might:

   ○ **A** charge high prices for tickets
   ○ **B** install metal detectors
   ● **C** rope off specific sections
   ○ **D** sell souvenirs at the door

10. Which of the following is NOT a *metaphor*?

   ● **A** He's as hungry as a bear.
   ○ **B** All the world's a stage.
   ○ **C** Time was the thief that had stolen her beauty.
   ○ **D** Duty was the chain that kept me shackled to home.

If students choose A for Item 2, point out that there is no judgment in verifying. Verifying involves proving something by checking the facts.

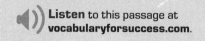

▶ **Watch** a video introduction to this passage at **vocabularyforsuccess.com**.

◀))) **Listen** to this passage at **vocabularyforsuccess.com**.

C **CCSS** Vocabulary: 4; Reading (Informational Text): 4, 6. (See pp. T16–17.)

Social Networking Grows Up

<personal narrative>

My mother moved to the United States from Iran when she was a teenager. In some ways, she is still a paragon of the traditional Iranian woman: She always wears a chador, or a head covering, veil, and shawl, in public and does not allow pork in her kitchen. She is also very strict. She used to get upset with me for wasting my time on such childish things as video games and social media, but ever since the Green Revolution, she has changed her mind—at least about social networking and microblogging.

You see, many of my mother's relatives still live in Iran. They often write and speak about politics, and my mother lives in ceaseless fear that the regime will target them as enemies. When the election results were announced in June 2009 indicating that Iran's President Ahmadinejad had won again, she knew immediately that there would be trouble.

Like many Iranians, she felt that the president had won unfairly. Sure enough, the country erupted in protests that came to be called the Green Revolution.

My mother's cousin Behzad was involved. He made an inflammatory speech calling for a regime change, which he posted on the Internet. She claimed this was a dangerous move, and somewhat surprising since Behzad was usually not so serious; he is more jaunty, even carefree. She feared one effect of this speech might be his arrest, which could result in torture or even death at the hands of the regime.

It was difficult to reach relatives on the phone. The revolutionary fervor alarmed the regime, and its efforts at containment included placing limits on traditional forms of communication. My mother finally succeeded

Iranians protesting the 2009 presidential election results

Explain that a personal narrative is a first-person account of something that actually happened to the writer.

in getting through, and her uncle gave her a social networking account to follow his posts. She had no idea how to do this; for once, she appreciated my gadget expertise.

Within hours, Behzad had posted a statement that he was fine, but the authorities were after him, and he would have to speak incognito from then on, via this electronic information network. His posts were mostly extremely short statements outlining the opposition's platform. They seemed designed to encourage outside support for the goals and policies of the opposition leader, Mir Hossein Mousavi. Occasionally, there was an image or a description of what was happening to the people. My mother said her cousin tended to exaggerate, and she prayed that his descriptions of the government's violence against protestors were hyperbole.

Then, Neda Agha Soltan was killed. A sniper shot the 27-year-old aspiring singer while she was walking down the street near a protest. How did this video affect my mother, you may wonder? Very deeply, as it did most Iranians. Demonstrators rallied across the country in protest. From then on, my mother was obsessed with social networking. She followed any and all posts about the Green Revolution, as though they could simulate actually being there with the marchers. Now to hear her talk, microblogging is the most exemplary method of communication ever invented.

VOCABULARY

paragon	effect	hyperbole
ceaseless	containment	affect
inflammatory	incognito	simulate
jaunty	platform	exemplary

TALK ABOUT IT

With a partner, answer the questions below. Use as many of the highlighted words in the selection as you can.

1. What was one *effect* of social networking on the writer's mother?

2. Why do you think the writer's mother called microblogging "the most *exemplary* method of communication"?

Below left: Iranian President Mahmoud Ahmadinejad

Below right: An Iranian woman with her cell phone

Word Meanings

For each highlighted word on pages 196–197, the meaning or meanings are given below.

For practice with synonyms, see page 206.

1. **affect** (uh-FEKT) **v.** to have an impact on. To *affect* something is to change it in some way through your actions. **SYNONYMS:** influence, modify; **v.** to pretend. In public, it is important to *affect* a polite demeanor even if you are feeling cranky. **SYNONYM:** fake

2. **ceaseless** (SEESS-less) **adj.** without end; constant. Something that is *ceaseless* never stops, such as Earth's spinning. **SYNONYMS:** continuous, uninterrupted

3. **containment** (kuhn-TAYN-muhnt) **n.** the process of keeping someone or something from spreading. The *containment* of a toxic spill requires a team of experts. **SYNONYMS:** restriction, limitation

4. **effect** (uh-FEKT) **n.** the change that results from an action. One *effect*, or result, of exercise is a decreased risk of heart disease. **SYNONYMS:** consequence, outcome

5. **exemplary** (eg-ZEM-pluh-ree) **adj.** worthy of being copied by others. An *exemplary* student has excellent study skills and can serve as a model to others. **SYNONYMS:** admirable, characteristic, representative

6. **hyperbole** (hye-PUR-buh-lee) **n.** an extreme exaggeration. You use *hyperbole* when you say something to make a point, such as telling someone "I'm starving" when you are actually just very hungry. **SYNONYM:** overstatement

7. **incognito** (in-kog-NEE-toh) **adj.** with an effort to hide one's identity; in disguise. The famous food critic went to the restaurant *incognito* so he would not receive special treatment. **SYNONYM:** unidentified

8. **inflammatory** (in-FLAM-uh-toh-ree) **adj.** likely to cause strong anger or outrage. An *inflammatory* speech is one that stirs up people's anger and can lead to a riot or rebellion. **SYNONYM:** rebellious; **adj.** likely to cause swelling. If you have an *inflammatory* reaction to a medicine, some part of your body swells up.

9. **jaunty** (JAWN-tee) **adj.** lively and spirited. An athlete who has just won a championship might have a *jaunty* air about her as she accepts the trophy. **SYNONYMS:** sprightly, peppy; **adj.** stylish, flashy. To wear your hat at a *jaunty* angle is one way to make a fashion statement. **SYNONYMS:** chic, showy

Watch a video introduction for each word at **vocabularyforsuccess.com**.

Listen to iWords at **vocabularyforsuccess.com**.

Refer to the online dictionary at **vocabularyforsuccess.com**.

10. **paragon** (PA-ruh-gon) **n.** an ideal example; a model of excellence or perfection. Someone who is a *paragon* of good health exercises regularly, eats the right foods, avoids stress, and gets enough sleep. **SYNONYMS:** model, ideal

11. **platform** (PLAT-form) **n.** the policies or goals of a group or person. The *platform* of a political party is the ideas that its candidates stand for. **SYNONYM:** philosophy; **n.** a structure that is built higher than the ground or surrounding area. A speaker might stand on a *platform* in order to be seen by the audience. **SYNONYMS:** stage, stand

12. **simulate** (SIM-yuh-late) **v.** to copy or reproduce the qualities or features of something in a way that seems real but is not. If a photographer wants to *simulate* a windy day, she might use a fan to blow on the models' hair and clothes. **SYNONYMS:** pretend, counterfeit

More on Meaning: Confusing Word Pairs

Some pairs of words can easily be confused because they sound alike. Such words are often used incorrectly. Compare these sentences:

Rainy weather will **affect** my mood.

I try to **affect** a confident manner when I go for a job interview.

The **effect** of the rainy weather was an abundance of crops.

In the first sentence, *affect* is a verb that means "to have an influence on." In the second, it is a verb meaning "to pretend." In the third sentence, *effect* is a noun that means "an outcome." The similar spelling and pronunciation cause people to confuse the words, but the first meaning of *affect* refers to the action of causing changes, and *effect* refers to the changes that occur.

Sometimes, a confusing word pair consists of words with meanings that are related.

Our flight will continue without **further** delay.

I will fly **farther** than you today.

In the first sentence, *further* means "additional." In the second sentence, *farther* means "greater." Both words express degree, but the word *further* applies to ideas or concepts, while *farther* applies to physical distance.

Challenge Choose one word pair below. Use each word correctly in a sentence.

fearful, fearsome   comma, coma
expand, expend

If students have trouble distinguishing the meanings of *fearful* and *fearsome*, review the meanings of the suffixes *-ful* and *-some*. Remind students to check a dictionary for the meanings confusing word pairs.

CCSS Vocabulary: 4.a., 5. (See pp. T16–17.)

vocabularyforsuccess.com   **199**

Word Talk

Each lesson word has been placed in a category. With a partner, discuss and list items that belong in each category. Compare your results with those of another pair of students.

C CCSS Vocabulary: 6. (See pp. T16–17.)

Things That Require *Containment*

a fire, an oil or chemical spill, a contagious disease, a flock of animals

Examples of *Hyperbole*

You sound a million miles away. I'm freezing. This suitcase weighs a ton.

How an Education Might *Affect* Your Future

by leading to better job opportunities, more money, and greater knowledge

Statements That Might Be *Inflammatory*

Students must be accompanied by parents in all stores. Theaters will be closed on Friday nights.

Reasons for a Political *Platform*

to make goals and ideas clear, to get votes, to inspire voters

Other Ways to Describe Someone Who Is *Jaunty*

cheerful, lighthearted, jolly, joyful, merry, relaxed

Things an *Exemplary* Employee Might Do

arrive on time, have a positive attitude, solve problems, work well with others

Ways to Live *Incognito*

wear a disguise, use an alias, hide movements

Examples of the *Effect* of a Major Storm

fallen tree branches, power outages, broken windows, flooding

Actions a Video Game Might *Simulate*

driving fast, flying a plane, riding a spaceship

Things That Are *Ceaseless*

waves washing up on a shore, a river flowing, time passing

Someone Who Might Be Considered a *Paragon*

teacher of the year, Olympic athlete, award-winning doctor, decorated soldier

Check for Understanding

Choose the lesson word that completes each sentence. Write the word on the line provided. Some words will be used twice.

affect	effect	incognito	paragon
ceaseless	exemplary	inflammatory	platform
containment	hyperbole	jaunty	simulate

1. The thing she disliked most about the beach was the _____ceaseless_____ wind, which blew her towel all over the place.

2. Her _____jaunty_____ attitude was attractive to the hiring committee, which was searching for fresh, confident teachers to add to the staff.

3. For his _____exemplary_____ courage and valor, the soldier was awarded a medal.

4. The candidate's _____inflammatory_____ language excited his base of supporters.

5. The _____platform_____ of this political party is: Minimum government, maximum freedom.

6. A/an _____paragon_____ of kindness, she spent all her time helping others.

7. The _____containment_____ of the huge fire required fire trucks from three towns.

8. Someone who is considerate thinks about how her actions will _____affect_____ others.

9. Not wanting to be recognized, the actor went _____incognito_____ in public.

10. It would be _____hyperbole_____ to say he's as skinny as a flagpole.

11. The _____effect_____ of the medicine was worse than the symptoms.

12. Astronauts train on machines that _____simulate_____ conditions in space.

13. The radio host was fired for his _____inflammatory_____ comments during the show.

14. Before the election, the newspaper published each candidate's _____platform_____.

If students complete Item 6 with *exemplary*, point out that "of kindness" requires a noun before it; *exemplary* is an adjective, so *paragon* is the correct answer.

Word Associations

Use what you know about the lesson word in italics to answer each question. Circle the letter next to the phrase that best answers the question. Be prepared to explain your answers.

1. Which would most likely need *containment*?

   a. a bright summer day
   b. a flu epidemic
   c. coupons for free food

2. Which of the following is *ceaseless*?

   a. the moon orbiting Earth
   b. an action-packed movie
   c. a football game

3. How might an ankle with an *inflammatory* injury look?

   a. swollen
   b. typical
   c. shrunken

4. Which is most likely to *affect* a person's grade?

   a. waiting patiently in line
   b. paying attention in class
   c. getting along well with siblings

5. Why might you stand on a *platform*?

   a. so a crowd can ignore you
   b. so a crowd can look down on you
   c. so a crowd can see you

6. What might a teacher do with an *exemplary* essay written by a student?

   a. tell the student it needs major revisions
   b. refuse to read it
   c. submit it to the school literary magazine

7. Which of the following is *hyperbole*?

   a. He tripped over his own feet.
   b. She's as light as a feather.
   c. She is a great swimmer.

8. What item of apparel would most likely look *jaunty* on the wearer?

   a. a dirty sweatshirt
   b. a pair of sunglasses
   c. a scuffed pair of shoes

9. In a movie, which of the following must a director *simulate*?

   a. an actor speaking
   b. a speeding car
   c. an alien invasion

10. What is an example of a *paragon*?

    a. a flawless diamond
    b. a broken chair
    c. a cracked window

11. In which situation do many people arrive *incognito*?

    a. a costume party
    b. a trip to the mall
    c. a dentist's appointment

12. Which is the most likely *effect* of your spreading a rumor?

    a. a decrease in your grade point average
    b. peace and quiet
    c. harm to someone's reputation

 CCSS Vocabulary: 4.a. (See pp. T16–17.)

Check Again

Use what you know about the lesson word in italics to complete each sentence. Be sure your sentences make sense.

1. A *jaunty* person is one who ___is easy and carefree, and perhaps wears bright, colorful clothes.___

2. If you make an *inflammatory* comment, you ___are sure to make people angry.___

3. The *ceaseless* hum of traffic ___never stops on this busy road.___

4. If a truck spilled chemicals on the highway, the *containment* would require ___emergency___ equipment to keep the spill from spreading.

5. One *effect* of volunteering at the community garden might be ___a harvest of delicious vegetables.___

6. Someone with an *exemplary* attendance record ___has never missed a day of school.___

7. In order for someone to be a *paragon,* ___he or she must be admired by others for a particular___ set of qualities.

8. A person needs a *platform* if ___he or she plans to run for elected office.___

9. A weather forecast of rain will likely *affect* ___your plans for outdoor activities.___

10. *Hyperbole* is a figure of speech that ___exaggerates for effect.___

11. You might need to go *incognito* if ___you don't want anyone to recognize you.___

12. In order to *simulate* a hurricane, you would need ___to recreate strong winds and rain.___

Write Your Own

Reread the passage on pages 196–197. Then, on a separate sheet of paper, write a one-paragraph response to the question, "What is the Green Revolution and how was it helped by social networking?" Use at least two words from the lesson word list and support your answer by referring to the text of the passage.

Word-Solving Strategies: Context Clues

Synonyms

Synonyms are a kind of context clue. Writers use synonyms, often in the same sentence, to provide a clue to the meaning of an unfamiliar word. Reread this sentence from "Social Networking Grows Up":

> She claimed this was a dangerous move, and somewhat surprising since Behzad was usually not so serious; he is more jaunty, even carefree.

The writer uses a comma to set off—and highlight—a phrase that includes a synonym for *jaunty*. In this context, the phrase "even carefree" has the same meaning as *jaunty*. As you encounter unfamiliar words, look for synonyms set off by commas or dashes.

Sometimes, a writer provides a synonym but does not set it off with punctuation. Look at this example:

> *The revolutionary fervor alarmed the regime, and its efforts at containment included placing limits on traditional forms of communication.*

The writer follows the word *containment* with the phrase "placing limits," which means the same thing, but without setting it off with punctuation.

BE CAREFUL!

Practice

Write six sentences using the five highlighted words from the paragraph below. When possible, use punctuation to signal a synonym.

> Some people refuse to join a social media site, because they fear they will get mired in reading frivolous posts—stuck on ridiculous, time-wasting updates. Others feel a compulsion, an absolute need, to stay connected with people. They can't stand the thought of being unable to log on to their favorite social media. It disconcerts them and makes them feel upset. They know social media is powerful, despite some of its disreputable aspects that cause some people to find it unrespectable.

1. I get mired down in everyday tasks, bogged down in my daily routine.

2. Their frivolous conversation included silly talk about who had lifted more weight at the gym.

3. He felt a compulsion, which some might call an obsession, to get good grades.

4. Getting lost disconcerts me and makes me feel totally confused.

5. The politician, having lost the respect and trust of the people, had become disreputable.

6. I feel a compulsion, or force, to finish reading this novel tonight.

CCSS Vocabulary: 4.a.; Reading (Informational Text): 4. (See pp. T16–T17.)

Practice for Tests

For a quiz and additional practice for this lesson, go to **vocabularyforsuccess.com**.

Fill in the bubble next to the answer that best completes the sentence or answers the question.

1. One quality of *exemplary* leaders includes:
   - ● **A** thinking about the people they lead
   - ○ **B** making the most money
   - ○ **C** having a lot of meetings
   - ○ **D** disregarding people's feelings

2. Something a friend might do that would *affect* your friendship negatively is:
   - ○ **A** eat lunch with you
   - ● **B** tell a lie about you
   - ○ **C** call you after school
   - ○ **D** joke around with you

3. Which of the following is NOT a *paragon*:
   - ● **A** an athlete who misses practice
   - ○ **B** a student who studies hard
   - ○ **C** a person who volunteers at a shelter
   - ○ **D** a person who picks up litter

4. Read this sentence.
   The city built a *platform* in the middle of the lake for swimmers and boaters.

   Platform means:
   - ● **A** a raised area
   - ○ **B** goals and policies
   - ○ **C** a type of shoe
   - ○ **D** a bridge

5. One *effect* of an earthquake is:
   - ○ **A** lightning and thunder
   - ● **B** the ground shaking
   - ○ **C** heavy downpours
   - ○ **D** strong winds

6. An example of something needing *containment* is:
   - ○ **A** a potted plant
   - ○ **B** a busy highway
   - ○ **C** a family gathering
   - ● **D** a chemical spill

7. Read this sentence.
   In a hydroponic garden, plants are grown in a solution that will *simulate* soil.

   Simulate means:
   - ● **A** copy or reproduce the features of
   - ○ **B** make more active or energetic
   - ○ **C** fool by disguise or trickery
   - ○ **D** improve the quality of

8. Someone who would most likely want to dress *incognito* is:
   - ○ **A** a local doctor
   - ● **B** a known criminal
   - ○ **C** a popular teacher
   - ○ **D** a political candidate

9. Something that is *inflammatory* will:
   - ○ **A** not catch on fire
   - ○ **B** have a soothing effect
   - ○ **C** likely go unnoticed
   - ● **D** stir up strong feelings

10. You often use *hyperbole* when you want to:
    - ○ **A** relate a serious story
    - ○ **B** make a good impression
    - ● **C** tell a funny anecdote
    - ○ **D** feel relaxed and content

If students answer B or C for Item 4, point out that three of the answers include correct definitions of *platform*, but only one is correct in the context of the sentence.

Synonyms and Antonyms

In the following Word Bank, you will find synonyms and antonyms for some of the words in Lessons 16–18. (Remember: Some words have both synonyms and antonyms.) Study these words; then complete the exercises below.

bold	**anonymous**	**commendable**	**deny**	**different**	**questionable**
alter	**circumstantial**	**confirm**	**sparse**	**outspoken**	**respectful**

A. For each sentence, fill in the blanks with a SYNONYM for the word in boldface.

1. I went to a **so-called** master chef to learn to cook, but I found his skills
   ___questionable___ when I saw him confuse the salt and sugar.

2. The young attorney had gathered **anecdotal** evidence he was sure would impress the jury,
   but his boss said he could not present it in court because it was ___circumstantial___.

3. Her grades are **exemplary**, and her extensive charitable work is also ___commendable___.

4. We know the new technology will **affect** athletes' performance, but just how it will
   ___alter___ the game, we do not know yet.

5. Delia got a/an ___anonymous___ note asking her to the dance, but how could she respond
   when the person who asked her was **incognito**?

B. For each sentence, fill in the blank with an ANTONYM for the word in boldface.

6. Janelle was extremely **diffident** and kept her opinions to herself, but her brother, who was
   ___outspoken___, said whatever was on his mind.

7. She claims that the two books are **analogous** in many ways, but I find them to be so
   ___different___ that her comparison does not make sense to me.

8. If he tries to ___deny___ that you were at the concert, you can show him your
   ticket stub to **verify** that you were there.

9. The toddler's **ceaseless** chatter nearly drove his mother crazy, but she knew when her child
   became a teen their communications would be ___sparse___ at best.

10. The twins were as different as could be: one was loud and **impertinent**, while the other
    was quiet and ___respectful___.

C CCSS Vocabulary: 4.a., 5, 6. (See pp. T16–17.)

Word Study: Proverbs

Some of the words in Lessons 16–18 have meanings related to proverbs. For example, *rhetoric* means "the use of speech to communicate well." The following proverbs offer advice about how to speak effectively: "Brevity is the soul of wit" and "Few words and many deeds."

Proverbs are brief, memorable sayings that state a common truth, such as "A fool and his money are soon parted" or "Lend your money and lose your friend." Use proverbs in your own writing to add interest to your work.

Practice

Read each sentence. Use context clues to figure out the meaning of each proverb in boldface. Then write the letter of the explanation for the proverb in the sentence.

___c___ **1.** Knowing that **he who hesitates is lost**, Keenan pointed his skis down the slope and took off.

___e___ **2.** Cheryl felt unprepared for the race, so her teammate said, **"If you can't take the heat, get out of the kitchen."**

___d___ **3.** Tina blamed Jess for starting the fight, but Leroy said, **"It takes two to make a quarrel."**

___g___ **4.** Grandpa listened to my plans for the summer and then warned, **"Don't bite off more than you can chew."**

___f___ **5.** Greg moped about his broken bicycle, until Dad got out his toolbox and said, **"It's better to light a candle than curse the darkness."**

___b___ **6.** Before the big race, Coach warned me not to start too fast, but **advice when most needed is least heeded**.

a. The child is very similar to his or her parent.

b. We often do not listen when we need help most.

c. Don't stop to think or you will lose your nerve.

d. No one can have a fight without an opponent.

e. It's better to quit if you can't handle the situation.

f. Instead of complaining, fix the situation.

g. Don't try to do more than you are able to accomplish.

Apply

Work with a partner to figure out the meaning of each proverb. (Use an online or print dictionary.) Then work together to write a sentence for each proverb.

1. You can't have your cake and eat it too.

2. Two wrongs don't make a right.

3. A friend in need is a friend indeed.

4. A picture is worth a thousand words.

5. Make hay while the sun shines.

6. One tree doesn't make a forest.

7. The squeaky wheel gets the grease.

8. A little knowledge is a dangerous thing.

Vocabulary for Comprehension

Read the following passage, in which some of the words you have studied in Lessons 16–18 appear in boldface type. Then answer questions 1–6.

Revolution in Bahrain

If you have any doubt about the power of the Internet to spark a revolution, then look no farther than Bahrain. This small, **albeit** wealthy, nation is made up of 33 islands located in the
5 Persian Gulf, off the coast of Saudi Arabia. Like its closest neighbor, Bahrain is rich with oil and governed by a royal family determined to maintain the **status quo**.

The members of the royal family have a habit of
10 **arbitrarily** taking large chunks of the choicest land on the islands for themselves. In 2011, a resident of Bahrain posted satellite images from the Internet showing side-by-side comparisons of the vast palaces and estates of the ruling
15 family and the crowded neighborhoods of poor citizens. To **confine** the many poor to such small areas, while **conversely** allowing just a few individuals to hoard huge swaths of prime waterfront property for their exclusive
20 enjoyment, was a situation that proved to be **inflammatory**. The images **eroded** respect for the ruling elite, and the **effect** was mass demonstrations and protests. The government found **containment** of the demonstrations to
25 be difficult, resulting in thousands of casualties. The citizens of Bahrain felt strongly that they needed to **revolutionize** their country.

If students choose C or D for Item 5, point out that the question is a NOT question and the answer should be the opposite of the word's meaning.

1. Another word for **albeit** (line 3) is
   ○ **A** because
   ○ **B** generally
   ● **C** nonetheless
   ○ **D** additionally

2. In sentence 3, **status quo** means
   ○ **A** the advantages of a group
   ● **B** the way things currently are
   ○ **C** the appearance of prosperity
   ○ **D** the goals of a group

3. Another word for **arbitrarily** (line 10) is
   ○ **A** quickly
   ○ **B** secretly
   ○ **C** greedily
   ● **D** randomly

4. The meaning of **confine** (line 16) is
   ● **A** limit
   ○ **B** reduce
   ○ **C** neglect
   ○ **D** maintain

5. Something that is **inflammatory** (line 21) will NOT
   ○ **A** catch on fire
   ● **B** calm people
   ○ **C** excite people
   ○ **D** cause a reaction

6. Another word for **revolutionize** (line 27) is
   ○ **A** rest
   ○ **B** resist
   ● **C** change
   ○ **D** manage

C CCSS Vocabulary: 4.a., 6; Reading (Informational Text): 4. (See pp. T16–17.)

LESSONS 16–18 ENRICHMENT

The Chemistry of 21st Century Adolescence

Watch a video introduction to this passage at **vocabularyforsuccess.com**.

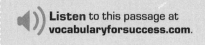**Listen** to this passage at **vocabularyforsuccess.com**.

C CCSS Vocabulary: 4; Reading (Informational Text): 4, 6. (See pp. T16–17.)

ADD and Food Additives: We Need More Science!

\<persuasive essay\>

Attention Deficit Disorder, or ADD, is a big problem in our schools today. Distracted, disruptive students make the peaceful ambience of an orderly classroom impossible to achieve. It's estimated that about 4.7 million American children, or 9.5 percent of boys and 5.9 percent of girls, have ADD. Some researchers, as well as parents, are convinced that food dyes and other additives worsen and possibly cause children's ADD symptoms. But much more evidence is needed to prove this connection.

Growing numbers of people, citing a 2007 study in Great Britain, are demanding that the government proscribe all use of food additives. In that study, scientists gave children ages 3 to 9 drinks containing food coloring and the preservative sodium benzoate. These children showed more symptoms of ADD than children who drank beverages containing no such additives. Nothing in the study, however, proves that food dyes and preservatives cause ADD. ADD's biochemistry—that is, the chemical processes that cause ADD—is not fully understood. Experts think that people with ADD have problems with the brain chemicals that carry nerve impulses. Studies have shown that, in people with ADD, the part of the brain that works to inhibit impulsive behavior is less active. Substances used in the study, like food colorings, might bring about ADD-like symptoms in children whose brain

chemistry is sensitive to them. However, those same substances may have no harmful effects on other children.

Should additives be banned, then, because of their possible effects on some people? That may be an example of throwing the baby out with the bathwater. Food dyes can make many foods look more appealing. Look at the red, yellow, and orange of fresh fruits and vegetables. These vibrant hues occur naturally, from pigments known as carotenoids. These same pigments give deciduous trees like maples their vivid coloration in the fall. The color of many processed foods is not appealing without food dyes. Butter is white. Pickles are a drab gray. As for preservatives, experts generally prescribe their use in foods to prevent spoiling. If preservatives prevent the growth of even one disease-causing pathogen, thereby protecting many people from serious illness, then it is not right to ban preservatives.

People who want the convenience, visual appeal, and safety of food containing dyes and preservatives should be able to make that choice. Those who wish to avoid such chemicals don't have to force everyone else to do without food additives. After all, they can buy organic food, food containing no additives, at both specialty markets and regular grocery stores.

Explain to students that a persuasive essay tries to convince the reader of the writer's point of view on a controversial topic. The writer has to give convincing reasons for his or her position in order to persuade the reader.

In the United States, the Food and Drug Administration says the food additives tested in the British study are safe. Without proof that dyes and preservatives are harmful, the imposition of a ban on these substances would be wrong. What's needed is more research. This research should be evaluated by an independent panel of experts who can make an informed ruling. Perhaps the United States could form a group similar to the Food and Drink Federation of the United Kingdom. This group of food producers works in part to ensure that food in the UK is safe for consumers. With more study and better communication, we'll all eventually be able to agree on a sane policy on food additives that makes sense for everyone.

Above: Organic vegetables at a farmer's market

Right: Food dye preparations

VOCABULARY

ambience	deciduous	organic
proscribe	prescribe	imposition
biochemistry	pathogen	panel
inhibit	thereby	federation

TALK ABOUT IT

With a partner, answer the questions below. Use as many of the highlighted words in the selection as you can.

1. How would you feel if the government were to *proscribe* food dyes and preservatives?

2. Do you prefer *organic* food to conventional food? Why or why not?

Word Meanings

For each highlighted word on pages 210–211, the meaning or meanings are given below.

For practice with synonyms, see page 240.

1. **ambience** (AM-bee-uhns) **n.** the tone, feeling, or character associated with a place, person, or thing. Emotional tone, visual qualities, sounds, smells, and other sensory details work together to create a specific *ambience*. **SYNONYMS:** aura, flavor

2. **biochemistry** (bye-oh-KEM-is-tree) **n.** chemical processes that happen inside living things. *Biochemistry* determines processes such as the function of organ systems in animals, photosynthesis in plants, and other processes. **SYNONYM:** chemistry of life

3. **deciduous** (di-SIJ-oo-uhss) **adj.** describing a tree or shrub that sheds its leaves seasonally. *Deciduous* trees in temperate regions of North America are generally full of colorful leaves during the autumn. **adj.** impermanent; temporary. Something that is *deciduous* does not last. **SYNONYMS:** ephemeral, fleeting, transient

4. **federation** (fed-uh-RAY-shuhn) **n.** a political or social group made up of smaller units that usually have a degree of independence. The United States is a *federation* of states. **SYNONYMS:** league, confederation, union, partnership, alliance, coalition

5. **imposition** (im-puh-ZISH-uhn) **n.** the act of establishing by authority or force. The *imposition* of a tax may be unpopular with citizens. **SYNONYMS:** levy, infliction, forcing; **n.** a burden or inconvenience caused by being overly demanding of someone's time or attention. Polite people want to stay overnight at friends' homes only if it is not an *imposition*. **SYNONYMS:** nuisance, strain, bother

6. **inhibit** (in-HIB-it) **v.** to prevent or restrain something from happening or a person from doing something or acting in a certain way. Preservatives in food *inhibit* the growth of mold and bacteria. **SYNONYMS:** impede, hinder, retard, curb, suppress, thwart

7. **organic** (or-GAN-ik) **adj.** describing food produced without the use of chemicals, drugs, and other artificial substances. *Organic* produce is grown without pesticides. **SYNONYM:** natural; **adj.** relating to living matter. Soil is part *organic* matter and part minerals. **SYNONYM:** biological; **adj.** fitting together harmoniously into a whole. A piece of art that is *organic* gives a sense of being complete. **SYNONYMS:** essential, integral, intrinsic, fundamental

CCSS Vocabulary: 4.c., 4.d. (See pp. T16–17.)

Watch a video introduction for each word at **vocabularyforsuccess.com**.

Listen to iWords at **vocabularyforsuccess.com**.

Refer to the online dictionary at **vocabularyforsuccess.com**.

8. **panel** (PAN-uhl) **n.** a group of people chosen to decide a particular issue. Sports competitions have a *panel* of judges. **SYNONYMS:** group, team, body, committee; **n.** a thin rectangular piece of wood or other material forming part of a building or vehicle. A car's door contains a side *panel*. **SYNONYMS:** section, board, pane, plate

9. **pathogen** (PATH-uh-juhn) **n.** an organism that causes disease. Bacteria and viruses are among the *pathogens* that can cause illness. **SYNONYM:** disease-causing agent

10. **prescribe** (pri-SKRIBE) **v.** to recommend an action or substance that is beneficial. A doctor may *prescribe* exercise for an overweight person. **SYNONYMS:** recommend, suggest; **v.** to give a direction or a rule. A government may *prescribe* certain rules, laws, and regulations. **SYNONYMS:** lay down, stipulate, order

11. **proscribe** (pro-SKRIBE) **v.** to forbid as harmful, especially by law. City ordinances may *proscribe* certain activities, such as littering and riding a bike on sidewalks. **SYNONYMS:** ban, prohibit, bar, outlaw, disallow

12. **thereby** (THAIR-bye) **adv.** as a result of that, in that way. People open bank accounts, *thereby* ensuring that their money is safe. **SYNONYM:** by that means

More on Meanings: Confusing Word Pairs

The English language contains numerous pairs of words that are commonly confused. The words may sound similar and have related meanings:

After a hot afternoon doing yard work, I **prescribe** lemonade and a long nap!

Our state is going to **proscribe** the use of cell phones while driving.

Prescribe and *proscribe* sound similar, and their meanings are related because they are nearly antonyms. *Prescribe* means "to recommend something," while *proscribe* means "to forbid something."

Other words may sound alike but have completely different meanings:

Darryl's family took in a paying **boarder**.

El Paso is on the **border** of Texas and Mexico.

Here, *boarder* is "a person who rents a room in someone's home," while *border* is "a political or geographical dividing line."

Challenge Choose one word pair below. Use both words correctly in the same sentence.

secede, succeed   *marshal, martial*
device, devise

Have students identify what makes these word pairs confusing. Point out that using memory aids, or mnemonic devices, can help students remember meanings.

Word Talk

Each lesson word has been placed in a category. With a partner, discuss and list items that belong in each category. Compare your results with those of another pair of students.

CCSS Vocabulary: 6. (See pp. T16–17.)

Things a Doctor May *Prescribe*

more rest, medications, more exercise, vitamins

Things That *Biochemistry* May Help Explain

how yeast makes bread rise, how photosynthesis occurs, why muscles hurt after excessive exercise

---

Words Associated with *Organic* Foods

healthy, safe, nutritious, from the earth

Things That a *Deciduous* Tree Does

turns color in the fall, loses its leaves, gets bare in winter, gets new leaves in the spring

---

Phrases You Might Use in Place of *Thereby*

and so, and for that reason

How You Might Protect Yourself Against *Pathogens*

wash your hands often, cook food thoroughly, don't share drinking cups, keep leftovers cold

---

Elements That Contribute to a Museum's *Ambience*

lighting, noise level, colors, decor

Things That People Might Want to *Inhibit*

spread of disease, viruses in a computer, poverty, coughing during a play

---

Topics That a *Panel* of Experts Might Talk About

climate change, nuclear disarmament, yesterday's football games, unemployment in America

---

Groups That Can Form a *Federation*

sports leagues, states, countries, professional associations

Conduct That a Movie Theater Is Likely to *Proscribe*

talking or texting on a cell phone, talking during the movie, kicking or putting your feet up on the seat in front of you

---

Types of *Imposition* That May Be Unpopular

higher taxes, early curfews, higher ticket prices for movies

Check for Understanding

Choose the lesson word that completes each sentence. Write the word on the line provided. Some words will be used twice.

ambience	federation	organic	prescribe
biochemistry	imposition	panel	proscribe
deciduous	inhibit	pathogen	thereby

1. Many different labor unions formed a/an _____federation_____ because they were more powerful when working together.

2. The neighbor's dog barked loudly in the morning, _____thereby_____ waking everyone in our house.

3. Rashida studied _____biochemistry_____ to learn more about how snake venom works.

4. Many people end up in the hospital each year from food poisoning caused by *E. coli*, a/an _____pathogen_____ found in meat and dairy products.

5. My quiet friend prefers neighborhoods with a peaceful, rural _____ambience_____.

6. While camping, James sealed all his food in a steel drum to _____inhibit_____ raccoons from stealing it.

7. _____Deciduous_____ trees are most common in places with distinct changes of season.

8. Natalie's parents gave her freedom, but they did _____proscribe_____ staying out late.

9. Congress convened a/an _____panel_____ to review official data about the economy.

10. One way to control pests in a/an _____organic_____ garden is with the use of nets.

11. The students heard there will be a/an _____imposition_____ of stricter dress code rules.

12. Staring at Nina's parrot made it anxious and would _____inhibit_____ it from talking.

13. I buried a key by the door, _____thereby_____ ensuring that I won't be locked out.

14. The doctor decided to _____prescribe_____ ice and elevation for Claude's sprained ankle.

If students complete Item 8 with *prescribe*, remind them to pay attention to context clues in the sentence. The words *but* and *staying out late* following *freedom* indicate that something is being forbidden (*proscribed*), not recommended (*prescribed*).

Word Associations

Use what you know about the lesson words in italics to answer each question. Circle the letter next to the phrase that best answers the question. Be prepared to explain your answers.

1. What do leaves on a *deciduous* tree do?

   a. stay red all winter
   b. drop in the fall
   c. lose their green in spring

2. Which of the following exclamations is meant to *inhibit* someone?

   a. "Wow!"
   b. "Halt!"
   c. "Perfect!"

3. Which of these is an example of something your school could *prescribe* for students?

   a. an announcement about a new school website
   b. a message about changes in the cafeteria menu
   c. a rule that all students wear uniforms

4. Which professional would need to know *biochemistry*?

   a. a doctor
   b. a lawyer
   c. an urban planner

5. What word best describes the *ambience* of a theater with red velvet curtains and lots of gold paint?

   a. relaxed
   b. convenient
   c. elegant

6. Which of these would most likely be described as *organic*?

   a. sugarless gum
   b. aerosol cheese
   c. grass-fed beef

7. How might houseguests make sure they're not an *imposition*?

   a. borrow the host's car
   b. make their beds
   c. help themselves to whatever is in the fridge

8. Which sentence is best completed with the word *thereby*?

   a. Baxter arrived early, _____ making sure he got a good seat.
   b. Bonnie had a cold, _____ her nose was stuffed.
   c. Burt explained methods _____ weeds could be controlled.

9. What might a *panel* be useful for?

   a. hiding a flaw in a plaster wall
   b. supporting a bridge
   c. forming part of a sidewalk

10. Which of the following sayings best represents the idea of *federation*?

    a. He who laughs last laughs best.
    b. Out of many, one.
    c. Every man for himself.

11. Which of these is a *pathogen*?

    a. a disease called malaria
    b. the protozoan that causes malaria
    c. the medicine that treats malaria

12. Why would a city *proscribe* bicycling on sidewalks?

    a. to hinder cyclists' fun
    b. to allow cyclists faster rides on streets
    c. to ensure the safety of pedestrians

216   **C** CCSS Vocabulary: 4.a. (See pp. T16–17.)

Check Again

Use what you know about the lesson words in italics to complete each sentence. Be sure your sentences make sense.

1. Coaches often *prescribe* weightlifting and cardio exercises to ___build strength and endurance.___

2. Because the Carter family's home was surrounded by *deciduous* trees, in the fall they ___had a lot of___ raking to do.

3. Lin wanted to change the *ambience* of her bedroom, so she ___painted it a brighter color.___

4. You wouldn't want any kind of *pathogen* to grow in your food because ___you wouldn't want to get___ sick from eating it.

5. To examine flooding problems, the city assembled a *panel* of ___damming experts and engineers.___

6. A group of athletic clubs formed a *federation* because ___they wanted to share ideas and pool resources.___

7. Svetlana locked her bike securely to a bike rack, *thereby* ___making sure it did not get stolen.___

8. Roger believed that his shyness might *inhibit* his social progress, so he ___took a course in public___ speaking.

9. When asked what activities she would *proscribe* to improve safety at the public pool, the director suggested ___running on slippery surfaces and horseplay.___

10. Hejun chose *organic* grapes to ___avoid exposure to pesticides.___

11. Dahlia studied *biochemistry* to prepare for a career in ___medical research.___

12. The *imposition* of parking restrictions along the parade route served to ___enable the parade___ to come off smoothly.

Write Your Own

Reread the passage on pages 210–211. Then, on a separate sheet of paper, write a one-paragraph response to the question, "Why are dyes and preservatives used in food?" Use at least two words from the lesson and support your answer by referring to the text of the passage.

Word-Solving Strategies: Context Clues

Embedded Definitions

Writers often define a difficult word within the body of the text. This technique is called an embedded definition. Read this sentence from "ADD and Food Additives: We Need More Science!":

ADD's biochemistry—that is, the chemical processes that cause ADD—is not fully understood.

Embedded definitions are usually signaled by punctuation, a phrase, or both. Dashes are often used to set off definitions. Words or phrases such as *or*, *that is*, *in other words*, and *which* are also often used. Here, the definition is set off by commas:

After all, they can buy organic food, food containing no additives, at both specialty markets and regular grocery stores.

An embedded definition may come before or after the term being defined. Here, "disease-causing" defines the term:

If preservatives prevent the growth of even one disease-causing pathogen, thereby protecting many people from serious illness, then it is not right to ban preservatives.

BE CAREFUL!

Although the word *or* often signals a synonym or a definition, it does not always. Read this sentence from the passage:

It's estimated that about 4.7 million American children, or 9.5 percent of boys and 5.9 percent of girls, have ADD.

Here, *or* signals further information on the figure 4.7 million, presenting it in percentages.

Practice

Write four sentences using each of the highlighted words in the paragraph below. Use embedded definitions as context clues in your sentences.

Should food be judged simply as sustenance—how well it provides energy and nutrition—or on its flavor and appearance? Connoisseurs favor the latter approach, and they've assiduous in evaluating the taste and texture of foods, carefully analyzing each bite. As for me, a pile of bitter and acrid greens has no appeal. I could let bugs eat all the garden greens, as long as I can eat pizza!

1. _____ Corn provided our main source of nutrition, giving us a basic level of sustenance. _____

2. _____ The art connoisseurs—expert judges of style—scoffed at the amateurs' watercolors. _____

3. _____ Johnny was assiduous, or precise and thorough, in his preparation for his hiking trip. _____

4. _____ The smoke that filled the room after the TV blew up was acrid—a bitter, biting smell. _____

C CCSS Vocabulary: 4.a.; Reading (Informational Text): 4. (See pp. T16–17.)

Practice for Tests

For a quiz and additional practice for this lesson, go to **vocabularyforsuccess.com**.

Fill in the bubble next to the answer that best completes the sentence or answers the question.

1. For pedestrian safety, you might *prescribe:*
   - ○ **A** jaywalking
   - ○ **B** riding bikes on the sidewalk
   - ○ **C** a higher speed limit
   - ● **D** an extra crossing guard

2. A plant that is *deciduous* is:
   - ○ **A** an orchid
   - ○ **B** a cactus
   - ○ **C** a pine tree
   - ● **D** an oak tree

3. Read this sentence.

   His allergy was a result of *biochemistry*.

   Biochemistry means:
   - ● **A** chemical makeup
   - ○ **B** personal food preferences
   - ○ **C** inherited tendencies
   - ○ **D** environment

4. An example of a *federation* would be:
   - ● **A** a national association of orchestras
   - ○ **B** fans of science fiction movies
   - ○ **C** your state government
   - ○ **D** graduates of the same college

5. Senator Wiggins wanted to make drinking water safer, so she proposed a bill that would *proscribe*:
   - ○ **A** the sale of "green" cleaning products in stores
   - ● **B** the use of pesticides near rivers
   - ○ **C** increased water testing
   - ○ **D** the building of more sewage treatment plants

If students choose A, C, or D for Item 5, review the meaning of *proscribe*. Point out that the thing being proscribed, or banned, has to be something that makes drinking water unsafe, not safer.

6. To achieve an *organic* expression of family life, the playwright would use staging that:
   - ○ **A** has black and white geometric shapes
   - ○ **B** is bare and brightly lit
   - ● **C** shows all the bedrooms of the home
   - ○ **D** has bleachers for a marching band

7. Read this sentence.

   The meeting with the *panel* of national park directors convinced Enrico to study forestry.

   Panel means:
   - ○ **A** platoon
   - ○ **B** meeting
   - ○ **C** association
   - ● **D** small group

8. If you like the *ambience* of a place, you like its:
   - ○ **A** advertising
   - ● **B** mood
   - ○ **C** price
   - ○ **D** aroma

9. One way to avoid picking up a *pathogen* in a locker room is to:
   - ○ **A** talk only to people you know
   - ○ **B** keep your belongings locked up securely
   - ● **C** never go barefoot
   - ○ **D** bring a change of clothes

10. To NOT *inhibit* something, you would:
    - ○ **A** stop it
    - ● **B** let it grow
    - ○ **C** make it end
    - ○ **D** stifle it

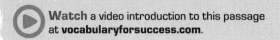
Watch a video introduction to this passage at **vocabularyforsuccess.com**.

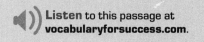
Listen to this passage at **vocabularyforsuccess.com**.

CCSS Vocabulary: 4; Reading (Informational Text): 4, 6. (See pp. T16–17.)

My Sunscreen Summer

\<journal entry\>

May 16 All my hard work acing AP chemistry, biochemistry, and advanced business has seemingly paid off! Silver & Ferris Inc., a company that makes every kind of cosmetic you can imagine, has offered me a summer internship. It's an honor and a great opportunity to have an internship in a real scientific lab where new products are created.

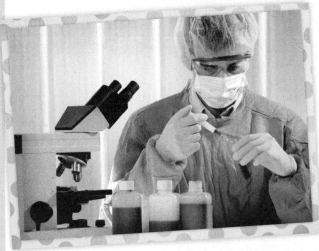

Testing sunscreen thickening agents at the lab

June 24 I've been on the job only a week now, and I'm already part of a team working on improving a moisturizing sunscreen. Sunscreens contain chemical substances that absorb or reflect the wavelengths of sunlight that cause sunburn. Sunburn can eventually lead to skin cancer, so I'm lucky to be working on something that might help reduce the incidence of this deadly disease. But while sunscreens can negate the harmful

effects of sun exposure, they can also block out the beneficial, cancer-fighting effects of Vitamin D from the sun. And some sunscreen ingredients, like artificial fragrances and petroleum products, may actually cause skin cancers. Our goal is to develop a natural, nontoxic sunscreen that protects while helping to heal previous sun damage. Talk about a challenge!

July 10 I'm learning a lot about moisturizers. A moisturizer is a preparation that helps hold water in the skin. The juice of the aloe vera plant is an excellent moisturizer. We're planning to incorporate an extract made from aloe vera juice into our new version of the sunscreen.

July 19 This week we worked on thickening agents for our sunscreen. We're experimenting with various polymers, which are substances made in labs from natural materials. The polymers we're testing expand when they're mixed up, making a nice, thick cream. I helped measure out the polymer, and I got to operate the machine that we use to agitate the mixture. But when we took it out of the machine, it was a lumpy mess. The only thing we accomplished was to coagulate the mixture. Back to the drawing board, as they say!

July 24 Whew, this is turning out to be challenging week! We've been having problems with our suppliers. The new polymers we

VOCABULARY

seemingly	extract	assurance
cosmetic	version	ambiguous
incidence	agitate	castigate
negate	coagulate	epiphany

needed for thickening our sunscreen didn't arrive on time. The lab director had me, of all people, call to find out why they were delayed. The person I talked to gave me assurance that the samples had been shipped, but when I asked for more information so I could track the package, his answers were really ambiguous. When I told the lab director that I couldn't get any information, he looked very upset. I was afraid he was going to castigate me, but he just went into his office and fumed silently for the rest of the day. He's under a lot of pressure to get the new formula to work.

August 9 We've been trying to get exactly the right formula of aloe, thickener, moisturizer, and sunscreen, but when we adjust one ingredient for a desired effect, it ruins another desired effect. But today I had an epiphany! I realized that if we used a small amount of beeswax, it could make the texture thick but smooth, the way we want it. I told the lab director; we tried it; and it worked. It's not perfect, but we're on the right track. We ordered in pizza and everyone toasted me with sparkling mineral water. I can't wait till I can get a real job here!

TALK ABOUT IT

With a partner, answer the questions below. Use as many of the highlighted words in the selection as you can.

1. Even though more people are using sunscreen to *negate* the harmful effects of sun exposure, the *incidence* of skin cancer has not decreased. What might be some reasons for this?

2. Have you ever had an *epiphany* that helped you solve a problem? Explain.

An aloe vera plant, useful for its skin-soothing qualities

A family walking along a beach is exposed to skin-damaging UV rays.

Word Meanings

For each highlighted word on pages 220–221, the meaning or meanings are given below.

For practice with synonyms, see page 240.

1. **agitate** (AJ-uh-tate) **v.** to stir briskly. If you *agitate* something, you shake it up. SYNONYMS: whisk, beat; **v.** to cause a person to feel nervous or troubled. A person who is easy to *agitate* gets upset at little things. SYNONYMS: perturb, disturb

2. **ambiguous** (am-BIG-yoo-uhss) **adj.** unclear, lacking in clarity. If you get *ambiguous* answers to a question, you will have to ask for clarification. SYNONYMS: vague, uncertain

3. **assurance** (uh-SHUR-uhnss) **n.** a statement intended to give confidence. If you want *assurance*, you need to be told that something will happen without a doubt. SYNONYMS: guarantee, promise; **n.** self-confidence. A sense of *assurance* while you take a test will help you perform better. SYNONYMS: nerve, poise, aplomb

4. **castigate** (KASS-tuh-gate) **v.** to scold severely. A parent may *castigate* a child for doing something that endangers her. SYNONYMS: reprimand, upbraid, berate

5. **coagulate** (koh-AG-yoo-late) **v.** to cause to change from a liquid to a solid or nearly solid state. Adding pectin to a boiling mixture of fruit and sugar causes the liquid to *coagulate* and become jam. SYNONYMS: thicken, congeal, jell, set; **v.** to form a thick mass or group by coming together. In normal circumstances, blood will *coagulate* around a wound to stop it from bleeding. SYNONYM: clot

6. **cosmetic** (koz-MET-ik) **n.** a product applied to the body to improve appearance. Eyeliner is a popular type of *cosmetic*. SYNONYM: makeup; **adj.** done for the sake of appearance. *Cosmetic* repairs to the roof made it look nice but didn't stop the leak. SYNONYMS: beautifying, external, outward, on the surface

7. **epiphany** (i-PIF-uh-nee) **n.** a simple, sudden, surprising insight. If you have an *epiphany*, you come to a realization about something. SYNONYMS: revelation, intuition

8. **extract** (EK-strakt) **n.** a solution in which the active ingredient is highly concentrated. Vanilla *extract* gives a strong taste and smell of vanilla. SYNONYMS: essence, distillate; (ek-STRAKT) **v.** to withdraw or remove, usually by force. To *extract* something, like a tooth, you have to pull it out. SYNONYMS: yank, dig out

C CCSS Vocabulary: 4.c., 4.d. (See pp. T16–17.)

Watch a video introduction for each word at **vocabularyforsuccess.com**.

Listen to iWords 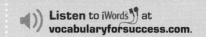 at **vocabularyforsuccess.com**.

Refer to the online dictionary at **vocabularyforsuccess.com**.

9. **incidence** (IN-suh-duhnss) **n.** the rate or frequency of something. The *incidence* of car accidents on that road showed that a guard rail needed to be built.
SYNONYMS: prevalence, extent, amount

10. **negate** (ni-GATE) **v.** to cause to be ineffective, to wipe out. One week of laziness can *negate* a semester's worth of hard work. **SYNONYMS:** nullify, reverse, undo

11. **seemingly** (SEEM-ing-lee) **adv.** done in a way that gives the impression of a particular attribute or characteristic. The *seemingly* wealthy businessman wore a dark suit and expensive shoes. **SYNONYMS:** apparently, outwardly

12. **version** (VUR-zhuhn) **n.** a form of something that differs from other forms of the same kind of thing. A particular singer's *version* of a song is different from another singer's version of the same song. **SYNONYMS:** sort, variety

More on Meanings: Denotation and Connotation

Denotation and connotation are two ways of looking at word meanings. Every word in the English language has a surface meaning—known as its *denotation*—which is what the word means according to the dictionary. But underneath this surface meaning is a word's *connotation*, or association. A connotation is made up of other meanings, or more accurately, attitudes and emotions that attach to the word based not only on its origin but also on tradition and usage.

Read these two sentences:

Mr. Gale would not let the clerk **castigate** his children for running in the store.

Mr. Gale would not let the clerk **admonish** his children for running in the store.

In both sentences, Mr. Gale is preventing a store clerk from correcting his children for running in the store. In the first sentence, Mr. Gale is seen as protecting his children from a mean clerk, because *castigate* has the connotation of a severe tongue-lashing. In the second sentence, though, Mr. Gale might be allowing his children to misbehave, since *admonish* has a gentler connotation: the store clerk might actually be looking out for the children's safety.

The connotation of words can be positive, negative, or neutral. If you don't know a word's connotation, consult an online dictionary and verify the word's meaning and its association.

Challenge Choose two of the words below. For each word, suggest two synonyms, each with a different connotation. Then use each synonym in a sentence that suggests its connotation.

absurd	*excursion*	*distress*
buy	*tread*	*forceful*

If students have trouble understanding the concept of connotation, review the nuances of positive and negative connotations of words.

C CCSS Vocabulary: 5.b. (See pp. T16–17.)

vocabularyforsuccess.com 223

Word Talk

Each lesson word has been placed in a category. With a partner, discuss and list items that belong in each category. Compare your results with those of another pair of students.

C CCSS Vocabulary: 6. (See pp. T16–17.)

Activities That Are *Seemingly* Good for You

jogging, eating vitamin-fortified breakfast cereal, eating reduced-fat snacks

Times When a Person May Need *Assurance*

when trying to make a difficult decision, when going in for surgery, when making up after an argument

Substances That Can *Coagulate*

blood, jelly, gelatin, custard

Exclamations That Signal an *Epiphany*

"Eureka!" "I get it!" "I see!" "That's it!"

Situations About Which More Than One *Version* of a Story Might Be Told

a car accident, an argument between friends, a conflict with a classmate or co-worker

Attributes of a *Cosmetic*

protects your skin, makes you look good, helps your complexion

Signs That a Person Is Being *Ambiguous*

clearing their throat, not making eye contact, not being direct

Things That Could *Negate* a Fun Camping Trip

running out of food, allergy attack, thunderstorm, an animal or insect invasion

Uses for an *Extract*

to put flavor in cooking, to put a scent into something, to add healing attributes to something

Things That Raise the *Incidence* of Flu

sharing utensils, not washing your hands, exposure to people who have the flu

Deeds for Which One Might *Castigate* Another Person

lying, stealing, being a hypocrite, saying something insulting

Things That You Typically *Agitate*

bottle of orange juice, can of paint, whipped cream in pressurized can

Check for Understanding

Choose the lesson word that completes each sentence. Write the word on the line provided. Some words will be used twice.

agitate	castigate	epiphany	negate
ambiguous	coagulate	extract	seemingly
assurance	cosmetic	incidence	version

1. The store had more than one _____version_____ of rice noodles, so I had to choose one.

2. A/an _____cosmetic_____ that has additional ingredients can help control acne.

3. One hungry rabbit can _____negate_____ weeks of careful gardening.

4. Mrs. Childs needed _____assurance_____ that her daughter was doing fine at camp.

5. A washing machine should _____agitate_____ clothes to clean them effectively.

6. After Paulette had her _____epiphany_____ about what her family meant to her, she no longer took them for granted.

7. Gretchen preferred the _____version_____ of the skirt with the elastic waist better than the one with the zipper.

8. A natural cure for headaches is a/an _____extract_____ of an herb called feverfew.

9. The document had the correct signatures, so it was _____seemingly_____ authentic, but it still had to be proven.

10. If I make a mistake, my boss shouldn't _____castigate_____ me in front of customers.

11. _____Ambiguous_____ statements from the twins about how the ketchup got onto the ceiling did not convince Mom of their innocence.

12. Bonnie's shampoo with avocado _____extract_____ made her hair smooth and shiny.

13. I dropped egg whites into boiling water to watch them _____coagulate_____ into clumps.

14. The rising _____incidence_____ of texting is in the news a lot these days.

If students answer *assurance* for Item 6, discuss the meanings of *assurance* and *epiphany*.

Word Associations

Use what you know about the lesson words in italics to answer each question. Circle the letter next to the phrase that best answers the question. Be prepared to explain your answers.

1. How might a person feel after having an *epiphany?*

   a. confused
   b. bewildered
   c. relieved *(circled)*

2. Which of these behaviors might *agitate* your best friend?

   a. giving the friend a present for no reason
   b. meeting the friend at a movie theater twenty minutes late *(circled)*
   c. inviting the friend to go to a concert

3. Which might be an alternate *version* of a written story?

   a. a movie *(circled)*
   b. a book
   c. a confession

4. Which is a *cosmetic* improvement?

   a. new paint on an old house *(circled)*
   b. a rebuilt car engine
   c. a cast on a broken arm

5. Which of the following best describes a way to *extract* something that is stuck?

   a. Turn upside down and shake gently.
   b. Grab it and yank hard. *(circled)*
   c. Heat it over a flame.

6. What would likely happen to a restaurant with a high *incidence* of food poisoning?

   a. It would get new customers.
   b. It would have its business license renewed.
   c. It would be closed down. *(circled)*

7. Which of these might signal that a person is being *ambiguous?*

   a. lack of eye contact *(circled)*
   b. a cheerful smile
   c. saying, "I love you"

8. How might a person express *assurance* when skiing?

   a. take the expert slope *(circled)*
   b. study the trail map
   c. wear a crash helmet

9. Which of these people is *seemingly* tired?

   a. the one who says "Boy, am I tired."
   b. the one whose shoulders are drooping *(circled)*
   c. the one who volunteers to help mow the lawn

10. What happens when blood starts to *coagulate?*

    a. It gets redder.
    b. It stops flowing. *(circled)*
    c. It spurts.

11. How might someone best *negate* the statement, "All apples are red"?

    a. Find a green apple. *(circled)*
    b. Say, "All bananas have brown spots."
    c. Peel a red apple.

12. What tone of voice would one likely use to *castigate* another person?

    a. questioning
    b. enthusiastic
    c. harsh *(circled)*

CCSS Vocabulary: 4.a. (See pp. T16–17.)

Check Again

Use what you know about the lesson word in italics to complete each sentence. Be sure your sentences make sense.

1. Molly had a *cosmetic* bag in which she kept _____ face cream, eye shadow, and mascara.

2. The *incidence* of bacterial infection went up after _____ the city stopped testing the water.

3. Mr. Kim could navigate the traffic on the busy expressway with *assurance* because _____ he had been a race car driver back in his native Korea.

4. The orange *extract* gave the dessert _____ a refreshing citrus flavor.

5. The pop *version* of the song differed from the original full-length version in that _____ it was much shorter.

6. Uncle Harry's answers to the questions were *ambiguous,* and we wondered _____ if he was hiding something that he didn't want to talk about.

7. If you leave the buttermilk out, it might *coagulate,* and if it does, _____ you won't be able to pour it.

8. After thinking about looking for a summer job for three months, Shawn had an *epiphany* that _____ maybe she should put in some applications.

9. The footbridge was *seemingly* solid, so _____ we walked over it carefully.

10. Natasha was a fair boss and would never *castigate* someone for _____ making an honest mistake.

11. You know I like to relax when I eat my lunch, so don't *agitate* me by _____ making me eat too fast.

12. It was simple to *negate* the heat of the summer by _____ jumping in the cool water.

Write Your Own

1. **What is the one thing that irritates you the most? Answer the question in a 10-word sentence using the word *agitate* in the fourth position.**

   Several things can agitate me, but the worst is rudeness.

2. **Write a 12-word sentence using the word *assurance* in the last position.**

   Steady confidence gives one the power to tackle any job with assurance.

Word-Solving Strategies:
Latin and Greek Roots

Latin Roots ag, ig: "move, act, or drive"

The roots *ag* and *ig* both come from the Latin *agere*, which means "to do, move, drive, lead, or act." Several words in this lesson have their origins in the Latin *agere*.

Agitate, which means "to move vigorously to and fro" or "shake," derives directly from the Latin *agitare*, or "to put in constant motion," which originates with *agere*.

Now let's look at the word *castigate*. This word derives from the Latin *castus*, or "pure," plus *agere*, "to do." You can see how the definition "to scold severely" comes from the idea of making someone pure by correcting him or her.

Another word is *coagulate*, from the Latin *coagere*, or "curdle." The prefix *co-* is derived from the prefix *com-*, which means "together,"

plus *agere*. Knowing this, you can figure out that *coagulate* means "to cause to come together."

A Third Example

Look at the word *ambiguous*. You can use the meaning of the prefix and the root to figure out the meaning of the word.

ambi- → about

agere → move or go

Its literal meaning is "to go about, or wander," which leads to the definition "to have a double meaning, to change or shift."

BE CAREFUL!

Some words may look like they have the same root, but that's not always so. You might think that *ig* in *ignored* is the same as the root *ig* in *castigate* and infer that the word originated in the concept of moving or doing. But you would be wrong. The *ig* in *ignored* is a combination of the prefix *-in*, meaning "not," and the Latin root *gno*, meaning "to know." The familiar meaning of *ignore*: "not knowing."

Practice

Read each sentence below. Then use what you know about the Latin root word parts *ig* or *ag* to write the meaning of the word in italics. Check your answers in a dictionary.

1. The *agenda* of the meeting was distributed a week ahead of time.

a list of actions to be taken

_____

2. Morris had to *fumigate* his apartment to get rid of termites.

the act of using fumes to drive out a pest

_____

3. Like a true *pedagogue*, Teresa didn't let the kids in class get away with a thing.

one who acts in a formal, strict manner

_____

4. *Navigation* on the inland waterways was easy with GPS.

figuring out the best course for moving

from place to place

Practice for Tests

For a quiz and additional practice for this lesson, go to **vocabularyforsuccess.com**.

Fill in the bubble next to the answer that best completes the sentence or answers the question.

1. A remark that is *seemingly* innocent:
   - ○ **A** will hurt someone's feelings
   - ○ **B** is quite humorous
   - ○ **C** is delivered with a wink
   - ● **D** sounds okay but might not be

2. A liquid that has had something added to it to make it *coagulate* will become:
   - ○ **A** yellow
   - ○ **B** steaming
   - ○ **C** clear
   - ● **D** thicker

3. You would add lemon *extract* to a cake recipe if you wanted to:
   - ● **A** give the cake a lemon flavor
   - ○ **B** sweeten the cake
   - ○ **C** make the cake moist
   - ○ **D** make the cake taste less like lemon

4. An example of a time that you might have to *castigate* someone is:
   - ● **A** when you see danger
   - ○ **B** when all is well
   - ○ **C** when you first arrive somewhere
   - ○ **D** when a project is successful

5. Read this sentence.

   One big wind can *negate* a week's worth of nest-building by the poor robins.

   Negate means:
   - ○ **A** turn around
   - ● **B** destroy
   - ○ **C** imitate
   - ○ **D** reinforce

6. Read this sentence.

   When asked why his cell phone bill was so high, Emilio's answer was *ambiguous*.

   Ambiguous means:
   - ○ **A** detailed
   - ○ **B** humorous
   - ● **C** unclear
   - ○ **D** brief

7. *Cosmetic* improvements to the playground equipment made it:
   - ○ **A** sturdier
   - ○ **B** easier to use
   - ○ **C** safer
   - ● **D** more inviting

8. If you need someone's *assurance* about something, you are looking for:
   - ○ **A** an objection
   - ● **B** a promise
   - ○ **C** permission
   - ○ **D** a review

9. Sheldon said that when he had the *epiphany*, it seemed as though:
   - ○ **A** a door had closed
   - ○ **B** a fog had descended
   - ● **C** a light had gone on
   - ○ **D** an era had ended

10. People who do NOT let things *agitate* them are generally:
    - ○ **A** loyal
    - ● **B** calm
    - ○ **C** sickly
    - ○ **D** upset

If students answer A, B, or C for Item 7, remind them that a cosmetic improvement is only superficial and changes only the looks of something; it does not increase sturdiness, ease of use, or safety.

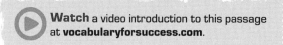
Watch a video introduction to this passage at **vocabularyforsuccess.com**.

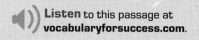
Listen to this passage at **vocabularyforsuccess.com**.

CCSS Vocabulary: 4; Reading (Informational Text): 4, 6. (See pp. T16–17.)

Reversing Antibiotic Resistance

\<debate\>

Moderator: Welcome to the state finals of the Senior Debate League. Our regional champions, Keith and Carmen, are here to debate a very important issue: antibiotic resistance. First, let's have some background. Antibiotics are drugs that target the causes of various afflictions: bacteria, fungi, and parasites. When researchers developed the first antibiotics in the 1940s, the drugs cured diseases that formerly led to suffering, permanent disability, and even death. But in recent decades, excessive use of antibiotics has led to the evolution of pathogens that are no longer killed by the antibiotics. As a result, all over the world antibiotics are increasingly failing to neutralize some infections that previously were easily cured.

Whereas our debaters agree on the adverse consequences of over-prescription of antibiotics, they disagree on how we should tackle this problem. Keith, let's hear from you first.

Keith: I don't mean to be facetious, but I'm really "bugged" by doctors who prescribe antibiotics when they know it's not appropriate. Doctors have too much leeway today for prescribing antibiotics. Many of their patients think antibiotics

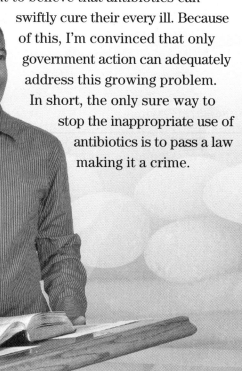

are a quick way to find relief from symptoms of the common cold, the flu, and other viral illnesses. Doctors know that not every toxin is the same; antibiotics kill bacteria but not viruses. Even though they know illnesses caused by viruses don't respond to antibiotics, doctors give in to their patients' demands. Because the doctors depend on their relationships with patients, they often are averse to saying "no," even when it's in the patients' best interest and in the best interest of society as a whole.

We can continue to educate doctors and the public, asking them to say "no" to the inappropriate use of antibiotics. But there is a clash between empiricism, or what scientific observation tells us, and stubborn belief, which is all too often based on "wishful thinking." People want to believe that antibiotics can swiftly cure their every ill. Because of this, I'm convinced that only government action can adequately address this growing problem. In short, the only sure way to stop the inappropriate use of antibiotics is to pass a law making it a crime.

Carmen: Control of antibiotic use needs to remain strictly voluntary. There is no way that a law could cover all the possible causes of a patient's symptoms. Doctors are well trained in the methodology of diagnosing illness— examining the patient, taking appropriate tests, and asking the right questions. This is the only way to determine the proper course of treatment. That is why the decision whether or not to prescribe an antibiotic needs to remain with the doctor. It is not the government's job.

Today, the government is running an educational campaign about the dangers of antibiotic resistance. Although this plan should be even more ambitious, it's a good attempt, and the basic approach does not need revision. When doctors and the public are made aware of the risks and consequences of antibiotic resistance, they will voluntarily change their behavior. They don't need a law.

Moderator: Thank you, debaters, for your intelligent arguments. Now our judges will decide on the winner. Only one of you will get to exult in being named state champion, but I want you to know that you can both be proud of your stellar performances.

VOCABULARY

excessive	facetious	methodology
neutralize	toxin	ambitious
whereas	averse	revision
adverse	empiricism	exult

TALK ABOUT IT

With a partner, answer the questions below. Use as many of the highlighted words in the selection as you can.

1. Do you think a law is needed to stop the *adverse* consequences of over-prescription of antibiotics? Why or why not?

2. What do you think will happen if antibiotic use continues to be *excessive* in our society?

A doctor discusses medication with a patient.

Word Meanings

For each highlighted word on pages 230–231, the meaning or meanings are given below.

For practice with synonyms, see page 240.

1. **adverse** (ad-VERSS) **adj.** causing harm or preventing success. *Adverse* usually applies to the outcome or effect of something dangerous or harmful. **SYNONYMS:** unfavorable, disadvantageous, injurious, hostile, negative

2. **ambitious** (am-BISH-uhss) **adj.** strongly desiring to achieve an outcome. An *ambitious* person works hard to accomplish a goal. **SYNONYMS:** determined, motivated; **adj.** made or created in order to satisfy high aspirations. An *ambitious* undertaking is one that is very difficult. **SYNONYMS:** demanding, challenging

3. **averse** (uh-VURSS) **adj.** strongly disliking or opposed to. When you are *averse* to something, you show your distaste for it and try to avoid it. **SYNONYMS:** ill-disposed, hostile, against

4. **empiricism** (em-PEER-uh-siz-uhm) **n.** a focus on observation and experimentation. *Empiricism* seeks results that are repeatable and testable. **SYNONYM:** experimental; **n.** a belief based on the idea that all knowledge comes from experience. *Empiricism* holds that a person can't believe something unless he or she has observed it firsthand.

5. **excessive** (ek-SESS-iv) **adj.** more than is necessary, appropriate, or customary. If something is *excessive*, it is far more than is needed or required. **SYNONYMS:** immoderate, overindulgent, unreasonable, extreme, lavish, superfluous

6. **exult** (ex-UHLT) **v.** to be very happy, especially after success. To *exult* is to express extreme joyfulness, usually after a tremendous achievement or fortunate event. **SYNONYMS:** rejoice, jubilate, celebrate, delight in, revel

7. **facetious** (fuh-SEE-shuhss) **adj.** slyly humorous; making a witty comment that says the opposite of what is really meant in order to point out the absurdity of something. If you look at a tacky holiday display and say, "Wow, that's classy," you are being *facetious*. **SYNONYMS:** flippant, glib, ironic, teasing, droll, mischievous

8. **methodology** (meth-uh-DAHL-uh-jee) **n.** a set of rules and processes used in an area of study or profession; a way of accomplishing a task. Most fields or disciplines have a specific *methodology*, or approach, for doing things. **SYNONYMS:** procedure, practice, skill

CCSS Vocabulary: 4.c., 4.d. (See pp. T16–17.)

▶ **Watch** a video introduction for each word at **vocabularyforsuccess.com**.

◀)) **Listen** to iWords at **vocabularyforsuccess.com**.

📖 **Refer** to the online dictionary at **vocabularyforsuccess.com**.

9. **neutralize** (NOO-truh-lize) **v.** to make something ineffective or chemically inactive. To *neutralize* something is to cancel out its effects. **SYNONYMS:** counteract, offset, nullify, negate

10. **revision** (ri-VIZH-uhn) **n.** a change or alteration to make something better. A *revision* is often made to improve a piece of writing. **SYNONYMS:** correction, edit, alteration, modification, redo

11. **toxin** (TOK-sin) **n.** a poisonous or disease-causing substance that is made by a living thing. A *toxin* can come from a venomous creature, such as a scorpion, or from microscopic organisms in the environment. **SYNONYMS:** poison, venom

12. **whereas** (wair-AZ) **conj.** in contrast to or in comparison with something else. *Whereas* is used to show a comparison based on difference. **SYNONYMS:** while, on the contrary, on the other hand, although

More on Meanings: Confusing Word Pairs

The English language contains many pairs of words that be confusing. The words *averse* and *adverse* are commonly confused. The words sound similar and have related meanings. *Averse* means "opposed to," usually with regard to someone's attitude. *Adverse* means "opposed or unfavorable," most often with regard to a situation, condition, or event.

I'm not **averse** to attending the dance, but I don't want to go without a dance partner.

The movie character faced an **adverse** situation, trapped by a tentacled monster.

Words that sound exactly alike but are spelled differently are called homophones. Homophone pairs, often confused, may have completely different, unrelated meanings:

Charitable organizations work to free people from the **yoke** of poverty.

When I eat an egg, I prefer the **yolk** to be firm, not runny.

Yoke means something that is burdensome or oppressive, while *yolk* is the yellow part of an egg.

Challenge

1. Choose two word pairs below. Use each of the words correctly in a sentence.

   lest, least   *magnet, magnate*
   continual, continuous

2. Choose one word pair below. Use both words correctly in the same sentence.

   rack, wrack   *assent, ascent*
   suppose, supposed

Point out word pairs here that sound exactly the same (homophones) and those that sound similar. Have students suggest memory aids to avoid confusing meanings of the homophones.

C CCSS Vocabulary: 4.a., 5. (See pp. T16–17.)

vocabularyforsuccess.com ➤ **233**

Word Talk

Each lesson word has been placed in a category. With a partner, discuss and list items that belong in each category. Compare your results with those of another pair of students.

C CCSS Vocabulary: 6. (See pp. T16–17.)

Words and Phrases That Could Be Used in Place of *Whereas*

on the other hand, in contrast, conversely, while

Times When a Person May *Exult*

after making a three-pointer to win a basketball game, after getting 100% on an exam, after winning an election

---

Reasons People May Be *Averse* to Going to the Pool

can't swim, dislike sitting in the sun, hate getting wet

Reasons a Menu Might Need *Revision*

new menu items being added, too many misspellings, price changes

---

Times People Are *Facetious*

when angry, when joking, when afraid to tell the truth

How a Body Might React to a *Toxin*

vomit, get fever and chills, break out in a rash, go into shock

---

Situations Where *Empiricism* Is Not Useful

when trying to figure out if you're really in love, when expressing an emotion, when writing a poem or song

---

How You Might *Neutralize* a Sore Throat

gargle, drink hot tea, drink a frozen drink

A *Methodology* for Choosing a Place to Eat

figure out how far you want to travel and how much you want to spend; ask friends or look online for recommendations; check restaurant menus online; read online reviews

---

Ambitious People

politicians, straight-A students, actors

Excessive Habits That Can Be Harmful

eating too much, staying up too late, spending too much money

---

Conditions That May Be *Adverse* to Having a Backyard Barbecue

lots of mosquitoes or wasps, a rainy day, too hot, unfriendly neighbors who will complain

---

Check for Understanding

Choose the lesson word that completes each sentence. Write the word on the line provided. Some words will be used twice.

adverse	empiricism	facetious	revision
ambitious	excessive	methodology	toxin
averse	exult	neutralize	whereas

1. A/an ____methodology____ that includes several stages of review usually gets good results.

2. Martha's mother used an oatmeal paste to ____neutralize____ her sunburn.

3. The grain in the farmer's silo had become tainted with a deadly ____toxin____.

4. Jacob's bicycling companions considered his "victory dance" to be a/an ____excessive____ reaction to making it to the one-mile mark.

5. Leena liked the polar bears at the zoo, ____whereas____ Mani was an admiring fan of the baby anteaters.

6. The latest ____revision____ of Michelle's party playlist includes less alternative music.

7. I will ____exult____ when I finally reach the top of that mountain.

8. Felicia showed how ____ambitious____ she was by carefully choosing only friends with wealth and powerful connections.

9. A good salesperson can't be ____averse____ to talking with others.

10. Shanté's deadpan expression made it hard to know whether she was being ____facetious____ when she called the cafeteria selection "a banquet fit for a queen."

11. Quin, a research scientist, values ____empiricism____ above intuitive approaches.

12. ____Whereas____ Omar had six pairs of sunglasses, Derek had only one pair.

13. These hives are an indication of my ____adverse____ reaction to Kara's guinea pig.

14. After my ____revision____, I was very pleased with my short story.

If students have difficulty answering Item 13, point out the word *reaction* after the blank and remind them that *adverse* applies to outcomes and effects.

Word Associations

Use what you know about the lesson words in italics to answer each question. Circle the letter next to the phrase that best answers the question. Be prepared to explain your answers.

1. Which describes a *facetious* statement?

    a. saying "please" when asking someone for a favor

    b. calling your neighbor's small, shy dog a "menacing beast"

    c. complimenting a friend on her really cool new jacket

2. When is the best time to do a *revision* of an essay for class?

    a. before you hand in the final draft

    b. as soon as you start writing

    c. when you're writing the first draft

3. Which of these is part of a person's *methodology* for raking leaves?

    a. the system of piling up leaves

    b. the size and shape of the yard

    c. the amount of leaf matter in the yard

4. What is a benefit of being *ambitious*?

    a. You'll have a lot of time to relax.

    b. You'll be very popular at school.

    c. You'll set and achieve goals.

5. What symptom indicates *excessive* eating?

    a. hunger

    b. upset stomach

    c. sore muscles

6. People who are *averse* to conflict might do which of the following?

    a. cut in front of other people in lines

    b. say nothing when they disagree

    c. help younger siblings with homework

7. What happens when you *neutralize* a tense situation between friends?

    a. The friends calm down.

    b. The friends go home.

    c. The friends become angrier.

8. What is the best way to complete the sentence, "I hold my breath when I'm nervous, *whereas* _____"?

    a. my chest gets really tight

    b. my sister bites her fingernails

    c. my brother hasn't learn to skate

9. Which is an example of *empiricism*?

    a. reading about an explorer's travels

    b. asking friends for a movie recommendation

    c. learning about a horse's gait by studying videos of it galloping

10. Which behavior creates *adverse* driving conditions?

    a. slowing for a yellow light

    b. having your car tuned up

    c. texting behind the wheel

11. Why might an insect produce a *toxin*?

    a. to fly faster

    b. to attract mates

    c. to defend itself against enemies

12. Which emotion do you feel when you *exult*?

    a. joy

    b. regret

    c. humility

CCSS Vocabulary: 4.a. (See pp. T16–17.)

Check Again

Use what you know about the lesson word in italics to complete each sentence. Be sure your sentences make sense.

1. The class officers thought that having three dances in one semester was *excessive*, so they ___canceled___ one of them.

2. Herman's mountain bike was very important to him, so he developed a *methodology* for ___keeping___ it tuned up.

3. Stacy decided she needed to make a *revision* to her hairstyle after ___she realized she'd worn the same___ style for five years.

4. Dogs love to go on walks on a leash, *whereas* cats ___just wander around on their own.___

5. The hazardous *toxin* found in the river came from ___a paint factory.___

6. My *adverse* reaction to scary movies comes out ___in my uncontrollable screaming.___

7. Brigit's *empiricism* made her an effective investigator because ___she made accurate observations.___

8. The volunteer supervisors said that anyone who is *averse* to preparing meat dishes ___can help with___ the salads.

9. When Doug was in the hospital, I knew he was being *facetious* when he said ___that he never knew___ food could be made bland in so many different ways.

10. Philip tried to *neutralize* his tension by ___closing his eyes and taking some deep breaths.___

11. I've worked hard on my art, and I know I will *exult* when ___I get a painting accepted into an art show.___

12. The marching band thought raising $5,000 was too *ambitious*, so they ___lowered their goal to $2,000.___

Write Your Own

Reread the passage on pages 230–231. Then, on a separate sheet of paper, write a one-paragraph response to the question, "Why is over-prescribing antibiotics a bad practice?" Use at least two words from the lesson word list and support your answer by referring to the text of the passage.

Word-Solving Strategies: Context Clues

Examples

When you come across an unfamiliar word in a text, read the surrounding content to see if there are **examples** that illustrate the word's meaning. Examples may be in the same sentence as the unfamiliar word or in a nearby sentence. Sometimes examples are introduced with punctuation, such as a dash, colon, or comma. Read this sentence from "Reversing Antibiotic Resistance":

> Doctors are well trained in the methodology of diagnosing illness—examining the patient, taking appropriate tests, and asking the right questions.

If you don't know what *methodology* means, you might look at the examples given after the dash: steps in the process of diagnosing illness. In other words, they are examples of a methodology, a system of procedures in a particular discipline.

BE CAREFUL!

A list of items that follows an unfamiliar word is not always an example:

> *Antibiotics are drugs that target the causes of various afflictions: bacteria, fungi, and parasites.*

Afflictions means "diseases," some of which are caused by bacteria, fungi, and parasites. Your peers may have knowledge of words that you lack, so try using your peers as resources.

Practice

Write the highlighted word and the example that is a clue to meaning in the first two columns. Write the meaning of the word in the third column.

The belief that antibiotics cure colds and flu is unfounded, based on incorrect assumptions rather than facts. People have a tenacious faith in antibiotics, clinging like vines to that faith. An antibiotic taken to cure a virus is merely a placebo, as effective as kissing a skinned knee. When people improve, they can't reconcile their "cure" with scientific evidence. They'll credit the antibiotic's effectiveness instead of the healing power of time and rest.

WORD	EXAMPLE	WORD MEANING
unfounded	based on incorrect assumptions	not based on fact
tenacious	clinging like vines	not easily letting go of or giving up on
placebo	kissing a skinned knee	a substance having no curative content
reconcile	"cure" with scientific evidence	to make one explanation consistent with another

CCSS Vocabulary: 4.a.; Reading (Informational Text): 4. (See pp. T16–17.)

Practice for Tests

For a quiz and additional practice for this lesson, go to **vocabularyforsuccess.com**.

Fill in the bubble next to the answer that best completes the sentence or answers the question.

1. A person could be exposed to a *toxin* when:
   - ○ **A** getting cold and wet in the rain
   - ○ **B** sitting at a computer too long
   - ● **C** eating improperly prepared food
   - ○ **D** eating a meal late at night

2. A person would most likely want to *neutralize*:
   - ● **A** a stain on a favorite shirt
   - ○ **B** a plane ticket to a tropical resort
   - ○ **C** an *A* on a final exam
   - ○ **D** an interaction with a friend

3. Read this sentence.

   When we asked Jan about her audition, her *facetious* response was, "If they wanted someone who forgets her lines, it went great!"

   Facetious means:
   - ○ **A** lengthy
   - ● **B** sarcastic
   - ○ **C** understanding
   - ○ **D** angry

4. In college, Ava was so *ambitious* that she:
   - ● **A** graduated in fewer than three years
   - ○ **B** had a wide variety of friends
   - ○ **C** failed science and math
   - ○ **D** got a part-time job

5. Connie wondered if her speech needed further *revision*, so she:
   - ○ **A** started over with a new topic
   - ○ **B** memorized the speech
   - ○ **C** read the speech aloud
   - ● **D** asked a friend to critique the speech

6. A person would definitely NOT *exult* when:
   - ○ **A** winning the lottery
   - ● **B** getting a speeding ticket
   - ○ **C** placing first in the science fair
   - ○ **D** being top student in the class

7. A sensible response to an *excessive* cell phone bill would be:
   - ○ **A** increasing texting
   - ○ **B** switching to a plan with fewer minutes
   - ● **C** limiting phone usage next month
   - ○ **D** telling all your friends

8. Read this sentence.

   Jake loved to snowboard, *whereas* Jude preferred cross-country skiing.

   Whereas could be replaced with the word:
   - ○ **A** because
   - ○ **B** now
   - ○ **C** or
   - ● **D** but

9. You might show that you are *averse* to brussels sprouts by:
   - ○ **A** adding a small squeeze of lemon juice
   - ○ **B** asking for seconds
   - ● **C** holding your nose and grimacing
   - ○ **D** buying them at the grocery store

10. Applying *empiricism* would be most useful when:
    - ○ **A** drawing a fantasy landscape
    - ○ **B** looking up a word in a dictionary
    - ● **C** examining asteroid fragments
    - ○ **D** deciding what to cook for dinner

If students choose A, C, or D for Item 3, review the meaning of *facetious*. Remind students that a facetious comment is ironic; what is said is intentionally different from what is meant.

Synonyms and Antonyms

In the following Word Bank, you will find synonyms and antonyms for some of the words in Lessons 19–21. (Remember: Some words have synonyms and antonyms.) Study these words; then complete the exercises below.

superficial	perturb	processed	atmosphere	lazy	refute
allow	soothe	earnest	extravagant	praise	asset

A. For each sentence, fill in the blank with a SYNONYM for the word in boldface.

1. Monica was **ambitious** about making the swim team, and her ____earnest____ training almost guaranteed she would succeed.

2. Aunt Marge always created a festive **ambience** around the holiday season, a cheerful ____atmosphere____ that made her get-togethers family favorites.

3. The street department completed a few **cosmetic** improvements to Gulf Parkway, with ____superficial____ touches such as new street signs and fifty potted palms.

4. To **negate** my entire argument, Pamela needed to ____refute____ only the main point.

5. Desiree's ____extravagant____ spending on jewelry did not seem **excessive** compared to her sister's tendency to buy new cars.

B. For each sentence, fill in the blank with an ANTONYM for the word in boldface.

6. Matthew wanted to ____allow____ dogs on the hiking trip, but if he let them come he would have had to **proscribe** taking them on the trails.

7. Oddly, soft music tends to **agitate** me, while hard-driving rock and roll always works to ____soothe____ me.

8. Junko was a/an ____asset____ to her host family; to avoid being an **imposition**, she always did more than her fair share of the chores.

9. To ____praise____ children for good behavior is better than to **castigate** them for being unruly.

10. Sometimes my mother can't help buying some ____processed____ foods, but most of the time everything she serves us is **organic**.

CCSS Vocabulary: 4.a., 5, 6. (See pp. T16–17.)

Word Study: Denotation and Connotation

Every word has a **denotation**, the literal meaning you find in a dictionary. Many words also have **connotations**, the positive or negative feelings that come to mind when you see or use the word. Neutral words are neither positive nor negative.

POSITIVE	NEGATIVE	NEUTRAL
truthful	blunt	straightforward
inquisitive	prying	curious

Synonyms share similar denotations but may have very different connotations. Here, all three of these words mean "intelligent," but each has a different connotation.

POSITIVE	NEGATIVE	NEUTRAL
brilliant	wily	smart

Be aware of words' connotations in order to choose the words that say exactly what you mean. For example, if you want to compliment a friend for staying calm during exams, tell her that she is *composed*. If you tell her she is *relaxed*, a synonym, it could suggest her calmness means she's unconcerned about her schoolwork.

Practice

A. Circle the word in parentheses that has the connotation (neutral, positive, or negative) given at the beginning of the sentence.

positive **1.** Our school paper published Aran's (silly, (witty)) essay about homecoming.

positive **2.** Conrad put forth some (interesting, (fascinating)) observations regarding the importance of a varied diet.

neutral **3.** Though he loves to read about science, Garrett also enjoys some ((effortless), unchallenging) reading now and then.

negative **4.** Dmitri said he was (upset, (anxious)) about going to the dentist.

neutral **5.** The (mouthy, (talkative)) 10-year-old next to me made the bus ride seem long.

positive **6.** Kind words can sometimes (appease, (comfort)) a disgruntled customer.

negative **7.** Ryan made an ((inept), amateur) attempt to fix the leaky faucet.

B. Work with a partner. Write a plus sign (+) if the word has positive connotations; write a minus sign (-) if the word has a negative connotation. Put a zero (0) if the word is neutral.

1. unplanned 0   **3.** charisma +   **5.** blemish −   **7.** merriment +

2. scrawny −   **4.** pacify +   **6.** shackle −   **8.** tedious −

Vocabulary for Comprehension

Read the following passage, in which some of the words you have studied in Lessons 19–21 appear in boldface type. Then answer questions 1–6.

The Story of Penicillin

Penicillin, a medicine that doctors **prescribe** to **neutralize** a large number of bacterial diseases, was the first antibiotic to be discovered. A number of researchers
5 contributed to the development of the drug, but the name Alexander Fleming is forever associated with penicillin because he was the first to recognize penicillin's antibacterial action. The discovery was a complete accident. In the
10 late 1920s, Fleming was growing various types of bacteria in glass dishes. One day he found that a dish of staphylococcus bacteria had been contaminated with a small growth of penicillium mold—the same mold that grows on bread and
15 gives blue cheese its flavor. Fleming noticed that the mold had worked to **inhibit** the growth of the

bacteria. He recognized the **adverse** effect it had on the bacteria.

But the medical field was far from putting
20 pencillium to use to help people. This was long before developments in the study of **biochemistry** that led to new treatments for **pathogens** and **toxins**. More than ten years passed before researchers started to perfect
25 the **methodology** to grow penicillium in large amounts and **extract** medicine from the mold.

Today penicillin is only one **version** among many types of antibiotics that cure deadly diseases, all thanks to a speck of mold growing
30 in Alexander's Fleming's lab.

1. In sentence 1, to **prescribe** a medication means to
   - ● **A** authorize its use
   - ○ **B** limit its use
   - ○ **C** warn against its use
   - ○ **D** prohibit its use

2. To **neutralize** (line 2) something is to make it
   - ○ **A** like something else
   - ○ **B** confusing
   - ● **C** ineffective
   - ○ **D** happen faster

3. Another word for **inhibit** (line 16) is
   - ○ **A** improve
   - ● **B** hinder
   - ○ **C** praise
   - ○ **D** encourage

4. When you follow a **methodology** (line 25), you follow a
   - ○ **A** hunch
   - ○ **B** tradition
   - ● **C** procedure
   - ○ **D** command

5. When you **extract** (line 26) iron from iron ore, you
   - ○ **A** erase it
   - ○ **B** tell it apart
   - ○ **C** sort it
   - ● **D** remove it

6. **Version** (line 27) is another word for
   - ● **A** type
   - ○ **B** brace
   - ○ **C** segment
   - ○ **D** choice

If students choose D for Item 1, review the differences between the commonly confused words *prescribe* and *proscribe*.

CCSS Vocabulary: 4.a., 6; Reading (Informational Text): 4. (See pp. T16–17.)

Using Context

Circle the word that best completes each sentence. Note that the choices are related forms of the vocabulary words in the box.

ambiguous	imposition	migratory
arbitrarily	incidence	neutralize
automate	infinitesimal	revelation
containment	inflammatory	rhetoric
eclectic	inhibit	satire
empiricism	metaphor	visualization

1. The art show was a (**visual**/metaphorical) feast, with eye-pleasing colors on every wall.

2. The door will open and the magician will (**reveal**/contain) a tiger where the lady used to be.

3. Emily feels no (incidents/**inhibitions**) about telling the world what she thinks.

4. Because of a senseless, (satirical/**arbitrary**) decision, Ana was not given the loan for her new business.

5. In a time of conflict, a speaker may (**inflame**/impose) a crowd to anger.

6. Known for his (**ambiguity**/eclecticism), Geraldo always seems to be saying opposite things at once.

7. The herdsmen of the far North followed the (**migration**/automation) of the caribou herds each spring.

8. This opinion article relies more on the writer's emotional, (empirical/**rhetorical**) tricks than on solid facts.

9. During WWII, Sweden decided not to take sides in the war and declared its (inflammation/**neutrality**).

10. There is an (**infinite**/incidental) number of ways to be happy—as well as to be unhappy.

Analogies

Read each sentence stem carefully. Then complete the sentence so that it makes sense. Use the relationship between the words in italics to help you.

1. An *aquatic* activity takes place in the water, while a *virtual* activity <u>occurs in an</u> <u>imaginary world.</u>

2. An *inquisitive* person asks valid questions, while an *impertinent* person <u>is rude and nosy.</u>

3. If you are *diffident*, you may not be noticed, while if you *exult*, <u>you will get attention.</u>

4. *Introspection* can slowly bring understanding, while an *epiphany* <u>may bring it in an instant.</u>

5. A *cosmetic* product may make you look good, while an *organic* product may <u>make you healthy.</u>

6. A *postulate* is what someone claims to be true, while *hyperbole* <u>is an exaggeration.</u>

7. A *ceaseless* process has no end, while a *cyclical* process <u>keeps coming back to the beginning</u> <u>and repeating.</u>

8. A *protagonist* usually has human flaws, while a *paragon* <u>is perfect in every way.</u>

Word Relationships

Read each question carefully. Think about the relationship between the two vocabulary words in italics. Then write an explanation that answers each question.

1. Why might a *vigilante* wish to travel *incognito*?

He or she would want to take action without being recognized.

2. How could one *negate* potentially *excessive* exposure to bright sunlight?

Apply sunscreen liberally and often, and wear a hat, a long-sleeved shirt, and sunglasses.

3. In what circumstances might a person be *averse* to a particular *ambience*?

The person might not feel comfortable in the specific surroundings.

4. How might *nanotechnology* *revolutionize* the world?

Nanotechnology might enable us to clean up the environment and invent personalized medical treatments.

5. How is a human being *analogous* to a *protozoan*?

Humans and protozoans are both living things: they move, ingest nutrients, excrete, and reproduce.

6. What force might *erode* a *vast* amount of a riverbank?

A flood or huge rainfall or other storm might erode a vast amount of a riverbank.

END-OF-YEAR REVIEW

Generating Sentences

Follow the directions to write sentences with the vocabulary words in italics. Be sure your sentences make sense both grammatically and in meaning.

1. Use the term *status quo* in an 11-word sentence.

   Nothing had changed; everything remained in accordance with the status quo.

2. Use the word *whereas* in a sentence about your activities.

   Whereas I used to play video games, now I work out at the Y.

3. Use the word *prescribe* in the fifth position in a question of at least 7 words.

   What did the doctor prescribe for your infection?

4. Use the word *castigate* in a sentence about feelings.

   It hurts my feelings when people castigate each other.

5. Use the word *allusion* in a sentence of 8 or more words about literature.

   The writer of the novel made an allusion that I couldn't understand.

Extend Your Sentence

Choose one of your sentences and turn it into a paragraph. Use at least four other words from Units 5–7 in your paragraph.

CCSS Vocabulary: 6; Writing: 2.d. (See pp. T16–17.)

The following is a list of all the words taught in the Lessons of this book.
The number after each entry indicates the page on which the word is defined.

Index